PIAGET: DICTIONARY OF TERMS

Original title: *Dictionnaire D'Épistémologie Génétique*, 1966
D. Reidel Publishing Company, Dordrecht, Holland

ANTONIO M. BATTRO

PIAGET: DICTIONARY OF TERMS

Preface by

JEAN PIAGET

Translated and Edited by

ELIZABETH RÜTSCHI-HERRMANN, DR. IUR.
and
SARAH F. CAMPBELL, PH.D.
Kendall College, Evanston, Illinois

PERGAMON PRESS INC.

New York · Toronto · Oxford · Sydney · Braunschweig

PERGAMON PRESS INC.
Maxwell House, Fairview Park, Elmsford, N.Y. 10523

PERGAMON OF CANADA LTD.
207 Queen's Quay West, Toronto 117, Ontario

PERGAMON PRESS LTD.
Headington Hill Hall, Oxford

PERGAMON PRESS (AUST.) PTY. LTD.
Rushcutters Bay, Sydney, N.S.W.

VIEWEG & SOHN GmbH
Burgplatz 1, Braunschweig

Printed in the United States of America
08 017039 0

PREFACE

Genetic epistemology is not to be confused with genetic psychology and the latter is not identical with child psychology. This last is the study of the child himself, whereas genetic psychology seeks within the study of the child the solutions to general problems, such as those of the mechanisms of intelligence, perception, etc., for it is only in analyzing the formation of such mechanisms that we can provide their causal explanation. In fact, in psychology as in biology, explanation is inseparable from development. Similarly, genetic epistemology has as its object the examination of the formation of knowledge itself, that is to say of the cognitive relations between the subject and objects: thus it bridges the gap between genetic psychology and epistemology in general, which it helps to enrich by considering development. But if epistemology always contains genetic psychological presuppositions (even in theories which pretend that they can neglect the subject and reduce its activity to a simple "Language"), which should be controlled by experiment and facts, it also involves the theory of knowledge from the considerations of logic or general algebra, etc., which do not pertain to psychology but to formal thought or pure deduction. Genetic epistemology is thus by nature an interdisciplinary research, where genetic psychology plays a necessary but not sufficient role.

Considering the complexity in the problems of genetic epistemology, it would be helpful and easier to study if we used a Dictionary which would provide the reader with a collection of definitions or references aiding him to get oriented in the reading of the texts. Twenty volumes have, indeed, been published in the "Etudes d'Épistémologie Génétique," and these "studies" (Etudes) do not pretend to exhaust the research in this field. Dr. A. M. Battro, who is a neurologist, as well as a psychologist and logician and who has participated in the work of our Center in Geneva, has been admirably prepared to accomplish this task. He has taken the initiative with a group of collaborators at Buenos Aires, and one day we received the manuscript of just this Dictionary as a surprise of which we had never dreamed ourselves. It is the fruit of this work which we have the honor and pleasure to present today to the public and we express our deep gratitude to him and to his co-authors. But there is much more to it, as we can easily discern by consulting his work, namely its importance and its inclusive information as well as the flexibility and ingenuity of the things which he has brought together. One can easily imagine the often fastidious work which was necessary to accomplish this task. But the result is here. The only criticism which we have been able to make is that he has centered his text too much on our own works. Genetic epistemology is not the accomplishment of a "school," but a tendency which more or less becomes apparent in various places and at different times. Now this tendency is affirming itself more and more and the work of Dr. Battro and his collaborators has certainly contributed vigorously to this movement.

JEAN PIAGET

INTRODUCTION

This *Piaget: Dictionary of Terms* is the result of a seminar of the Science Division (University of Buenos Aires, 1962–63) on the theory of psychology and knowledge of Professor Jean Piaget.

The great number of research works by the Geneva group led us to compile a vocabulary of the most important terms which we find in the several thousand pages of the works by Piaget and his collaborators.

The Dictionary could thus be useful to psychologists and philosophers interested in the genetic method, but the reading of the Dictionary would certainly be insufficient for adequate understanding of the problems of genetic epistemology without direct consultation of the texts and personal reflection on the theoretical and experimental problems.

The goal which we have set for this work has been that of providing a tool for study. We organized the various terms in a way to permit better understanding of their different relationships. Several times we cite the text *in extenso* when the interest of the term leads us to do so. The commentaries which are ours are of simple connectives or summaries. Opposite terms are indicated "opp.," the insertion of words for the sake of syntax are noted between brackets [ ]. Capital initials and numbers in parentheses refer to the books and articles consulted (*see* Bibliography). We have taken, with a few exceptions, only notions and terms found in the actual Piaget texts. The choice of text quotations was made with regard to their function in the Dictionary. The quotations from the works of Professor Piaget have been reproduced with the gracious consent of Presses Universitaires de France, Armand Colin bookshop, Centre de Documentation Universitaire, and Delachaux & Niestlé.

Those who have collaborated in the compiling of this dictionary are: Alicia Casullo, Enrique Colignon, Eva Giberti, Emilia Ferreiro, Celia Jakubowicz, Martha Accinelli.

A. M. B.

TRANSLATORS' AND EDITORS' NOTE

We have translated directly from the passages selected by Professor Battro, staying close to the original French in our attempt to preserve what Piaget actually said when he used the particular terms in his special way.

The reference given at the end of each term is to the original French edition as listed in the Bibliography and indicated by initials. We have added in brackets [ ] and bigram initials the references as translated into English, where such translations are available.

We used American spelling (behavior, organization, etc.) and made the consistent translation of the word "schema" (plural "schemas") in accordance with only some of the previously established habits of Piaget's various translators.

Several cross-references have been added.

In all, we have attempted to extend to readers of English what Professor Battro intended as a useful tool and to safeguard Professor Piaget's own statements.

BIBLIOGRAPHY

JEAN PIAGET

Books

A.I. *Les relations entre l'affectivité et l'intelligence dans le developpement mental de l'enfant.* C.D.U., Paris, 1962.

C.P. *La causalité physique chez l'enfant.* F. Alcan, Paris, 1927.
[*The child's conception of physical causality.* Paterson, New Jersey: Littlefield, Adams, 1960.] [Co Ph Ca]

C.R. *La construction du réel chez l'enfant.* 2e éd., Delachaux & Niestlé, Neuchâtel, 1950.
[*The construction of reality in the child.* (Trans. M. Cook). London: Routledge and Kegan Paul, 1955.] [Co Re]

D.Q. (Avec B. Inhelder): *Le développement des quantités physiques chez l'enfant.* 2e éd., Delachaux & Niestlé, Neuchâtel, 1962.

E.G. I *Introduction à l'épistémologie génétique. I. La pensée mathématique.* Presses Universitaires de France, Paris, 1949.

E.G. II *Introduction à l'épistémologie génétique. II. La pensée physique.* Presses Universitaires de France, Paris, 1950.

E.G. III *Introduction à l'épistémologie génétique. III. La pensée biologique, la pensée psychologique et la pensée sociologique.* Presses Universitaires de France, Paris, 1951.

F.S. *La formation du symbole chez l'enfant.* 2e éd., Delachaux & Niestlé, Neuchâtel, 1959.
[*Play, dreams and imitation in childhood.* (Trans. C. Gatteno and F. M. Hodgson). New York: Norton, 1962.] [Pl Dr Im]

G.N. (Avec A. Szeminska): *La genèse du nombre chez l'enfant.* Delachaux & Niestlé, Neuchâtel, 1941 (2e éd., 1950; 3e éd., 1964).

[*The child's conception of number.* (Trans. C. Gatteno and F. M. Hodgson). London: Routledge and Kegan Paul, 1952. (2nd ed., 1961; 3rd ed., 1965). New York: Norton, 1965.] [Co Nu]

G.S.   (Avec B. Inhelder et A. Szeminska): *La géometrie spontanée de l'enfant.* Presses Universitaires de France, Paris, 1948.

[*The child's conception of geometry.* (Trans. G. A. Lunzer). London: Routledge and Kegan Paul, 1960; New York: Harper, 1964.] [Co Ge]

G.S.L.   (Avec B. Inhelder): *La genèse des structures logiques élémentaires. Classifications et sériations.* Delachaux & Niestlé, Paris–Neuchâtel, 1959.

[*The early growth of logic in the child (Classification and seriation)* (Trans. G. A. Lunzer and D. Papert). London: Routledge and Kegan Paul, 1964; New York: Harper, 1964.] [Ea Gr Lo]

I.H.   (Avec B. Inhelder): *La genèse de l'idée du hasard chez l'enfant.* Presses Universitaires de France, Paris, 1951.

J.M.   *Le jugement moral chez l'enfant.* Presses Universitaires de France, Paris, 1957.

[*The moral judgment of the child* (Trans. Marjorie Gabain). New York: Harcourt, 1932 (2nd éd., Glencoe, Illinois: Free Press, 1948, Paperback 1965).] [Mo Ju]

J.R.   *Le jugement et le raisonnement chez l'enfant.* 4e éd., Delachaux & Niestlé, Neuchâtel, 1956.

[*Judgment and reasoning in the child.* New York: Harcourt & Brace, 1926 (2nd ed., 1938); Paterson, New Jersey: Littlefield, Adams, 1964.] [Ju Re]

L.E.A.   (Avec B. Inhelder): *De la logique de l'enfant à la logique de l'adolescent.* Presses Universitaires de France, Paris, 1955.

[(With B. Inhelder): *The growth of logical thinking from childhood to adolescence* (an essay on the construction of formal operational structures). (Trans. A. Parsons and S. Milgram). 3rd ed., London: Routledge and Kegan Paul, 1968.] [Gr Lo Th]

L.P.   *Le langage et la pensée chez l'enfant.* 4e éd., Dela-
            chaux & Niestlé, Neuchâtel, 1956.
            [*The language and thought of the child* (Trans.
            M. and R. Gabain). 3rd ed., London: Routledge and
            Kegan Paul, 1959.] [La Th]
M.P.   *Les mécanismes perceptifs. Modèles probabilistes, an-
            alyse génétique, relations avec l'intelligence.* Presses
            Universitaires de France, Paris, 1961.
            [*Mechanisms of Perception* (Trans. G. N. Seagrim).
            New York: Basic Books, 1969.] [Me Pe]
M.V.   *Les notions de mouvement et de vitesse chez l'enfant.*
            Presses Universitaires de France, Paris, 1946.
            [*The child's conception of movement and speed*
            (Trans. G. E. T. Holloway and M. J. Mackenzie).
            New York: Basic Books, 1970.] [Mo Sp]
N.I.   *La naissance de l'intelligence chez l'enfant.* 3e éd.,
            Delachaux & Niestlé, Neuchâtel, 1959.
            [*The origins of intelligence in children* (Trans. M.
            Cook). New York: International University Press,
            1952 (2nd ed., New York: Norton, 1963).] [Or In]
N.T.   *Le développement de la notion de temps chez l'enfant.*
            Presses Universitaires de France, Paris, 1946.
P.I.   *La psychologie de l'intelligence.* A. Colin, Paris, 1947.
            [*The psychology of intelligence* (Trans. M. Piercey
            and D. E. Berlyne). London: Routledge and Kegan
            Paul, 1950. (Reprint: Paterson, New Jersey: Little-
            field, Adams, 1960).] [Ps In]
R.E.   (Avec B. Inhelder): *La réprésentation de l'espace chez
            l'enfant.* Presses Universitaires de France, Paris, 1948.
            [*The child's conception of space* (Trans. Langdon and
            Lunzer). London: Routledge and Kegan Paul, 1956;
            New York: Norton, 1967.] [Ch Co Sp]
R.M.   *La représentation du monde chez l'enfant.* F. Alcan,
            Paris, 1938.
            [*The child's conception of the world* (Trans. Joan and
            Andrew Tomlinson). New York: Harcourt & Brace,
            1929. (Reprint: New Jersey: Littlefield, Adams, 1963).]
            [Co Wo]
S.E.A.   "Les stades dans le développement de l'enfant et de

l'adolescent" dans P. A. Osterrieth, J. Piaget, R. de Saussure, J. M. Tanner, H. Wallon, R. Zazzo, B. Inhelder et A. Rey, *Le problème des stades en psychologie de l'enfant*. Presses Universitaires de France, Paris, 1956.

T.L.   *Traité de logique. Essai de logistique opératoire*. A. Colin, Paris, 1949.

T.O.L.   *Essai sur les transformations des opérations logiques. Les 256 opérations ternaires de la logique bivalente des propositions*. Presses Universitaires de France, Paris, 1952.

T.P. I   (Avec P. Fraisse): *Traité de Psychologie Expérimentale Tome I. (Histoire et Méthode)*. Presses Universitaires de France, Paris, 1963.
[(With P. Fraisse and M. Reuchlin): *Experimental Psychology: its scope and method. I. History and Method*. London: Routledge and Kegan Paul, 1968.]

E.E.G. I   (Avec E. W. Beth et W. Mays): *Epistémologie génétique et recherche psychologique* (Etudes d'épistémologie génétique I). Presses Universitaires de France, Paris, 1957.

E.E.G. II   (Avec L. Apostel et B. Mandelbrot): *Logique et équilibre* (Etudes d'épistémologie génétique II). Presses Universitaires de France, Paris, 1957.

E.E.G. III   (Avec L. Apostel, B. Mandelbrot et A. Morf): *Logique, langage et théorie de l'information* (Etudes d'épistémologie génétique III). Presses Universitaires de France, Paris, 1957.

E.E.G. IV   (Avec L. Apostel, W. Mays, A. Morf et B. Matalon): *Les liaisons analytiques et synthétiques dans les comportments du sujet* (Etudes d'épistémologie génétique IV). Presses Universitaires de France, Paris, 1957.

E.E.G. V   (Avec A. Jonckheere et B. Mandelbrot): *La lecture de l'expérience* (Etudes d'épistémologie génétique V). Presses Universitaires de France, Paris, 1958.

E.E.G. VI   (Avec J. S. Bruner, F. Bresson et A. Morf): *Logique et perception* (Etudes d'épistémologie génétique VI). Presses Universitaires de France, Paris, 1958.

E.E.G. VII   (Avec P. Gréco): *Apprentissage et connaissance* (Etudes d'épistémologie génétique VII). Presses Universitaires de France, Paris, 1959.

E.E.G. X (Avec M. Goustard, P. Gréco et B. Matalon): *La logique des apprentissages* (Etudes d'épistémologie génétique X). Presses Universitaire de France, Paris, 1959.

E.E.G. XI (Avec P. Gréco, J. B. Grize et S. Papert): *Problèmes de la construction du nombre* (Etudes d'épistémologie génétique XI). Presses Universitaires de France, Paris, 1960.

E.E.G. XII (Avec D. E. Berlyne): *Théorie du comportement et opérations* (Etudes d'épistémologie génétique XII). Presses Universitaires de France, Paris, 1960.

E.E.G. XIV (Avec E. W. Beth): *Epistémologie mathématique et psychologie. Essai sur les relations entre la logique formelle et la pensée réelle* (Etudes d'épistémologie génétique XIV). Presses Universitaires de France, Paris, 1961.
[Evert W. Beth and Jean Piaget, *Mathematical epistemology and psychology* (Trans. W. Mays). Dordrecht, Holland: D. Reidel, 1966.]

E.E.G. XV (Avec L. Apostel, J. B. Grize et S. Papert): *La filiation des structures* (Etudes d'épistémologie génétique XV). Presses Universitaires de France, Paris, 1963.

E.E.G. XVII (Avec P. Gréco, B. Inhelder et B. Matalon): *La formation des raisonnements récurrentiels* (Etudes d'épistémologie génétique XVII). Presses Universitaires de France, Paris, 1963.

Articles

(1) "La psychoanalyse et ses rapports avec la psychologie de l'enfant." *Bulletin de la société Alfred Binet* **20** (1920) 18–34, 41–58.

(2) "La pensée symbolique et la pensée de l'enfant." *Archives de psychologie* **18** (1923) 273–304.

(3) "Les traits principaux de la logique de l'enfant." *Journal de psychologie* **21** (1924) 48–101.

(4) "De quelques formes primitives de causalité chez l'enfant." *Année psychologique* **26** (1925) 31–71.

(5) "La première année de l'enfant." *The British Journal of Psychology* **18** (1927) 97–120.

(6) "Les trois systèmes de la pensée de l'enfant." *Bulletin de la société française de philosophie* **28** (1928) 97–141.

(7)   "Retrospective and prospective analysis in child psychology."
      The British Journal of Educational Psychology (1931)
      130–139.
(8)   "Le développement intellectual chez les jeunes enfants."
      Mind **40** (1931) 137–160.
(9)   "Esprit et réalité." *Annuaire de la société suisse de philoso-*
      phie **1** (1940) 40–47.
(10) "La fonction régulatrice du groupement dans le développe-
      ment mental: esquisses d'une théorie opératoire de l'intelli-
      gence." *Compte rendu des séances de la société de physique*
      et d'histoire naturelle de Genève **58** (1941) 198–203.
(11) "Le mécanisme du développement mental et les lois du
      groupement des opérations. Esquisse d'une théorie opératoire
      de l'intelligence." *Archives de psychologie* **28** (1941) 215–285.
(12) "Les trois structures fondamentales de la vie psychique:
      rythme, régulations et groupement." *Revue suisse de psy-*
      chologie **1** (1942) 9–21.
(13) "Une expérience sur le développement de la notion de temps."
      Revue suisse de psychologie **1** (1942) 179–185.
(14) "Le problème neurologique de l'intériorisation des actions
      en opérations réversibles." *Archives de psychologie* **32**
      (1949) 241–258.
(15) "La langage et la pensée du point de vue génétique." *Acta*
      psychologica **10** (1954) 51–60.
(16) "Motricité, perception et intelligence." *Enfance* **2** (1956)
      10–14.

A

1. **Abstraction**

"... abstraction consists in adding relations to perceptual data and not merely in deducing such relations from them. If we recognize the existence of common properties such as square or round, large or small, 'flat' or three dimensional, etc., it means that we construct schemas which are related to the actions of the subject as well as to the properties of the object ... In a still more general way the common properties upon which a classification is based are 'common,' to the extent that the action of the subject makes them common, as well as to the extent that these objects are suitable to be made common." G.S.L. 247. [Ea Gr Lo 246]

2.1 **Abstraction, simple** opp.*

2.2 **Abstraction, constructive**

(2.1) "... it is one thing to deduce from the perceived objects the property x in order to unite them in a class which has only this quality x. This would then be a process which we shall call simple abstraction and simple generalization (that which is used by classical empiricism). It is a different thing [2.2] if we recognize in an object a property x and utilize it as an element in a different structure than in the above mentioned perceptions. We shall then call it 'constructive' abstraction and generalization." M.P. 395. [Me Pe 317]

2.1 **Abstraction, empirical** (or **simple**)

"Abstraction starting from the perceived objects – which we shall call 'empirical abstraction' (with the hypothesis that non-perceivable objects are products of operations) ... consists simply in deriving the common characteristics from a class of objects (by combining abstraction with generalization only)..." E.E.G. XIV 203.

2.11 **Abstraction, simplifying**

"No geometrical figure ... is realized in its pure form in the physical world [abstraction]. It is therefore a construction which replaces an imperfectly perceived figure by a perfectly conceived one." E.E.G. XIV 161.

"Often we reason [wrongly] as though geometrical forms were attached to the objects like their weight or their color." R.E. 39. [Ch Co Sp 25]

2.2 **Abstraction, reflecting** (or **constructive**)

"... abstraction starting from actions and operations – which we

*The opposite is the next term.

1

shall call 'reflecting abstraction' ... is necessarily constructive." E.E.G. XIV 203.

"... it consists in deducing from a system of actions or operations on a lower level, certain characteristics through which reflecting (somewhat in the physical sense of the term) upon actions or operations at the higher level are assured, because it is possible to be aware of processes of a previous construction only by means of reconstruction on a new level."

"... reflecting abstraction proceeds by reconstructions which feed back, by integrating them, to the previous constructions." E.E.G. XIV 203. Cf. E.E.G. XIV 217; E.E.G. XIV 223.

"In the abstraction of [geometrical] forms ... there is an abstraction in connection with the action, or from the coordination among the subject's actions..." R.E. 40. [Ch Co Sp 25]

2.21   **Abstraction, reflecting from logico-mathematical experience**
"... (a) logico-mathematical experience consists of observing the results of actions performed upon any objects; (b) the results are determined by the schemas of the actions that are carried out on the objects; (c) but in order to observe (or 'read') these results, the subject has to carry out other actions (of reading) using the same schemas as those the products of which have to be examined. However, (d) the knowledge acquired is new for the subject; that is (although, in principle, a simple deduction might have been able to replace experience) the experience teaches him what he had not been aware of before. We thus must conclude (e) that abstraction by which the subject draws new knowledge (consciously) of the results of his action involves partly a construction, which has the effect of translating the schema and its implications in preoperational terms or of conscious operations, of which the latter handling will allow replacing through deductions the empirical experiences or procedures which thus became useless." E.E.G. XIV 253.

"... transforms behavior by differentiating it and consequently ... adding something qualitative, though isolated by abstraction." E.G. I 72.

3.   **Abstraction and consciousness**
"To make an abstraction from the appropriate point of view is to become conscious." R.E. 278. [Ch Co Sp 235]

4.   **Abstraction starting from internal coordinations (hereditary)**
"This does not necessarily mean that the operations were preformed in an innate form, but that they could be interpreted in the sense of a

progressive abstraction from borrowed elements beginning with hereditary functioning and regrouped thanks to new constructive combinations." E.G. I 25.

5.   **Abstraction — the inverse operation of logical multiplication**
"Abstraction is the inverse operation of logical 'multiplication'." D.Q. 308.
"Setting aside K_2, the product $K_1 K_2$ comes back to being K_1." T.L. 119–120.

6.   **Abstraction and symbolism**
"To the double mechanism of 'condensation' and 'displacement' in the symbol [according to Freud] could correspond, respectively, 'generalization' and 'abstraction' in thought. Abstraction is a kind of displacement." L.P. 152. [La Th 158] (*See* **Generalization** and **Symbolism**.)

7.   **Abstraction from qualities** (origins of number)
There is "abstraction from qualities ... in the beginning of enumeration where each element is considered as a unit independently of its qualitative properties..." E.E.G. XIV 193–194.

8.   **Abstraction belonging to successive forms of causality (historical and psychogenetic)**
"... each transformation of causality leads not only to a new hierarchy of scales of approximation, which finally decrease the degree of validity of earlier causal forms, but also to relegating, either in the domain of phenomenal appearances or of egocentric relations, certain aspects of the characteristics sacrificed." E.G. II 290.

1.   **Accommodation and experience**
We must "distinguish in intellectual activity ... a time corresponding to what experience is (accommodation as such)." N.I. 241. [Or In 275]
"There is accommodation when the 'environment acts on the organism'." P.I. 13. [Ps In 8]

2.   **Accommodation** opp. **Assimilation**
For the "accommodation of the schemas ... there is ... a third possibility (*tertium*) between applying and not applying a schema of assimilation: i.e., to modify it." E.E.G. VII 44.
"In the first place it designates an activity. Even though the modification of the assimilating schema is imposed by the resistances to the objects, it is not imposed as such by the object, but by the reaction of the subject which tends to create this resistance (it can therefore proceed by reflex or by trial and error, etc.). But in the second place,

3

if accommodation is still an activity consisting in differentiating an assimilatory schema, it is derived, or secondary, only with regard to the assimilation." E.E.G. VII 44.

"The pressure of things always results, not in passive submission, but in a simple modification of the action directed toward them." P.I. 14. [Ps In 8] Cf. N.I. 245.

3.   **Accommodation, acquired** (Example)
"For example, if a child systematically sucks his thumb, no longer because of a chance encounter, but because of coordination between hand and mouth, we may speak of acquired accommodation." N.I. 49. [Or In 48]

Acquisition (Mechanisms)
"(1) internal maturation of the nervous system [e.g.: walking];
(2) learning as the result of experience;
(2a) physical [e.g.: notion of weight];
(2b) logico-mathematical [e.g.: commutativity of addition];
(3) through language and educational or social transmissions [e.g.: spoken enumeration];
(4) through progressive equilibrium [e.g.: conservation of matter] instead of limiting himself to judgments about configurations alone, [the child] starts to reason about transformations and this in a more and more reversible fashion (in the sense of introducing inverse transformations)." E.E.G. XIV 210.

1.   **Action**
"All action applied to objects accommodates itself to them, i.e., it undergoes as a negative the imprint of the things on which it molds itself. The essence of the action is naturally not in this imprint; it is in the modification imposed on the object, i.e., the assimilation of the latter to the schemas of the subject." R.E. 540. [Ch Co Sp 455]

"Df. 1. Action is all behavior (externally observable, including the clinical interview) seeking a goal from the point of view of the subject under consideration." E.E.G. IV 43.

"Action" has to be "defined as a reequilibration of behavior in the event of change of environment." E.E.G. IV 44.

1.1   **Action, beginning of**
"Df. 2. An action begins at a moment t if, before this moment t, a change in the environment makes it improbable to reach state e, and if it is not followed by any compensatory measure, in the experiment, whereas after that moment t, it is." E.E.G. IV 44

4

1.2 **Action, termination of**
"Df. 3. An action ends at the moment t if, after t, changes in the environment decrease the probability of reaching state e, or if they are no longer followed by their effects, or if they are followed by returning toward e, reached at t." E.E.G. IV 44.

1.3 **Action, result of**
"Df. 18. We shall say that the result of an action is related to a schema, if this result consists in introducing a type I property in the object on which this action was applied." "Df. 19. The result of the action is said to be related to the object, if this result consists in introducing a property of type II in the object on which this action was applied." E.E.G. IV 56. (*See* **Property** 2.1, 2.2.)

1.4 **Action, minimal**
"Df. 4. An action is minimal, if, in the situation in which it was effected, no sub-behavior of this behavior is an action." E.E.G. IV 44.

1.5 **Action, fractional**
"Df. 5. A fractional action is any action which is part of a compound action (we shall also use the terms of coordinated action and of coordinations of actions instead of fractional actions and compound actions)." E.E.G. IV 44.

1.61 **Action, logico-mathematical**
"Df. 20. We shall call logico-mathematical all action capable of introducing type I properties into objects." E.E.G. IV 57

1.62 **Action, physical**
"Df. 21. We shall call physical all action the result of which is related to its object." E.E.G. IV 59.

2. **Action and operation**
"... without the activity of the subject, that which explains progressive reversibility of actions and intuitions up to complete reversibility in operational mechanisms, the actions are not transformed into operations and they will not succeed in becoming 'grouped' into mobile and coherent systems." M.V. 262. [Mo Sp 284]

3. **Action and abstraction**
"Therefore we must say, and this at all levels, that action — common starting point for imaged intuitions and operations — adds something to reality instead of simply extracting from it (or as we say to 'abstract') the elements of its own construction." M.V. 31. [Mo Sp 32]

5

4. **Action, virtual and object**
   "A reality which remains simply 'at the disposition' of action without existing in the objective 'groups' of displacement is not then an object: it is solely a potential act." C.R. 42. [Co Re 44]

5. **Action, interiorized**
   "We call interiorized an action carried out in thought on symbolic objects ... either by representation of its potential unfolding and application to its real object evoked by mental images (it is then the image which plays the role of the symbol), or by direct application to the symbolic systems (verbal signs, etc.)." E.E.G. II 44–45. (*See* **Notion, concrete.**)

1. **Activities, perceptual**
   We use the "collective term of perceptual activities (for there are many distinct ones which are not necessarily at the same level)." M.P. 172. [Me Pe 133] (*See* **Intelligence, perceptual.**)
   It is "one aspect of sensory-motor intelligence ... a limited aspect in the case where the object enters into direct and actual relations with the subject." P.I. 135. [Ps In 112]
   "Indicated at first by the introduction of decentration." P.I. 98. [Ps In 81]
   It is the "origin of decentrations, of transports (spatial and temporal), of comparisons, of transpositions, of anticipations, and, in a general way, of the more and more mobile analysis tending toward reversibility." P.I. 103. [Ps In 85]

2. **Activity, perceptual and perceptual schemas**
   "Consists essentially to assure the mutual passage of perceptions, in other words to establish likenesses and differences between the successively perceived relations. It leads thus to something other than simple perception: to the formation of 'perceptual schemas,' which are already schemas of transformation and not just the readings of static relations." E.G. I 182.
   Perception is a sign related to the perceptual schema; it "is only a point of reference for the real action in order to connect the perceived forms, that is in relation to the perceptual activity ... moreover perceptual schemas are only the particular case of assimilatory sensory-motor schemas." E.G.I. 183.

3. **Activity, exploratory**
   "Exploratory activity [is] a prolongation of the relating of centrations..." M.P. 175. [Me Pe 137]

6

"Exploratory activity is thus activity, on any level, which directs movements of observing and choice of posture or centering, while examining the perceived figure." M.P. 176. [Me Pe 137]

4. **Activity, perceptual** opp. **Elementary or "pure" perception**
"... pure perception itself obeys the proportionality laws (Weber's law, law of relative centrations, etc.) but perceptual activity assumes the becoming conscious of that proportionality..." R.E. 432. [Ch Co Sp 365 note]

5. **Activity, sensory-motor**
"We call those activities sensory-motor which involve only perception, attitudes (feeling) and movements, and sensory-motor intelligence the capacity to resolve the practical problem by means of these activities, before the appearance of language." E.E.G. II 46.
"The only difference between perceptual and sensory-motor activities is that the first are specialized in function of various sensory organs (ocular movements, etc.) whereas the second apply to poly-sensory realities and bring about the entire action, notably by co-ordination of vision and manual activities." E.E.G. II 86.

5.1 **Activity, sensory-motor assimilatory**
"Sensory-motor activity is first assimilatory, i.e., in the confusion of impressions which assail him, the newborn searches first to retain and find again those which fit the functioning of his organs." F.S. 87. [Pl Dr Im 83]

6. **Activity, operational**
There is the "problem of knowledge in biological terms of the relation between the organism and the environment, or in psychological terms the connection between operational activity of the subject and experience." E.G. I 25.

1. **Adaptation, organic**
"Mutual penetration between some part of a living body and a sector of the external environment." P.I. 14. [Ps In 8]
There is adaptation "when the organism is transformed as a function of the environment, and that variation effects an increase of exchanges between him and the environment which favor his survival." N.I. 11. [Or In 5] Cf. P.I. 13.

2. **Adaptation, mental or intellectual**
"Mediate exchanges between the subject and the object take place at ever increasing spatio-temporal distances and according to even more complex paths." P.I. 14. [Ps In 8–9]

"As everything else is a progressive equilibration between an assimilatory mechanism and a complementary accommodation." N.I. 13. [Or In 7] Cf. N.I. 12, 357; P.I. 14; (10) 203.

"The things which require an adaptation on our part, those which consequently excite our consciousness, are always first changes which intervene in the outside world, as opposed to chance changes in the work of thought." J.R. 119. [Ju Re 144]

"The agreement of thought and things and the agreement of thought with itself expresses the double functional invariance of adaptation and organization. Now these two aspects of thought cannot be disassociated; it is in adapting itself to things that thought becomes organized and it is in organizing itself that the thing structures itself." N.I. 14. [Or In 8]

"From the point of view of knowledge this means that the activity of the subject is relative to the composition of the object just as the latter implies the former. It is the affirmation of the irreducible interdependence between experience and reason." N.I. 21. [Or In 14]

3.1 **Adaptation, (state)**
"... is confused with the group of relations between the organism and the environment if the organism survives; that is, it becomes the same as life itself." E.G. III 81.

3.2 **Adaptation, (process)**
It is "the passage from a less stable equilibrium to a more stable equilibrium between the organism and the environment." E.G. III 81.

"The idea of adaptation is only an extension of functioning, including the exchanges between the organism and the environment. An organism is said to be adapted if those exchanges favor its normal functioning, and not adapted if they interfere." E.E.G. I 70.

4. **Adaptation** as a mobile external equilibrium (between the environment and the organism) and **Functioning** as mobile internal equilibrium. E.E.G. I 71.

4.1 **Adaptation, hereditary**
"Hereditary adaptation allows no experience outside its own characteristic exercise." N.I. 48. [Or In 47]

4.2 **Adaptation, reflex**
"... the reflex is to be understood as the organized total of which the characteristic is to survive while functioning, consequently to function sooner or later itself (repetition) by incorporating those objects

which favor its functioning (generalized assimilation) and by discriminating the situations necessary for certain specific modes of its activity (motor recognition)." N.I. 39. [Or In 38]

4.3 **Adaptation, acquired**
"Acquired adaptation implies learning related to new data of the outside environment at the same time as incorporation of the objects to schemas differentiated in such a way." N.I. 48–49. [Or In 47–48]

5. **Adaptation, inactive** (in play and imitation) opp.
Adaptation, active (in intelligence). Cf. F.S. 94. [Pl Dr Im 89]

1. **Addition, logical**
"Inclusion or logical addition (union or exclusion of objects as elements of classes)." D.Q. 332.
"Logical addition ... is nothing other than union of elements into a class or of two classes into a total class." D.Q. 266.

2. **Addition, partitive or infralogical**
"Partition or partitive addition (sectioning or union of parts) ... is infralogical, that is to say the 'whole' which determines its upper limit is the individual object ... and it envisions the parts and the whole as spatial or temporal elements." D.Q. 332.

Adherences, subjective
We observe five classes of subjective tendencies: (1) *Magical beliefs*: the world is full of tendencies or intentions for intimate connection with ourselves. (2) *Animism*. (3) *Artificialism*. (4) *Finalism*. (5) *Notion of force*: things possess a force and that implies internal energy and substantial analogy with our own muscular force. C.P. 231–232. [Co Ph Ca 244–245]

1. **Affectivity**
"By this term we understand: appropriate spoken sentiments and in particular emotions; various tendencies, consisting of 'higher emotions,' and in particular the will." A.I. 2.

2.1 **Affects, intra-individual**
"... energy elements, which are the interests, strivings, affects of all kinds which enter into intra-individual behavior: that is what we call intra-individual affects, which regulate behavior in general." A.I. 157.

2.2 **Affects, inter-individual**
"... behaviors related to people; their affective or energetic aspect constitutes the group of inter-individual affects, from the most primitive inter-individual sympathies to moral sentiments and the organization of tendencies which we have called the will." A.I. 157.

9

Analogy

"Two classifications or two divisions, two series or two placements 'are analogues' if they obey the same operational rules and one could bring about a biunivocal correspondence between their respective operations but the grouping notions are different." (11) 267.

"Clearly there is analogy where there is 'horizontal décalage'." (11) 267. (*See* **Décalage**.)

1. **Analysis, psychological, retrospective or functional**

"The same question as 'why should the cave be so black' fits both Isaacs' and [Piaget's] schemas. For Isaacs it results from an anticipation due to prior experience and frustrated by the actual experience..." (7) 138.

2. **Analysis, psychological, prospective or structural**

"But this does not hinder [for Piaget] analyzing that which the child understands by 'black' by 'should ... be' by 'why,' etc. We become aware that these notions have a different structure from the corresponding adult notions ... Consequently, structure is later than function. It has a history partly independent and is therefore a sort of crystallization of past functioning." (7) 138.

1. **Analytica I**

"Df. 28. Analytica I is by nature all action composed in a way that the truth of its result has for necessary and sufficient condition the significance of the component actions." E.E.G. IV 67.

"... an action is Analytica I when the truth of its result is entirely determined by the meanings at the moment of observation (as in the example cited where equality of sums b of $B_1 = 5$ and of $B_2 = 2 + 3$ is understood as the result of the equality of the numbers a at the moment of actual counting)." E.E.G. IV 68.

2. **Analytica II**

Action is "analytica II when b is inferred from a previous observation of a without actual observation. (For example, when the subject having established $B_1 = B_2$ by visual correspondence or counting, etc., then deduces that $B_1 = A_2 + A_2$ if B_2 is divided into A_2 and A_2 but without new observation)." E.E.G. IV 68.

"Df. 29. Analytica II is by nature all action composed such that the truth of its result is entirely determined (= necessary and sufficient condition) by inference from the significance of the actions which compose it." E.E.G. IV 69.

Analytica II is included in analytica I and thus in Logico-Mathematics. Cf. E.E.G. IV 69. (*See* **Synthesis**.)

"And"

We must distinguish "... the 'and' of serial addition (the non-commutative operation +) and the 'and' of simple union (the commutative +)." N.T. 262.

Angle and co-univocal correspondences

"An angle is a system of relations determined by the progressive diversion of two straight lines from their point of intersection and it is precisely the appropriate correspondence of the gradual separation which results finally in the co-univocal correspondence ... Because it is tied to the existence of straight lines, an angle does not exist in nature any more than the straight lines which determine it ... similarly the angles are constructed by action, before becoming operations, and do not emanate from the object in the way that heat and weight do." G.S. 268. [Co Ge 207]

1. **Animism**

It is "the tendency that the child has to ascribe life and consciousness to inanimate beings." R.M. 117. [Co Wo 132]

Animism "to us means the tendency to consider things as living and having intention." R.M. 160. [Co Wo 170]

"Animism exists much more in the child, for orientation of the mind and the schema of explanation, than for consciously systematic beliefs." R.M. 182. [Co Wo 188]

"The child ascribes to things moral attributes rather than psychological." R.M. 222. [Co Wo 224]

2.1 **Animism, diffuse**

"We call diffuse animism the general tendency of children to confuse the living and the inert..." R.M. 236. [Co Wo 234]

2.2 **Animism, systematic**

"We call systematic animism the group of explicit beliefs which the child has. The clearest one of them is that children believe that the heavenly bodies follow them." R.M. 236. [Co Wo 234]

1. **Anticipation**

"Retroaction becomes ... anticipation as this is the rule in sensory-motor learning and ... proceeds simply from repetition of retroactions." E.E.G. I 71.

2.1 **Anticipation, intuitive**

It is a "partial regulation due to the decentering of the initial intuition..." M.V. 158. [Mo Sp 169]

"It is that kind of mental experience which makes up the articulated intuition, more mobile than the static intuition of the initial perceptual simple reconstructions." M.V. 22. [Mo Sp 22]

11

2.2 **Anticipation, representative**
It is "a true decentration of intuition … it is only a representative progress (an intuition 'articulated' by its decentration)." N.T. 97.
Apperception, simple (synonym for simple perception)
"… The notion of an angle is not at all the product of a simple apperception." R.E. 412. [Ch Co Sp 348]

1. **A priori** opp. **Innate idea**
"… the *a priori* is included under the necessary form of structures only as a term of evolution of ideas and not their origin; while it is hereditary, *a priori* is thus the antithesis of what used to be called 'innate ideas'." N.I. 10. [Or In 3] Cf. J.M. 323.

2. **A priori**
"… is neither a principle, from which real actions could be derived, nor a structure from which the mind can become conscious as such, but a collection of functional relations, implying the distinction between disequilibrium of fact and an equilibrium of right." J.M. 323–324. [Mo Ju 399]

2.1 **A priori** (for epistemology)
"For epistemology, such concepts could be *a priori* only if one understands by *a priori* naturally not an innate idea, but a norm toward which reason can tend only in accordance with its degree of purification." J.M. 253. [Mo Ju 317]

2.2 **A priori** (for psychology)
"… From the psychological point of view, which is one of fact and no longer of right, an *a priori* norm has existence only in the form of equilibrium; it constitutes the ideal equilibrium toward which the phenomena tend, and we still have to know, given the facts, why they have such a form of equilibrium and not a different one." J.M. 253. [Mo Ju 317–318]

Arithmetization, progressive, of a series of numbers
"(a) From 1 to 7 or 8 [elements] a series is quasi-structured, with coordination between the succession and the iteration, which permits the solution to former problems for such small numbers…"
"(b) From 8 to 14 or 15, we speak of an ordered series of equidistant terms; that is, if the ordinal–cardinal correspondence is generally still recognized, the succession and the iteration are usually dissociated; iteration is not being used for the required predictions. (c) From 15 to 30 or 40 one has only an ordered series. Iteration is no longer recognized and the order is usually found only in reciting the entire series; the successors of a number are more

easily found than its predecessors." "(d) Beyond 30 or 40, order is no longer assured." E.E.G. XI 23–24.

1.1 **Artificialism, diffuse** (First period)
"We might say that nature is directed by people or at least gravitates around people." R.M. 392. [Co Wo 370]

1.2 **Artificialism, mythological** (Second period)
"... appears from the moment when the child asks questions about the origin of things or answers questions which we put to him. From then artificialism, up to then diffuse, is narrowed down to a certain number of myths which we have collected. Thus the sun is not seen simply as dependent on man, but as made by man by means of a stone or a match." R.M. 393. [Co Wo 371]
"As for mythological artificialism, we can presume ... that it is the problem of the origin which triggers its appearance." R.M. 399. [Co Wo 377]

1.3 **Artificialism, technical** (Third period)
"The child continues to attribute to man the general arrangement of things, but by limiting his action to the operations which can be technically achieved. As for the rest, there are things which, set going by man, have completed their nature thanks to natural processes." R.M. 396. [Co Wo 373] [for the child of 7–8 to 9–10 years].

1.4 **Artificialism, imminent** (Fourth period)
"In other words, nature is the heir of man and manufacturer like a workman or artist." R.M. 397 [Co Wo 375] [for the child of 7–8 to 9–10 years].

2.1 **Artificialism, infantile, implicit and transcendent**
"... infantile artificialism is more implicit than systematic, and transcendent much more than imminent; it considers things as the product of human manufacturing much more than it attributes to them the manufacturing activity." R.M. 255–256. [Co Wo 253]

2.2 **Artificialism, Aristotelian**
"... is imminent as well as transcendent; manufacturing activity is attributed to nature (conceived it is true as demoniacal) as well as by divine means." R.M. 255. [Co Wo 253]

1. **Assimilation**
"The act of assimilation is the first fact which encompasses in a totality the functional need, repetition and that coordination between the subject and the object which indicates implication and judgment." N.I. 46. [Or In 44]

"... objective changes in movements and external positions by the appropriate movements such that the subjective modification results from the fact that perception or the understanding of those movements and external positions is necessarily related to the appropriate 'point of view'." "... assimilation of the actual data and previous data for making the same action; i.e., the same schema is successively applied to them." F.S. 288. [Pl Dr Im 274]

"If the whole action is assimilatory and if to assimilate means to integrate the objects (or their exterior connections) to the schemas of action, the whole action related to that object will transform its properties or its relations." E.E.G. V 57.

2. **Assimilate, to**

"To assimilate, psychologically as well as biologically, is to reproduce oneself by means of the external environment; that is, thus to transform perceptions to the point of rendering them identical to the appropriate thought, i.e., to previous schemas. To assimilate is thus to conserve and in a certain sense to identify." J.R. 142. [Ju Re 174]

"Assimilation appears then to create a fixed element, a uniform manner of reacting in relation to the development of things."

"... is the fusion of a new object to an already existing schema." J.R. 143. [Ju Re 174–175] Cf. C.P. 321–327.

"... assimilation constitutes a process common to organic life and to mental activity, thus a notion common to physiology and to psychology." N.I. 43. [Or In 42]

"... assimilation takes into consideration the primitive fact generally admitted to be the most elementary of mental life: repetition." N.I. 44. [Or In 43]

"... the notion of assimilation includes from the start in the mechanism of repetition that essential element by which activity is distinguished from passive habit: coordination between the new and the old, which anticipates the process of judgment." N.I. 44. [Or In 43]

2.1 **Assimilation, biological**

"... is an incorporation of the substances and energies in the organization of the body itself..." E.E.G. III 123.

"Assimilation is ... the same functioning of a system of which organization is the structural aspect." N.I. 359. [Or In 410]

"Physiological assimilation is entirely centered on the organism; it is an incorporation from the environment into the living body and

14

the centripetal character of this process has progressed so far that the incorporated elements lose their specific nature by being transformed into substances identical to those of the body itself." N.I. 360. [Or In 412]

2.2 **Assimilation, mental**
"... elementary mental assimilation, or incorporation of objects into the schemas of the appropriate activity..." E.G. III 123.
"... incorporation of objects into the schemas of behavior, those schemas are nothing other than the catcher of the actions susceptible of being actively repeated." P.I. 13. [Ps In 8]
"... the criteria for the mental assimilation are... [1] the existence of schemas, [2] the fact that a contribution of the subject impinges on the data furnished by the object and [3] the fact that an inferential element impinges on the observation." E.E.G. V 68.

2.3 **Assimilation, rational**
"... rational assimilation or incorporation of objects into the system of operations." E.G. III 123.
"Rational assimilation, such as revealed in judgment, does not destroy at all the incorporated aspect in the subject, since in manifesting its activity it yields to the reality of it." N.I. 360–361. [Or In 412]
"... assimilation is an act of judgment in so far as uniting the experiential contents of the logical form." N.I. 359. [Or In 410]

3.1 **Assimilation, deforming** opp.

3.2 **Assimilation, equilibrated**
"... assimilation of an object to its appropriate activity and construction of relations as a function of that assimilation, at first deformed then little by little equilibrated with complementary accommodation of the schemas of assimilation to the real." E.G. II 14.

3.11 "In the primitive stages ... assimilation, wanting to be too complete, destroys at the same time the object to assimilate and the schema which assimilates ... The process is thus not reversible." J.R. 144. [Ju Re 176]

3.12 "In non-directed thought, at first, assimilation is always deforming." J.R. 143. [Ju Re 175]

3.13 "In directed intelligence of the child ... several phenomena are analogous to deforming assimilation ... for example, ... 'syncretism' ... 'condensation'." J.R. 143. [Ju Re 175]

3.2 "... tends to assure a permanent accommodation to all the new

15

combinations of experience. Equilibrium, finally achieved between assimilation and accommodation, thus explains reversibility of the operational grouping, which is at one and the same time deduction or assimilation which is indefinite and can perpetually be accommodated to new situations." M.V. 172. [Mo Sp 185]

4. **Assimilation, deductive**
    "... the accommodation to experience and alternating deductive assimilation ... in a movement of which the rhythm can vary but from which the cyclic character attests a correlation always closer between the two terms. This is, in effect, under the pressure of the need (thus of the principal schema of assimilation) and of schemas tried out by initial means how groping accommodation starts searching for new means and how it finally constructs new schemas susceptible of being coordinated with the old ones." N.I. 283. [Or In 325]

4.1 **Assimilation (judgment and concept)**
    "... assimilatory judgment is the active element of the process from which the organizing concept is the result..." N.I. 359. [Or In 410]

4.2 **Assimilation and implication**
    "... assimilation is the bond of union between motor organization and implication..." N.I. 355. [Or In 405]
    "Particular moment in the intellectual activity answering to what would be deduction in reflective thought." N.I. 241. [Or In 275]

5.1 **Assimilation from the point of view of consciousness**
    "... new objects which present themselves to consciousness do not have their own qualities which can be isolated. Or else they have been assimilated right away to such an existing schema: thing to suck, to look at, to grasp, etc. Or they are vague, nebulous, because unassimilable, and thus they create a discomfort from which there emerges sooner or later a new differentiation of the schemas of assimilation." N.I. 129. [Or In 141]

5.2 **Assimilation from the point of view of behavior**
    "From the point of view of behavior assimilation presents itself as cycles of movements or acts involving each other and closing again on themselves." N.I. 129. [Or In 141]

5.21 **Assimilation of objects to classes**
    "... before 'categorization' on a higher level, which is an assimilation of perceived objects to the classes in the proper sense, there exists an assimilation to those schemas, either sensory-motor or simply perceptual..." E.E.G. VI 55.

16

5.22 **Assimilation to the schemas of action**

"... the meaning of the result of a series of actions depends effectively only on the senses of the actions themselves (to order and to join together), or their coordinations, and not by the properties of the objects." E.E.G. I 33.

"... To assimilate an object to a schema means conferring to that object one or several meanings and it is that attribution of meaning which thus requires, even when it takes place by observation, a system of more or less complex inferences. In brief, one could say that assimilation is an association accompanied by inferences." E.E.G. V 59.

6. **Assimilation, functional**

"... it is the total relationship from need to satisfaction. From the point of view of behavior, this relation is nothing other than the operation by which a mechanism already organized is strengthened by functioning and functions in using outside data; it is then functional assimilation." N.I. 151. [Or In 170]

7. **Assimilation, reproductive**

"... the reproduction appropriate to an act of assimilation always implies the incorporation of an actual datum to a given schema, and the schema is constructed by the repetition itself." N.I. 44. [Or In 43] Cf. P.I. 121.

"... reproductive assimilation is the circular reaction or imitation of itself..." F.S. 53. [Pl Dr Im 49]

7.1 **Assimilation (reversible reproduction)**

"... any act of assimilation, that is, any relationsh'ρ between organization of the subject and external environment, presupposes a system of operations ordered in 'groups'; in effect, assimilation is always reproduction; that is, it implies a reversibility, or a possible return to the point of departure, which precisely defines the 'group'." C.R. 182. [Co Re 209–210]

8. **Assimilation, recognitive**

"... that elementary recognition consists, in the strictest sense of the word, in an 'assimilation' of the group of data presented to a defined organization already having functioned and giving way to an actual discrimination thanks only to its past functioning." N.I. 38. [Or In 37] Cf. P.I. 121.

"... recognitive and reproductive assimilation at the same time as the beginning of imitation of others by circular incorporation from the model to the circular schema..." F.S. 53. [Pl Dr Im 49]

9.   **Assimilation, generalizable**
Contains an "incorporation of more and more varied objects to a schema of a reflex." N.I. 35. [Or In 34] Cf. P.I. 121.

10.   **Assimilation, mediate**
"... mediate assimilation, by intelligently coordinated indices, which is imitation of movements known by, but invisible to, the subject." F.S. 53. [Pl Dr Im 49]

Associativity
When "the same result is obtained by two different routes [and it is] ... nevertheless recognized as 'the same'." D.Q. 330.

1.   **Atomism**
"Atomism forms at its beginning the prototype of intensive quantification since it has for its only goal the explanation of conservation." D.Q. 335.
"Early atomism consists of a schema of composition." D.Q. 116. Cf. D.Q. 139.

1.1   **Atomism, primitive**
"The first form of atomism [is] that of particles of substance, weightless and without appreciable volume." D.Q. 135.
"The atoms of our subjects are nothing other than particles themselves but cut down in size and having become entirely invisible." D.Q. 136–137. Cf. D.Q. 116.

1.   **Attitude, antigenetic**
"... always comes back to locating a virtual preforming at the beginning of actual knowledge." E.G. I. 34.

2.   **Attitude, infantile toward children and toward the adult**
"... are essentially different: the first is made of cooperation; the second is made of intellectual submission." L.P. 55. [La Th 250]

3.   **Attitude, empirical or intuitive**
"... at a certain level of development the empirical attitude or sometimes intuitive fact so completely obstructive to the operational grouping that it then results in the monstrous and contradictory product of irrepresentable representations or of intuitions which cannot be intuited." M.V. 15. [Mo Sp 14]

Autonomy opp. **Heteronomy**
Between "anomy proper to egocentrism and heteronomy proper to constraint," we find autonomy: "disciplined or self-disciplined activity, equidistant from inertia [anomy] or from forced activity" [heteronomy]. E.G. III 269.

Awareness (*See* **Realization, conscious**)

1. **Axioms**
    "... the axioms of logistics appear to the psychologist as the expression of a simple 'conscious realization' of the operational mechanism as such." T.O.L. VII.
2. **Axiomatic and concrete thought**
    "... the ties which connect axiomatic to concrete thought are not to be found in their content ... but in the form itself ... in the connection between formal axiomatic coordinations and the coordinations from which they proceed genetically, which is the bond between abstract and concrete." E.G. I 233.

B

1.1 **Behavior** (such as adaptation or readaptation)
    Behavior is "all behavior — which is concerned with an act unfolding outwardly as well as one interiorized within thought." P.I. 8. [Ps In 4]
1.2 **Behavior** (as a particular case of exchange between the exterior world and the subject)
    Physiological (material) exchange and psychological exchange (functional). P.I. 8. [Ps In 4]
1.3 **Behavior, social**
    "There are three types of behavior: motor behavior, egocentric behavior (with exterior constraint) and cooperation. To these three types of social behaviors there correspond three types of rules: the motor rule, the rule due to unilateral respect and the rule due to mutual respect." J.M. 61–62. [Mo Ju 86]
2.   **Behavior and intelligence**
    "Possessing an energetic or emotional aspect and structural or cognitive aspect." P.I. 9–10. [Ps In 5]
2.11 **Behavior, intelligent** (First group)
    "Those of which the aim is in some way imposed by the exterior environment." Circular reactions, primary, secondary, tertiary; understanding of indices, exploration. N.I. 279. [Or In 321]
2.12 **Behavior, intelligent** (Second group)
    "... is formed by the behavior of which the aim, to the contrary, originates from a spontaneous intention of the subject himself." N.I. 279–280. [Or In 321]
    "... consists of three distinct types: 'application of known means to

19

new situations,' 'discovery of new means by active experimentation,' and 'invention of new means by mental combination'." N.I. 280. [Or In 322]

2.21 **Behavior, phenomenistic** (in the development of the notion of an object at the fourth stage: 8–12 months)
"... phenomenistic because the object remains dependent on its context and not isolated because of a shifting endowed with permanence." C.R. 60. [Co Re 65]

2.22 **Behavior, dynamic** (in the development of the notion of object at the fourth stage: 8–12 months)
"They are dynamic on the other hand, since the object remains in the prolongation of the effort and of the feeling of efficiency connected with the action through which the subject finds it again." C.R. 60. [Co Re 65]

3. **Behaviors** (classification)
(1) hereditary organic (instinct), (2) sensory motor structures (can be acquired), (3) representative structures (thought). P.I. 143 (note). [Ps In 119 (note)]

3.1 **Behavior, verbal**
"... is an action, without doubt having become smaller and remaining inside ... which simply replaces things by their signs and movements by their evocation." P.I. 43. [Ps In 32]

4. **Behaviors, experimental**
"The essence of the experimental behaviors (which are scientific, technical or moral) lies also not in a common faith but in the rules of mutual control." J.M. 278. [Mo Ju 346]

5. **Behavior of support**
"... consists in bringing distant objects closer by retracting the supports upon which they rest." N.I. 245. [Or In 280]

1. **Belief** (definitions)
"Df. 23a. For a subject considered at a given moment a proposition is to be accompanied by belief if that subject acts according to this proposition."
"Df. 23b. A proposition is taken as true if it is accompanied by belief. A proposition is held false if after a plan of action has been created, this action is discarded." E.E.G. IV 61.
"Df. 24. The subject believes more or less in a proposition according to the kind, number, and resistance of the obstacles which he is prepared to overcome in order to continue his action in accordance with said proposition."
"Df. 25. A belief is called provoked by observation if it has as

necessary condition an adequate perceptual contact with an object (the term contact means that this object comes into one of the subject's sensory fields) at the moment of triggering of the perception." E.E.G. IV 62.

"... a belief is a disposition to act in a certain way in the presence of certain objects; i.e., according to our terminology, it expresses a schema..."

"(1) The resulting disposition to act must be obtained by relating the dispositions to act [premises] and only by them.

(2) The resulting disposition to act must be obtained by applying certain initial schemas (premises) to objects of other initial schemas, or by applying combinations of parts of the initial schemas to their objects or by other analogous proceedings."

"Df. 26. A belief is said to be provoked by inference when it results in relating the initial schemas (in the sense of conditions 1 and 2 of the preceding remark." E.E.G. IV 64.

2.1 **Belief, suggested**
"If a child makes an effort to answer a question, but if the question is suggestive or if the child simply tries to satisfy the examiner without using his own reflection, we call it a suggested belief." R.M. XVI. [Co Wo 10]

2.2 **Belief, triggered**
"If a child responds with a reflection by drawing the response from his own reserves without suggestion, but if the question is new for him, we call it a triggered belief." R.M. XVI. [Co Wo 11]

2.3 **Belief, spontaneous**
"Finally, if the child does not need to think in order to answer a question, but if he can give a ready-made answer because it is already formed or formable, it is a spontaneous belief." R.M. XVII. [Co Wo 11]

C

1. **Categories, fundamental or regulatory**
"... appear to us definable from the static point of view through the notions of totality and of relations, and from the dynamic point of view through those of ideal and value." N.I. 15. [Or In 10]

2. **Categories essential to the thought of the child (3 to 7–8 years)**

2.1 "Explanatory function: Causality. Reality. Time and Place.

2.2   Mixed function: Motivation for acts. Justification of rules.

2.3   Implicitory function: Classification. Name. Number. Logical relations." L.P. 206. [La Th 237]

3.   **Categories, real**

There is "the process of relating between a universe more and more external to the self and intellectual activity progressively internalized which explains the evolution of real categories, i.e., the notions of object, space, causality, and time." C.R. 312. [Co Re 356]

3.1   **Categories, the most "real"**

Those "which express further the centrifugal process of explanation and accommodation..." "... (those which imply further the activity of reasoning, and *hic* and *nunc* inherent in experience, like causality, substance or object, space and time; thus each works as an indissociable synthesis of data and deduction)..." N.I. 17. [Or In 11]

3.2   **Categories, the most "formal"**

"... they make possible assimilation of things to intellectual organization and the construction of implications. They can lead to an indefinite, deductive elaboration, like logical and mathematical relations." N.I. 17. [Or In 11]

1.   **Causality, infantile** (origin)

1.1   **Precausality**

A.

(1) Psychological (of motivation).

(2) By pure finality.

(3) Phenomenistic.

(4) Of participation.

(5) Magical causality (through efficacy).

B.

(6) Moral causality.

(7) Artificial causality.

(8) Animistic causality.

(9) Dynamic causality ... Once animism as such is eliminated, there still remain in things forces susceptible of explaining their activity and their movements.

1.2   **Causality, strict**

(10) By environmental reaction or 'antiperistasis.'

(11) Mechanical causality proper means explanation by contact and transmission: the wind pushes the clouds, the pedals move the bicycle, etc.

(12) Causality by generation: As soon as the child gives up con-

sidering the stars and clouds as made by man he tries to conceive them as being born from each other. It is this kind of relation which we call generation.

(13) By identification of substance: Let us suppose that identification starts when the bodies being born from each other are no longer endowed with power to grow like living things.

(14) By condensation and rarefaction: This way the matter is more or less condensed or rarefied.

(15) By atomistic composition: The bodies are considered composed of more or less dense or separated particles.

(16) By spatial explanation: The explanation of why water rises if solid bodies are put into it refers (around 9–10 years) to the volume of the submerged body. C.P. Sec. IV §2. [Co Ph Ca 258–266]

2.   **Causality of the possible**

"From the physical point of view, only the real has a causal character, since the virtual or the possible plays a positive role only in the mind of the physicist. In other words, the possible is only an instrument of deduction or of calculation whereas causality is exclusively real. Now the situation in an operational equilibrium is very different, since in this domain the real and the possible are both psychological; i.e., both are located in the mind of the subject and interfere causally with each other in the heart of the constituent mechanisms of the mental life of this subject." "... In a state of psychological equilibrium the possible (structurally as well as materially) play a causal role as much as the real operations. We may even say that all mental life is completely dominated by this kind of causality of the possible." L.E.A. 231. [Gr Lo Th 262–263]

2.1   **Causality of the operational possible**

"Causality of the possible becomes manifest in form of a kind of action of implicit schemas upon explicit operations, being determined not only by acts of thought which were really performed, just preceding the new operation, but by the totality of the operational field which is constructed of the possible operations." L.E.A. 234. [Gr Lo Th 265] Cf. L.E.A. 294.

2.2   **Causality of the materially possible**

"... the causal function of the materially possible is the conducting of the hypothesis which permits the subject to surpass what he perceives or conceives, with the belief in the real in order to start in the direction of that which can be perceived without actual decision as to verification." L.E.A. 231. [Gr Lo Th 263]

3.   **Causality and constancy**
"... causality [is a] particular variety of constant aiming at the conservation of a movement of one moving thing to another..." M.P. 262. [Me Pe 206]
"... causality is finally to be conceived as intelligence in so far as it is applied to temporal relations and organizes a durable universe." C.R. 276. [Co Re 315]

4.   **Causality, noetic** opp. **Practical causality**
"Just as the object of primitive physics and geometrical space reflect the phenomena to the practical object and space, it could be that noetic causality consists in conscious realization of practical causality, but in a conscious realization it is not limited to prolongation of the last stage to which sensory-motor intelligence leads, and thanks to a totality of décalages, it repeats stages analogous to those which we observe on the initial plane." C.R. 193. [Co Re 221]

5.   **Causality, elementary**
"... the initial universe is not a net of causal sequences, but a simple collection of events surging as a prolongation of the activity. Efficiency and phenomenism are thus the two poles of this elementary causality from which are absent physical spatiality and a feeling of a self acting on behalf of interior cause." C.R. 191–192. [Co Re 220] Cf. C.R. 246.

5.1   **Causality by efficacy**
"When there are no spatial relations between A and B, A is held to produce B to the extent that A is a manifestation of the voluntary activity or of the personal power of the child or of the subject in general." (4) 33.

5.2   **Causality, phenomenistic**
"When an event A is held to produce an event B simply because A and B were perceived together and without any spatially intelligible or personally effective relations." (4) 33.

6.   **Causality and activity**
"... the logico-mathematical operations consist in actions performed by the subject on objects, whereas causality adds to these actions (which it also understands) analogous actions attributed to the object as such; in causality thus the transformations of the object become operations in as much as they are encompassed in the composition of the very operation of the subject." E.G. II 278.
"What else indeed is causality if not the spatio-temporal coordination of movements of which time itself is one of the dimensions?" N.T. 7.

24

Cause

"... we define cause as deduction from laws..." E.G. II 322. Cf. E.G. II 317.

"The process followed by causal explanation consists in inserting real modifications into a group of possible operational transformations, from which they thus draw their intelligibility in becoming particular cases." E.G. II 347.

"... 'cause' is not to be looked for at the level of 'law,' but rather at the level of deduction from a law starting from one or from a group of others, thus at the level of deductive construction..." T.P. I 126.

"... cause is a logical coordination (2) 'projected' into a real coordination (3)." T.P. I 128.

1. **Centration**

   It is the "fixation of the sense organs." M.V. 206. [Mo Sp 222–223] (*See* **Decentration**.)

   "Perceptual space is then not homogeneous, but it is centered at any moment, and the centration zone corresponds to a spatial dilation, whereas the periphery of this central zone is more contracted farther away from the center." P.I. 88. [Ps In 72]

   Centration (Ct) is therefore not an entity because it is "reducible to relation complexes. Centration corresponds to a space of which the different regions can be dilated or contracted according to probabilistic mechanism to be established..." M.P. 9. [Me Pe xxi] (*See* **Temporal effects**.)

2. **Centration, privileged**

   It is a "deforming assimilation." M.V. 169. [Mo Sp 181] Cf. M.V. 170.

3. **Centration, enveloping**

   "... concerning tachistoscopic experiments ... centrations which, starting from a necessary fixation point, contain the relations which generate an illusion, i.e., the total of deforming and deformed elements of a figure." M.P. 135. [Me Pe 100]

4. **Centration of action** (*See* **Egocentrism** and **Centration**)

   "... in the case of beginning sensory-motor intelligence, it is distorted (falsified) by a centration which is no longer perceptual only, but which is constituted by the application point of the momentary action visualized in its totality (perceptions, movements and affectivity)." N.T. 124.

5. **Centration on the body itself**

   "... there is [a] relatively complex development [of the group of motor displacements] (with decentration after an initial state of centration on the body itself, where the group is yet impossible because of lack of autonomous paths of mobile objects and of object permanence)." E.E.G. I 46.

6.   **Centration, real** opp. **Virtual centration**
"Beside real centrations and decentrations, we have to distinguish virtual centrations and decentrations due to action during the time of mutual perceptions..." N.T. 123. (*See* **Decentration** 6.1.)

7.   **Centration, aberrant**
"... beside equally adapted infantile centrations there is a large number which we shall call aberrant..." [which do not fixate the object to be perceived]. M.P. 177. [Me Pe 139]

1.   **Chance**
"... chance consists of that which, in reality, remains irreducible to reversible operations. And these operations above are able to grasp that which resists them." I.H. 11.
"... chance is opposed to order; the subjects not yet in possession of the operations susceptible of disclosing a true causal order are not capable either of recognizing the existence of fortuity: everything appears to them halfway between suspected but not established order and not dangerous but simply capricious arbitrariness." I.H. 86.
"... the idea of chance implies thus that of combinatory operations of which the fortuitous fact constitutes a fraction of the accomplishment." I.H. 174.
"... chance is making an inventory of the possibilities as such, once the possible has been distinguished from the real and the necessary. So, on one hand, the distribution of the total group becomes predictable, and on the other hand, each isolated case acquires a probability by being a fraction of this totality." I.H. 242.

2.1 **Chance, physical**, opp.
2.2 **Chance, logico-mathematical**
"... indetermination in comparison with spatio-temporal operations (physical chance) or by correspondence with logico-arithmetic operations (random drawing from among a collection, or logico-mathematical chance)." I.H. 236.

Change of scale
"Change of scale consists (1) in extending further the field of application of actions, therefore the field of equilibrium (2) in utilizing new actions which create a more mobile equilibrium and (3) in finding greater stability and permanent conditions of equilibrium, but at the cost of more pronounced abstraction which neglects certain charac-

teristics of reality to the sole benefit of the ones affected by the structuration. The change of scale occurs therefore in the direction of a better equilibrium..." E.E.G. II 112.

"... the succession of structures, as function of scale changes, follows the same laws of equilibrium as the constitution of each particular structure..." E.E.G. II 115.

Character of the individual

"The schema is conserved in so far as the mode of reaction and the group of those schemas in which we would call the character of the individual." A.I. 94.

Circle, fundamental epistemological, of subject and object

"... the object is never known except through modifications which the actions of the subject exert on it. On the other hand, the subject never knows of itself except through transformations which the object provokes in his actions." E.E.G. I 84. (*See* **Reductions 2.1** and **2.2**.)

Circle of sciences

"... psychology connects biology with mathematics, explaining the formation of abstract beings starting from living behaviors, in the same way as physics connects mathematics with biology preparing the explanation of organized structures starting from material realities which are mathematically interpreted. The sciences thus come full-circle." E.G. III 131.

"The real explains the mind through physics and biology; the mind explains the real through psychology and mathematics." (9) 46.

1.   **Class**
"... is a union of terms (individual or subclasses) considered as equivalents independently of their differences..." G.N. 121. [Co Nu 94] "A class is the totality of terms which can be substituted for each other in discussion assigning a truth value to a propositional function." T.L. 53 (df. 8).

2.   **Class, logical**
"... a logical class and ... its division into subclasses or into component elements ... is a system of unions (additive or multiplicative) and of disjunctions (logical subtractions or divisions)." D.Q. 272–273.

"... is the union of individuals which jointly present the same quality." G.N. 217. [Co Nu 177]

2.1   **Class, logical** opp. **Perceptual aggregate**
"There exists an essential difference which separates groups or perceptual aggregates from logical classes; whereas in the latter

27

there is an exact correspondence between the predicates or relations considered in understanding and in the distribution in extension of the elements thus qualified. The perceptual aggregates on the other hand contain no regular correspondence between the perceived qualities of their elements and their grouping in the more or less extended totalities." G.S.L. 17. [Ea Gr Lo 8]

3.   **Class, intensive**
They "consist of the weakly structured and the semistructured classes." T.L. 72.

"When in a system of classes, the properties characterizing the total class (B) cannot be composed, through the defining operations, starting from the characteristic properties of one of the subclasses (A), the quantification of the system remains intensive." T.L. 75.

3.1   **Class, weakly structured**
"... classes as well as the individuals belonging to one of them (for example B) are connected to each other by the possession of certain common properties ($\xleftrightarrow{b}$) belonging to that class, without any given operation permitting to construct, starting from these properties ($\xleftrightarrow{b}$) the qualities ($\xleftrightarrow{c}$), etc., belonging to the classes C, etc., in which the class B is included, nor the qualities ($\xleftrightarrow{a}$) belonging to classes A included in B." T.L. 69. (df. 11).

3.2   **Class, semistructured**
"We call 'semistructured' the ordered classes $A \to B \to C$ ... the same as the asymmetrical relation ($\to$), uniting an element A of that class to an element C, constituting the sum of the partial relations $(A \to B) + (B \to C)$, but without any given operation being permitted to compose the relation $A \to C$ from the single relation $A \to B$ (i.e., without its being possible to transform $A \to B$ into $B \to C$ or into $A \to C$)." T.L. 70. (df. 12).

4.   **Class, structured**
"We call 'structured classes' such classes starting from which properties (relations) which characterize a subclass A, one may, by means of the given operations, combine the characteristic relations from other subclasses A' as well as the relations defining the total class B (or reciprocally combine the properties of A or of A' starting from those of B)." T.L. 70. (df. 13).

5.   **Class of equivalent actions**
"... two actions are said to be equivalent when the subject establishes the same relations between the same objects or between more and

28

more different objects (including the relations between those objects and his own body)."

"Df. 7. The schema of an action corresponding to a class of equivalent actions from the subject's point of view is the common structure which characterizes that equivalence." E.E.G. IV 46.

1. **Classification**

"... on all levels of development there exists classifying behavior either at the differentiated state, or the classifications remain inherent in other forms of action; either the subject would distribute the objects in collections, or else he would act on them in any fashion (knowing, balancing, etc.) but his actions would imply the classifications as well..." E.E.G. XIV 183.

2. **Classification by convenience** (partitive)

"... to classify by empirical convenience the cradle in the same collection as the baby would result in uniting not only the two similar elements (by resemblances) but one element (the baby) and one of his more or less constant attributes (the cradle). Then, that union constitutes a new relation between the parts of a total object, thus a partitive belonging and not an inclusive one..." G.S.L. 43–44. [Ea Gr Lo 37]

3. **Classification, simple**

"... a system such that the classification is not a properly constituted group. The group belonging to its subject is limited to the collection of the disjointed parts $(A, A', B',$ etc.)." T.O.L. note 197.

Co-displacement

A correspondence "of order between two displacements reduced to the overtaking model." M.V. 172. [Mo Sp 184]

"... operations of co-displacement, i.e., the correspondence between placements and displacements..." M.V. 258. [Mo Sp 280]

Coherence, preoperational

"Acquisitions due to a process of equilibrium distinct from learning in the strict sense." E.E.G. VII 37–38.

1. **Collection, figural**

"... when a child arranges the elements to classify them into groups according to spatial configurations..." G.S.L. 26. [Ea Gr Lo 18]

1.1 **Collection, figural, Types of**

"(1) The alignments (of a single dimension), continuous or discontinuous. (2) The collective objects: figural collections in two or three dimensions formed by similar elements and constituting a unity of a single member of the geometrical structure. (3) Complex objects: the same characteristics but collections formed from heterogeneous elements. Two varieties: geometrical structures and forms of empirical meaning." G.S.L. 28. [Ea Gr Lo 20]

2. **Collection, nonfigural**

"... collections not yet forming classes because inclusions are missing but no longer containing any definite figure connected to its properties" [in comprehension and in extension]. G.S.L. 27, note 1. [Ea Gr Lo 19]

Combinative

"At the level where hypothetico-deductive operations are formed (i.e., reasoning on a proposition considered as an hypothesis independently of the truth of its content) one watches the construction of a new structure which results in a second form of union (or 'combination') between the structures with inversions $[N]$ and the structures with reciprocity $[R]$." E.E.G. XIV 194.

The first form is the general synthesis of number with groupings of classes (where N is understood as the inverse operation $A - A = 0$) and the groupings of asymmetrical relations (R is understood as the relation of order with permutation of the domain and of its codomain.)

The propositional combinative derives genetically from a generalization of elementary additional grouping of vicariance. E.E.G. XIV 196.

$(A_1 + A_1' = A_2 + A_2' = ... = B)$. For example, $A_1 =$ Frenchmen, $A_1' =$ strangers to France, $A_2 =$ Chinese, $A_2' =$ the strangers to China, $B =$ everybody. Cf. T.L. 114.

The discovery of the notion "any ('any number' and 'any operation') is connected with [the] combinative in formation from the development of the vicariance." E.E.G. XVII 14.

The hypothetico-deductive operations (11–12 years to 14–15 years) present "the new fundamental character of combinative operation ... because the 16 binary operations of bivalent logic of propositions is constructed by combinations of the four basic combinations $(p . q \lor \bar{p} . q \lor p . \bar{q} \lor \bar{p} . \bar{q})$ which by themselves only constitute the elementary 'grouping' of a simple multiplicative nature." E.E.G. XIV 187–188.

Combinative (Example). **The four ways of implication**

$p \supset q = pq \lor \bar{p}q \lor \bar{p}\bar{q}$ (normal disjunctive form)

Inversion $N(p \supset q) = p \cdot \bar{q}$

30

Reciprocity $R(p \supset q) = \bar{p}\bar{q} \vee p\bar{q} \vee pq = q \supset p$

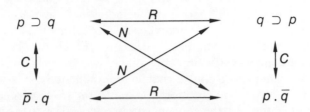

T.L. 272.

(1) the direct operation with its inverse cancels itself

$(p \supset q) . (p . \bar{q}) = 0$

(2) the direct operation with its reciprocal gives the equivalence

$(p \supset q) . (q \supset p) = (p . q) \overset{?}{\underset{c}{=}} (p . q)$.

E.E.G. XIV 195.

The structure which regulates the propositional operations is precisely the *INRC* group. (*See* **Commutative *INRC* group of 4 elements.**)

Commutativity

"We have to recognize that at an initial level of development certain logico-mathematical truths which then would give way to immediate deductive evidence are at first accepted only through the intermediary of an experimental constant ... We can at first recall the one of commutativity in general: the fact that $2+3 = 3+2$ or that 5 elements counted from left to right or from right to left give the same results, is accepted at first only upon observation. The sum is not conceived with evidence as independent of order, whereas at a later level the fact is understood as necessary analytically from the moment when one neither adds nor takes away any unit." E.E.G. XIV 247.

Complementarity

"Df. 3. We call complementarity a' the differences between the members of class A' and those of class A if they resemble each other under B; for example, first cousins of A are the grandsons of the same grandfather (thus are the Bs) but do not have the same father as the As, thus $a' = b$ not a..." G.S.L. 16. [Ea Gr Lo 7]

Composition, additive, of classes

"It is ... the inclusions of partial classes in a total class." G.N. 200.

1. **Comprehension**

"Df. 1. In a system of classes A, A' and B such that $B = A + A'$ and

31

$A \times A' = 0$ (A' thus being the complement of A under B, since A and A' are disjoint), we call 'comprehension' of those classes the totality of qualities common to the individuals in each of these classes and the totality of differences distinguishing the members of one class from those of another." G.S.L. 16. [Ea Gr Lo 7]

1.1 **Comprehension and extension**
"Whereas 'comprehension' based on resemblances is assured as soon as we have sensory-motor assimilation from perception of common qualities and the elementary abstraction tied to the practical finalities, the extension of concepts is accessible to the subject only through the intermediary of a precise symbolism and also if the verbal signs are subordinate to a system of well regulated quantifications." G.S.L. 282–283. [Ea Gr Lo 283]

2. **Comprehension of indices**
"... this constitutes a term intermediary between judgment and reasoning: it is judgment to the extent that it is immediate assimilation of the index, and reasoning to the extent that this assimilation is full of predictions, i.e., virtual deduction. But this intermediary finds its equivalent in verbal thought; the majority of judgments are implied reasonings." N.I. 235. [Or In 268]

3. **Comprehension, verbal**
"... bearing on the causal or logical connections." L.P. 104. [La Th 88]

3.1 **Comprehension, global**
"That is the manner by which the reproducer has understood the whole account of the explainer." L.P. 104. [La Th 88]
"We distinguish therein on one hand the implicit and explicit understanding and on the other hand the understanding of the explainer in relation to the adult and the understanding of the reproducer in relation to that of the explainer." L.P. 105. [La Th 88–89]

3.11 **Comprehension, explicit**
"... that which the child spontaneously reproduces." L.P. 105. [La Th 89]

3.12 **Comprehension, implicit**
"This means that which the child has understood without his necessarily being able to explain it." L.P. 105. [La Th 88]

4. **Comprehension, operational, of duration**
"... to understand the duration of an interval between states equals coordinating distinct speeds." E.G. II 37.

1. **Concept**
   "Df. 14. A concept is the understanding of the meaning of a term."
   E.G. IV 51.

2. **Concept and schema**
   A concept "is nothing but a schema of action or operation, and it is by performing the actions bringing about *A* and *B* that one observes whether they are compatible or not." P.I. 41. [Ps In 30]

3. **Concepts, infantile**
   "... infantile concepts are a product of juxtaposition and not of the synthesis of a certain number of elements yet disparate and which will only progressively become related." J.R. 129. [Ju Re 157]
   "... their apparent unity would be that which gives syncretism to the diverse elements, i.e., a subjective unity, not susceptible to initiating logical reasoning." J.R. 130. [Ju Re 157]

1. **Conditions for passing from a sensory-motor level to a reflexive one**
   "(1) the increase in speeds permits the knowledge tied to the successive phases of the action to be molded into a simultaneous totality. (2) Conscious realization is no longer simply derived from the results of an action but from the separate steps themselves... (3) multiplication of distances permits to prolong the actions which are related to the realities themselves by the symbolic actions leading to representations and thus passing the limits of space and immediate time." P.I. 145. [Ps In 121]

2.1 **Conditions, elementary axiomatic**
   We call "elementary axiomatic conditions those axioms necessary and sufficient for formally deducing a system." E.E.G. XIV 268.

2. **Conditions, elementary genetic**
   Elementary genetic conditions are "the starting structures as well as the actions or operations permitting the passage of these structures to those whose formation we have to explain." E.E.G. XIV 268.
   Configuration
   It is a "structure not depending on a single object but on a totality of elements related by a total simple form; it is another image. It is thus no more an image of an object, but is the image of a schema and an image which, in intuitive thought, is necessary for the existence of the schema..." F.S. 259. [Pl Dr Im 243]

1. **Consciousness**
   Df. "Consciousness is — essentially a system of meanings." E.E.G. I 81.

"... the most general characteristic without doubt of the states of consciousness is to imply the 'meanings' of the cognitive aspect (capable of being expressed as true or false) or the affective aspect (values) or, more probably, both at the same time. Then, neither the connection between meaning nor the relation of significate to signifier arises from causality. We would speak thus of 'implication in the larger sense' for characterizing those two sorts of connections including the second (which one can call 'designation'), and our hypothesis is that the mode of proper connection with the phenomena of consciousness is implication in the larger sense, of which implication in the narrow sense is a particular case." T.P.I. 150.

2. **Consciousness of the rule**
   "Consciousness of the rule, i.e., the manner by which children of different ages represent the compulsory character, sacred or decisive, the heteronomy or autonomy appropriate to the rules of the game." J.M. 2. [Mo Ju 14–15]

3. **Consciousness of legality**
   "... certain physical events (the alternation of night and day ...) are reproduced with sufficient precision for giving rise to consciousness of 'legality' or all the means for favoring the appearance of the motor schemas of prediction." J.M. 32. [Mo Ju 51–52]

4. **Consciousness of values**
   "The value or the interest of intermediate acts which serve as means is subordinated to the value of its goal..." N.I. 134. [Or In 149]

5. **Consciousness of the ideal**
   "The act to be accomplished is part of a real totality of previously organized acts." N.I. 134. [Or In 149]

6. **Consciousness, primary or protoplasmic**
   "... the primary consciousness or the consciousness of 'that which is desirable,' of 'that which is painful,' is directly projected upon reality, by absolute realism, then by immediate realism and only through découpage of this real will there come about the double feeling of objective data and of its own emotion which evaluates them." R.M. 112. [Co Wo 127]
   "If we say that childish thought proceeds from the real to the objective, we say that originally the child places on the same plane all the contents of consciousness, without distinguishing the self from the exterior world. This means especially that the construction of a notion of reality presupposes a successive separation of that protoplasmic consciousness into two complimentary universes, the

34

objective universe and the subjective universe." C.P. 275. [Co Ph Ca 242]

1. **Conservation (substantial) of the object**

"At first it means prolonging the coordinations of habit, then the object is constructed by intelligence, and it constitutes the first invariant thereof." P.I. 133. [Ps In 110]

1.1 **Conservation of the whole**

"... the property of concrete operation, as well in the area of logical 'groupings' as those of partitive composition, is precisely to assure the free mobility of its parts at the heart of the whole necessarily conserving itself as union of its elements (real or virtual)." G.S. 414. [Co Ge 327]

2. **Conservation and group**

"The discovery of a notion of conservation by the child is always the expression of the construction of a (logical or infralogical) 'grouping' or of a (mathematical) 'group' of operations." G.S. 354. [Co Ge 278]

"We observe ... that once the conservation is formed, it is based simply on identity." G.S. 138. [Co Ge 102]

"... conservation constitutes a necessary condition for all rational activity..." G.N. 6. [Co Nu 3]

2.1 **Conservation, quantitative**

"Quantities which are conserved are invariants of groupings or of groups." D.Q. 214. (*See* **Invariance**.)

3. **Conservation, affective**

"... that elementary reciprocity which starts at the same time as the beginnings of socialization depends on the beginning of reciprocity which already existed at the sensory-motor level." A.I. 79.

4. **Conservation, collective**

"... reversibility of thought thus is connected with collective conservation, outside of which individual thought would enjoy only an infinitely more restricted mobility." P.I. 196. [Ps In 164–165]

1. **Constancy, perceptual**

"A perceptual constancy is recognized by three characteristics: conservation of a property perceived in spite of the transformation of other properties of an object or figure; a 'double phenomenon' permitting at the same time the perception of the conserved and transformed properties; and in compensation permitting the assurance of constancy as function of the transformations in the inverse sense of nonconstant properties." M.P. 297. [Me Pe 234]

There is assured "by sensory-motor assimilation 'transporting' or 'transposing' the involved relationships where there is modification of position or of removal of perceived objects." P.I. 135. [Ps In 111]

2. **Constancy, simple**
"... simple constancies (applied to the conservation of a property of a single object and not to the conservation of a movement transmitted from one object to another, as in perceptual causality..." M.P. 303. [Me Pe 239]

Constraint (*See* **Cooperation**)

1. **Construction of number**
"... consists in equalizing differences; that means, reuniting into one operational totality the class and asymmetrical relation. The numerous terms are thus at the same time equivalent between each other in what they share of a class, and different one from another by their numerical order, and in which they can take part in an asymmetrical relationship." G.N. 122. [Co Nu 95]
"The hypothesis from which we started ... is that this construction (of number) is correlated with the development of logic and that at the prelogical level there corresponds a prenumerical period." G.N. II. [Co Nu viii]

2. **Construction and reflection**
"The genetic process is thus simultaneously constructive and reflexive, and the reflexive factor is in part constructive, just as the constructive factor is itself in part reflexive: the reflexive part enriches retroactively the ultimate element, while the construction incorporates it effectively into a new combination." E.G. III 300.

2.1 **Constructivism**
"... the formal obligation of constantly transcending the systems already constructed to assure non-contradiction converges with the genetic tendency to pass constantly the already achieved constructions by filling in the gaps..." E.E.G. XIV 324.

1. **Contents** opp. **Form**
"The 'content' of operational connection consists of the data, or the terms capable of substituting for them, while 'form' is that which remains unchanged in the course of such substitutions." T.L. 41. (df. 4)

2. **Content, extralogical**
"We shall call 'extralogical content' the terms which are incapable of playing the role of contents." T.L. 42. (df. 6)

3. **Content of a physical proposition**
    "The content of a physical proposition, in other words the fact which it expresses, contains itself a form which encompasses a content of a lower scale, which again contains a new form, and so on, but with more pronounced indifferentiation as you descend on the scale. E.E.G. V 97.

4. **Content of time** opp. **Time**
    "... it is the content only of time, i.e., the events of reality, exterior or psychological, which are irreversible, whereas time itself as organizing schema consists in a system of reversible operations." N.T. 263.

1. **Contradiction, logical and psychological**
    "From the logical point of view, there is a first and undefinable notion which can be described simply by showing the moral impossibility of simultaneously affirming the contradictory propositions. But, from the psychological point of view, there is a problem because one does not see how the mind gets to the point which wants to avoid the contradictions nor which are the conditions of non-contradiction. The psychological structure (and not logical) of thought no more than the structure of any natural phenomenon cannot be non-contradictory from the start, if we define non-contradiction by the entire accountability or the mutual dependence of the parts or of the movements; it is too evident that at the heart of the organism, for example, there coexist a mass of antagonistic tendencies in an unstable equilibrium and the development of one leads to the destruction of the others. It is understood that the elementary psychological life, instinctive or affective, follows the same necessity." J.R. 139. [Ju Re 170] Cf. J.R. 141.

2.1 **Contradiction by amnesia**
    "The child hesitates, as it often happens to us too, between two opinions ... There are good reasons for each one of these opinions, but instead of choosing one or refusing to make a statement, the child will affirm both, one after the other." J.R. 134–135. [Ju Re 164]
    "... this is the generality of infantile amnesia." J.R. 136. [Ju Re 165]
    "This contradiction is not really due to amnesia, but to insufficient consciousness which is analogous." J.R. 137. [Ju Re 167]

2.2 **Contradiction by condensation**
    "'Condensation' is therefore the result of overdetermination: the same concept would then not be a 'system' but a heterogeneous and

contradictory conglomeration, the result of a 'participation' among several realities at once." J.R. 137. [Ju Re 167–168]

Conviction (*See* **Belief**)

1. **Cooperation** opp. **Constraint**

"In any field we have to distinguish between two types of social relations: constraint and cooperation. The first implies an element of unilateral respect, of authority and of prestige; the second is a simple exchange between equal individuals." J.M. 41. [Mo Ju 61] Cf. J.M. 272.

"Constraint of tradition imposes opinions or customs, and that is the end. Cooperation does not impose anything if not the very procedures of intellectual or moral exchange. (Synnomic of Baldwin as opposed to syndoxic.)" J.M. 50. [Mo Ju 73]

Constraint opp. **Cooperation** (unilateral respect opp. mutual respect)

"The big difference between constraint and cooperation, or between unilateral and mutual respect, is that the first imposes ready-made beliefs or rules to be adopted all together, and that the second imposes only a method of mutual control and verification, in the intellectual domain, of discussion and justification, in the moral domain." J.M. 70. [Mo Ju 97]

2. **Cooperation**

"... cooperation consists of a system of operations by which the activities of the subject acting upon objects and the activities of the subjects acting upon each other are in reality reduced to one and the same collective system, in which the social and logical aspects are inseparable in form as well as in content." E.G. III 263. Cf. P.I. 195; J.M. 48.

"... cooperation appears as the limiting term, as ideal equilibrium to which any constraining relation tends..." J.M. 65. [Mo Ju 90]

2.1 **Cooperation and personality**

"Cooperation is therefore a factor of personality, if we understand by personality neither the unconscious self of infantile egocentrism nor the anarchic self of egoism in general, but the self which finds its place and submits itself, in order to be respected, to the norms of reciprocity and of objective discussion." J.M. 69. [Mo Ju 95–96]

1. **Coordination**

"... is the multiple assimilation constructing an increasing number of relations between complex 'action × objects'." N.I. 363. [Or In 415]

"... coordination or organization external to the schemas..." N.I. 216. [Or In 245]

2. **Coordination or reciprocal assimilation**

There is a tendency of two schemas "to assimilate each the domain of the other, which is the same as saying they assimilate reciprocally. It is this reciprocal assimilation (total or partial) which forms the coordination of schemas." E.E.G. VII 44.

"Now in order for two schemas, so far isolated, to be coordinated to each other in a single act, the subject has to plan to reach a goal which is not directly accessible, and besides it has to include in this intention schemas which so far are related to other situations." N.I. 187. [Or In 211]

"We have second degree assimilation when there is coordination of two schemas of assimilation (e.g., vision and sucking) and there is second degree accommodation as long as it prolongs the chain of acquired associations." N.I. 61. [Or In 62]

"... there is coordination between schemas if these latter can function alone in other situations..." N.I. 119. [Or In 129]

3. **Coordination, partial**

"This means simple conjunction of two partly independent schemas." N.I. 95. [Or In 101]

4.1 **Coordinations, general, of action** opp.

4.2 **Particular (specialized) actions**

"The mathematical notions appeared to us as due to general co-ordinations of action [4.1] as opposed to particular actions which differentiate the objects from each other and lead therefore to abstraction of their properties, because of physical data [4.2]. But since the specialized actions have to be coordinated as the more general ones, any mathematical framework contains a possible physical content, even if this framework should go beyond this content and any formed physical notion is related to a mathematical coordination." E.G. II 10.

"As opposed to the general coordinations of the action from which logic, number and space derive [4.1] the particular actions intervening in the construction of notions of time, speed and force seem to contain already these realities because of subjective experience. There is an interior duration, a kinesthetic experience of speed, and above all a feeling of muscular force [4.2]. On the other hand, if logic and number are obviously tied to our activity, space seems more remote from our physical nature than time. It is therefore paradoxical to attach time to the object and space to the subject, and it would seem that in a genetic epistemology based on analysis of action, time, speed and force should emanate directly from the activity of the subject." E.G. II 11.

5. **Coordinations, sensory-motor** (up to about 2 years)
"... in which we distinguish in a practical and not representative form certain relationships and certain generalizations. They lead to a schematism which constitutes without doubt the substructure of the later logical structurations and to the formation of an elementary invariant (schema of the permanent object), which represents the starting point of the later forms of conservation." E.E.G. I 27.

6.1 **Coordination, rectangular and**
6.2 **Coordination, triangular**
"Either we coordinate [6.1] distances by biunivocal correspondence according to two dimensions at once and we obtain a rectangular figure (or a reference system of measure); or else [6.2] we coordinate distances according to two dimensions [co-univocal multiplication of relations] by having correspond to each of them a larger one starting from a given point and we obtain a triangular figure by successive increase of the (normal) opening lines." G.S. 267. [Co Ge 206]

1. **Correlation, direct**
"$p \cdot q \vee \bar{p} \cdot \bar{q}$, if taken alone, express equivalence between p and q; that is a term by term correspondence between the concurrent values in case of seriation. We shall speak in this case of perfect positive correlation." L.E.A. 288. [Gr Lo Th 324]

2. **Correlation, inverse**
"But the two other associations $p \cdot \bar{q} \vee \bar{p} \cdot q$, if taken alone, express the mutual exclusion of p and q. That is an inverse correspondence or a perfect negative correlation." L.E.A. 288. [Gr Lo Th 324]

3. **Correlation, null**
"On the other hand, if the 4 associations have been realized and if they correspond to an equal numerical distribution of the events stated by propositional conjunctions there is null correlation." L.E.A. 288. [Gr Lo Th 324]

Correlative (C)
"We shall call 'correlative' of an operation the operation which is obtained by substituting, in the normal corresponding form the ($\vee$) for the (.), and reciprocally, but without changing the signs." T.L. 269. (df. 34)

$$\text{Example: } p \vee q = (p \cdot q) \vee p \cdot \bar{q} \vee (\bar{p} \cdot q)$$
$$C(p \vee q) = (p \vee q) \cdot (p \vee \bar{q}) \cdot (\bar{p} \vee q)$$

40

1. **Correspondence** opp. **Parallelism** (between logic and experience)
   "There is not parallelism but correspondence between this experimental knowledge and logistics, as there is correspondence between a schema and the reality which it represents. Each question raised by one of the two disciplines corresponds then to a question of the other." P.I. 40. [Ps In 30]

2.1 **Correspondence, intuitive or qualitative**
   There are "different types of correspondence distinguished at least by their relation with the idea of equivalence which they involve: ... the inferior types are of intuitive order—because the equivalence of the collections is recognized only if their correspondence is perceived by visual (or audial, etc.) contact and ceases as soon as it is no longer in the same perceptual field." G.N. 77. [Co Nu 65]
   "We shall call ... intuitive all correspondence based on perceptions only (or eventually on representative images) and which therefore is not conserved outside of the actual perceptual field (or of its clear memory)." G.N. 84. [Co Nu 70]

2.11 **Correspondence of two logical classes**
   "... means simply that ... two classes have the same hierarchic structures, the same classifying composition, but not the same number." G.N. 225. [Co Nu 182]

2.2 **Correspondence, quantifying or operational**
   There are "... different types of correspondence which can be distinguished at least by their relation with the idea of equivalence which they involve. The superior type may be qualified as 'quantifying correspondence' because it arrives at the notion of necessary and durable equivalence of the corresponding collections..." G.N. 77. [Co Nu 65]
   "Operational correspondence is ... formed of relations of an intellectual order and its distinctive sign is their conservation, independent of actual perception as well as the mobility of its composition, in one word its 'reversibility'." G.N. 84. [Co Nu 70]
   "The quantifying correspondence presupposes in addition to the simply perceptual correspondence, even if it is qualitatively exact, a superior operation which is equalization of differences; that means a coordination of displacements such that the latter are compensated by becoming reversible." G.N. 67. [Co Nu 56]

2.21 **Correspondence, numerical**
   "Will be ... the one which disregards the qualities of the parts and considers them as so many units..." G.N. 84. [Co Nu 70]

3. **Correspondence, logical**
"Relation of relations of part to whole." M.V. 280. [Mo Sp 302]
"Double comparison of parts to whole." M.V. 281. [Mo Sp 303]

4. **Correspondence, serial and ordinal**
"... serial and ordinal correspondences establish qualitative or numerical correspondences of two similar series..." D.Q. 238. Cf. G.N. 124.

1. **Couplings, perceptual**
"Couplings" in the widest sense are "the relations introduced between the encounters by assimilation to the schemas. The encounters are ... what is discovered about the objects in connection with any action, and the couplings are the manner in which these discoveries are structured by the subject." E.E.G. II 116. (*See* **Encounter** and **Law of relative centrations**.) Perceptual coupling is established between two objects (2 parallel lines L_1 and L_2, one extending further than the other, for example).

1.1 **Resemblance** (R)

1.2 **Difference** (D)

1.3 **Reciprocal difference** (D')

1.4 **Resemblance between differences** (D'') M.P. 142. [Me Pe 105]
$$R + D + D' + D'' = S; L_1 = L \max$$

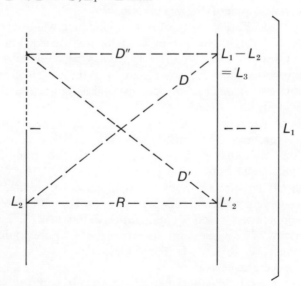

2.1 **Couplings, initial or automatic couplings**
"Initial couplings for few encounters, thus in very short times of

42

presentation, constitute only the factual correspondences 1 to n between the 'encounters' due to the centrations of the subject. The coupling does not contain thus from the subject's point of view any activities distinct from those of centration." M.P. 125. [Me Pe 91]

"Automatic couplings correspond to the weak effects of centration when the couplings are still almost 'complete' and to the strong effects of centration when they become less and less complete." M.P. 125–126. [Me Pe 92]

2.2   **Couplings, terminal or active (decentrations)**

"Terminal couplings on the other hand can correspond to a larger number of encounters which consist in a homogenization of the number of encounters between two elements L to be compared, resulting in an activity which is properly called one of the subject constituted by explorations which become more and more systematic and especially by 'transports' attached to movements of the eye which connect L_1 to L_2 and reciprocally." M.P. 125. [Me Pe 91]

"... 'Active couplings' (corresponding to progressive 'decentration,' that means to a gradual coordination of centrations) ... [The difference between 2.1 and 2.2] explains the variation in the probabilities of the coupling between T_0 and longer and longer times." M.P. 126. [Me Pe 92]

3.1   **Coupling, complete**

"If the encounters were, in effect, homogeneous or of the same density on all the elements L, the couplings would always be by definition 'complete,' and neither one nor the other of these two notions would add anything to the one of encounters (and on the other hand, the effects of centration would be limited to increasing or decreasing without deforming anything)." "We shall say that there is 'complete coupling' between the encounters on L_1 and L_2 at a given moment T if $\Sigma \alpha N = \Sigma \beta N$." M.P. 121. [Me Pe 88]

(αN and βN are the number of encounters for L_1 and L_2 respectively.)

3.2   **Coupling, incomplete**

As far as "encounters are heterogeneous on L_1 and L_2 we have to translate the heterogeneity of densities into terms of correspondences, that is what incomplete ... couplings mean" when $\Sigma \alpha N \leq \Sigma \beta N$. M.P. 121. [Me Pe 88]

Criticism and mockery

"Their function is ... to satisfy the intellectual instincts like aggressiveness, self-love, emulation, etc." L.P. 30. [La Th 24]

"This group includes all the remarks about the work or the behavior

of others … which are specific in relation to any given interviewer …
These remarks are more affective than intellectual; that means they
affirm superiority of the self and denigrate others." L.P. 19. [La Th
10]

D

Datum, immediate
"… even in the most prescientific field, and the most embryonic, no
immediate data exist." E.G. II 16.
1.   **Décalage, in comprehension, or vertical**
"… the child is not able to reflect from the start in words and in
notions on the operations which he already knows how to perform
in acts, and, if he cannot reflect upon them, it means that he is forced,
in order to adapt himself on the collective plane and on the conceptual plane on which his thought moves from there on, to redo the
work of coordination between assimilation and accommodation,
which has been accomplished before in his former sensory-motor
adaptation to the physical and practical universe." C.R. 317.
[Co Re 341] Cf. C.R. 323.
"… décalages in comprehension due to the passage of one plane of
activity to another." For example, from the plane of action to that of
representation. C.R. 330. [Co Re 371] Cf. (3) 66.
"It is the phenomenon of repetition with décalage from one level to
the other which we shall call 'vertical décalages'." (11) 251.
"They mark the successive reequilibria of the same system of actions
or of notions in the course of his development." (11) 263.
2.   **Décalage, horizontal, or décalage in extension**
"… originating from the problems located on the same plane but
showing increasing complexity." C.R. 323. Cf. C.R. 315, 330.
"Horizontal décalages happen at the same level of development but
between different systems of actions and notions." For example:
conservation of the notion of quantity of matter before conservation
of the notion of weight; where such groupings of action are the same
(simple or vicariant addition of parts) but they do not apply to
qualitatively different contents (substance and weight). (11) 263.
(*See* **Analogy**.)
"Express the differences of speed between vertical décalages of
distinct notions." (11) 270.

44

1. **Decentration and objectivity**

"The more he can decentrate himself the more active is the subject, or, to say it better, his decentration is the very measure of his effective activity on the object..." E.G. II 15.

"It is impossible at any level to separate the object from the subject. Relations exist between the two only, but these relations may be more or less centered or decentered, and it is this inversion of direction which makes up the transition from subjectivity to objectivity." E.G. II 16.

1.1 **Decentration and operation**

"To decenter is to reverse the relationships themselves and to construct a system of reciprocities which is qualitatively new in relation to the starting action." E.G. II 112.

"Decentration ... is only the inverse (or interior aspect, that is to say related to the subject) of the operational coordination." E.G. II 85.

"... Progressive decentration of action itself, i.e., elimination of egocentrism profiting the closed and regulated 'composition,' by the fact that the initial actions become reversible and operational." D.Q. 339.

"To decenter means 'to group'..." E.G. II 112.

2. **Decentration (coordination of centrations)**

"Coordination of centrations is decentration." M.V. 206. [Mo Sp 222–223] Cf. M.P. 155; M.V. 171. (*See* **Centration.**)

3. **Decentration (assimilation)**

"Decentration is assimilation by relating the assimilated objects." M.V. 169. [Mo Sp 182]

4.1 **Decentration, perceptual (regulation)**

"Decentration constitutes – by definition, a regulation; that is to say it tends either to diminish an error by augmenting the inverse error or to have them tend to a state of equilibrium which is a compromise between the two, or, at most, in their cancellation." N.T. 123.

"On the whole, we may say that the intuitive regulation prolongs the perceptual regulation. Perceptual decentration comes from the regulated movements executed by the subject in order to reach the object (fixation of centrations, i.e., decentration)." M.V. 206. [Mo Sp 222–223]

4.11 **Decentration, relative**

"Relative decentrations, i.e., establish simple reciprocal compensa-

45

tions of deformations *P*, without absolute diminution of their arithmetic sum..." M.V. 171. [Mo Sp 183]

4.12   **Decentration, absolute**
"... due to absolute decentrations which diminish the total value of deformations *P* because the interval between points of centration is itself decentered." M.V. 171. [Mo Sp 183]

4.2   **Decentration, intuitive**
"Intuitive decentration comes from ... regulation of forms of the entire action..." M.V. 206–207. [Mo Sp 223]
"... is translated ... as a regulation which tends in the direction of reversibility from the transitive composition and from associativity, therefore, on the whole from survival by coordination of points of view." P.I. 166. [Ps In 139]

4.3   **Decentration, affective**
"... interest in sources of pleasure conceived from now on as distinct from the action itself." A.I. 36.

4.4   **Decentration, intellectual**
"... permits to achieve reality by a continuous process of application of operations to objective transformations, or ... of exteriorization of these operations (for example, in connection with explanations of survival in different forms); [it is] in solidarity with and complementary to the interiorization process which leads to conscious realization of operational structures." E.E.G. I 67.

4.41   **Decentration of thought**
"Not only in relation to perceptual centration but in relation to the whole action itself." P.I. 146. [Ps In 122]

5.1   **Decentration, general, or of totality** opp.

5.2   **Decentration, local**
"... these are the perceptual activities which are responsible for local decentration, at the same time as, by their generalization, they bring about these global forms of decentration mentioned ... for example, in connection with systems of reference." M.P. 372. [Me Pe 299]
Decentration of a totality is a "... refounding [of the] system of perceptions and evaluations." L.P. 68–69.

6.1   **Decentration, virtual,** opp.

6.2   **Centration, actual**
(6.1) consists of "anticipating or reconstructing the centrations which could be real or which have been, in such a fashion as to

46

relate them to actual centration [6.2]." N.T. 123. (*See* **Centration 6.**)

1.   **Deduction**
"Deduction begins when the construction is formed at the interior of achieved 'groupings' or 'groups'." D.Q. 338.

2.1   **Deduction, formal**
"... it consists in drawing conclusions, not from direct observation or from such judgment that one appears without reservations (and which we incorporate in the reality such as we see it), but from judgment which one simply assumes, i.e., one admits without believing or seeing what it entails." J.R. 61. [Ju Re 69]

2.2   **Deduction, causal**
"... consists in ... a fusing of the physical modification with the operational transformation by subordinating the real to the possible, and by conferring to the generalizations of real legal relations a character of necessity or of probability, as function of this very subordination." E.G. II 348.

1.   **Development of mental activity**
"... it is the function of distance which gradually increases with exchanges, i.e., from equilibrium between assimilation of the realities more and more distant from action and accommodation of the latter to the former." P.I. 14. [Ps In 9]

1.1   **Development I: Sociogenetic and cultural**
"One of these aspects is sociogenetic and cultural: it is development I, collective, following from generation to generation forming new generations before being relieved in their continuous march." E.E.G. XV 12.

1.2   **Development II: Psychogenetic**
"Another aspect is psychogenetic: it is development II, at the same time organic (nervous system) and mental which leads from birth to adolescence; that is to say to the point of introduction of the individual into adult society." E.E.G. XV 12.

Dichotomy
Constitutes the "natural form of logical separation (independent of the equality of the complementary classes)..." G.S. 401. [Co Ge 316]

Disanthropomorphization of physics and **Deconcretization of mathematics**
"... physics is disanthropomorphized, thus liberated from the ego-centric subject, whereas mathematics is deconcretized, thus is

freed from the apparent object, and accordingly the more they are engaged in opposite directions, the better they are adjusted to each other." E.G. II 18. Cf. E.G. I 66.

1. **Discontinuity, relative**

"Df. 34. We say that a behavior evolves according to a relative discontinuity of degree n if following n refinements of measures we do not find more behaviors which present intermediate values after the nth refinement." E.E.G. IV 83.

2. **Discontinuity, absolute**

"Df. 35. We say that behavior evolves according to an absolute discontinuity if the behavior is present or absent, but cannot be graded." E.E.G. IV 83.

Discovery

"A discovery is the encounter between a subject and an object, until now unknown by him, but which existed as such before this encounter..." E.E.G. XIV 219.

1. **Discussion, primitive**

"As much as justification remains implicit and as the child progresses by successive affirmations which are not interconnected, there is primitive discussion." L.P. 91. [La Th 68]

It "is equivalent on the level of thought to dispute on the level of action: a simple clash between desires and contrary opinions." "It makes its first appearance on the average according to our material around 5 or $5\frac{1}{2}$ years." L.P. 32. [La Th 70]

"They consist simply of shocks of contrary affirmations, without explicit demonstrations." L.P. 29. [La Th 26]

2. **Discussion, true**

"Beginning from the moment when the speakers limit themselves to affirming their contrary opinions instead of teasing or criticizing or threatening." L.P. 90. [La Th 68]

"There is a demonstration (thus a true discussion) when the child connects his affirmation and the reason which he gives for the validity of that affirmation by a term of conjunction (for example: since, because, then, etc.) and makes explicit the fact of this demonstration." L.P. 90–91. [La Th 68]

1. **Displacement**

"It is at first for the child only a change of 'placement,' that is to say of order, but owing to the permutations of the objects that are themselves in order and not simply to the inversion of direction of the course of the ordering subject." G.S. 487. [Co Ge 390–391]

"The changes of order constitute the displacement as such." M.V. 93. [Mo Sp 99–100]

"A simple change of order is only a displacement." M.V. 153. [Mo Sp 165]

"The operations of displacement (or change of placement)." M.V. 258. [Mo Sp 279]

"A change of position (displacement)." M.V. 275. [Mo Sp 298]

2. **Displacement of equilibrium**

"In the domain of intuitive thought as in that of perception ... during each modification of exterior sensory data, we have 'displacement of equilibrium'; i.e., it intervenes from the 'transformations not compensated' or not entirely compensated by the decentrations or regulations. Perceptual equilibrium, and to a lesser degree intuitive equilibrium, are thus comparable to a statistical system in which the chance transformations ... modify at any moment the totality, but the latter cannot result from an additive composition." N.I. 178.

In the case of non-permanence of conditions of equilibrium the latter is accompanied by the appearance of displacements of equilibrium "with a tendency to moderate the factor of disturbance according to the principle of Le Châtelier." E.E.G. II 39. (*See* **Equilibrium, permanent**.)

Dispute

"The clash of contrary actions." L.P. 80. [La Th 53]

Distance

"We use ... the term 'distance' in the case of linear measure from straight lines measured not on the object but on the open space: distance is thus defined expressly according to linear intervals between objects." G.S. 95. [Co Ge 69]

"... distances are nothing but symmetrical intervals extracted from the grouping of asymmetrical relations of placement (order) and of displacement (change of order). Once achieved this is a grouping of operations under its qualitative form." G.S. 116. [Co Ge 85]

"... distance implies relations between independent objects located in space and the space or homogeneous and common environment become for it the true geometrical object." G.S. 121. [Co Ge 88]

Double transport (*See* **Transport**)

1. **Duration**

"... consists in the general interval between two states." M.V. 273. [Mo Sp 296]

"Contrary to the successive order, which is asymmetric ... duration appears logically as an interval between successive terms and consequently as a symmetrical relationship." N.T. 282.

"Between any two successive points of co-seriation we can separate out an interval having these points as limits and which will not by definition be a duration; if the two points are not successive the duration is null (simultaneity)." N.T. 55.

1.1 **Duration, lived**

"Lived durations are nothing but—the times passing in the intervals between events." N.T. 265.

"... in lived duration during the act itself, time is contracted (as far as consciousness is concerned) as a function of speed..." E.G. II 29.

1.2 **Duration evaluated by memory**

"... whereas in duration, evaluated by memory, the well-spent times are increased, whereas empty times are condensed." E.G. II 29.

2. **Duration, interior**

"Interior duration is ... only the time of an action itself; then if you say action you mean the relation between the subject and objects on which he acts." N.T. 207.

E

Echolalia

It is "the repetition of syllables or words. The child repeats for the pleasure of speaking ... It is one of the last states of babbling of babies..." L.P. 18. [La Th 9]

Eduction of correlates, the

"... the qualitative operation is called 'eduction of correlates' (Spearman) ... it is only the relation by logical multiplication of relations (equals the correspondence between correspondences)." M.V. 280. [Mo Sp 304]

Effects, field or primary

"... the perceptual observable effects in a single or momentarily same field of centration are said to be 'primaries'." "... those effects, which we also call 'field effects'..." M.P. 19. [Me Pe 3]

"To attribute to the term of 'primary' a sense relative to hierarchy more than to temporal succession and to remember that any centration, with the 'primary' effects that it includes, is always inserted in the context of movement of regard and thus always subordinated to one activity." "... the term 'primary' keeps the meaning of 'common to all levels' and 'relative to the local effects of centration'." M.P. 254. [Me Pe 199]

"The field effects contain ... two differentiable aspects without too much artificiality: an aspect of signalization, of which the extreme border is furnished by the accommodating 'encounters' acting upon the object and an aspect of schematization or of internal organization." E.E.G. VI 109.

"... field effects do not constitute anything more than the product of sedimentation of [perceptual] activities, once automatic (sedimentation bearing upon the deformations as well as on structures)." M.P. 262. [Me Pe 206] (*See* **Perceptions, Primary.**)

Effects, temporal, of centration

"... there are two kinds: (1) the first is an effect of duration; the overestimation due to the centration on an element increases with the duration of presentation up to a stabilization. (2) The second variety ... known as temporal error, belongs to the order of succession in time; of two elements presented for the same duration but successively (all or in part), the last perceived is overestimated." M.P. 103. [Me Pe 72–73] (*See* **Centration 1.**)

1. **Effort (behavior)**
    "Effort is a behavior, as has been well shown by P. Janet founded upon the analysis of J. M. Baldwin and J. Philipe, and it is precisely a behavior or a regulation of acceleration." E.G. II 63. Cf. E.G. II 91.

2. **Effort (feeling)**
    "... that is to say the conscious realization more or less adequate of the behavior of acceleration." E.G. II 63.
    "It is the expression of the resistance felt by the organs in contact with the object, and it is through an elaboration derived from that peripheral impression that we attribute effort to ourself and to the will." E.G. II 63.

1. **Egocentrism**
    "Egocentrism is an effect characterized by an undifferentiation between the subject and his exterior world, and not by the exact knowledge which the subject has of himself: instead of leading to an effort of introspection or reflection upon the self, infantile egocentrism is on the contrary ignorance of the interior life and deformation of the self as well as ignorance of objective relations and deformations of things." N.T. 206.
    "... egocentrism is opposed to objectivity, as far as objectivity means

relativity on the physical plane and reciprocity on the social plane."
L.P. 70. [La Th 271]*

"Egocentrism is ... on one hand, prior to satisfaction on the objective observation (from which the character of initial thought of the child, which remains midway between play and adaptation) and, on the other hand, is the deformation of reality as function of the action itself and of the point of view itself. In both cases, he is naturally unconscious of himself, which means essentially there is a dis-association of subjective and objective." ... "'The child thinks of the optative rather than of the indicative' [H. Wallen] which could constitute the definition of egocentrism from the functional point of view." F.S. 301, note 1. [Pl Dr Im 285]

"... egocentrism means the absence of consciousness as well as absence of objectivity about himself, whereas taking possession of the object as such accompanies the conscious realization of himself."
C.R. 6. [Co Re xii]

1.1 **Egocentrism and society**

The child "plays individually with social material; that is egocentrism." J.M. 21. [Mo Ju 37]

"Egocentrism appears to us as an intermediate between socialized and purely individual behavior." J.M. 20. [Mo Ju 35–36]

"Infantile egocentrism, far from consisting of asocial behavior, always goes along with adult constraint. Egocentrism is not pre-social except in relation to cooperation." J.M. 41. [Mo Ju 61]

"Egocentrism is presocial in the sense that it marks transition between the individual and the social, between a motor stage and a quasi-solipsism of the baby and the stage of true cooperation."
J.M. 66. [Mo Ju 91]

"Egocentrism as confusion of the self with the exterior world and egocentrism as lack of cooperation thus are one and the same phenomenon." "Egocentrism and imitation are one and the same."
J.M. 67. [Mo Ju 93]

"Infantile egocentrism is thus in its essence an undifferentiation between the self and the social environment." J.M. 68. [Mo Ju 93]

"Egocentrism is by definition the confusion between the self and the other." J.M. 200. [Mo Ju 251]

*Editors' note: Chapter II [L.P., pp. 47–77] of the French edition, revised in 1947, appears in the English edition cited [La Th] as Chapter VI, "The measure of ego-centric language in verbal communication between the adult and the child and in verbal exchanges between children," pp. 239–281; that chapter, and consequently many definitions dealing with egocentrism, do not appear at all in the 1955 Meridian paperback edition with which many American readers are familiar.

"Undifferentiation between the other and the self." L.P. 50. [La Th 243]

"We call egocentrism the undifferentiation of one's point of view and that of others, or the activity itself and the transformations of the object." L.P. 67. [La Th 267]

"Social egocentrism is an epistemic attitude as well as purely intellectual egocentrism; it is a way of understanding others, as egocentrism in general is an attitude toward objects." L.P. 71. [La Th 273]

"... Social egocentrism succeeds sensory-motor egocentrism and reproduces the phases thereof, but, as the social and the representative are interdependent there seems to be a regression when the mind simply fights the same battles on a new planc in order to make new conquests." C.R. 323. [Co Re 368]

1.2 Egocentrism and consciousness

"Egocentrism is not thus in its origin either a phenomenon of consciousness (consciousness of the egocentrism destroys egocentrism), nor a phenomenon of social behavior (the behavior manifests egocentrism indirectly but does not constitute it), but a sort of systematic and unconscious illusion..." L.P. 68. [La Th 268]

"It is somehow the totality of precritical and consequently preobjective attitudes of knowledge." L.P. 68. [La Th 268]

Egocentrism "is the spontaneous attitude of individual thought which is directed toward the object without being conscious of the perspective itself." L.P. 74. [La Th 276]

2.1 Egocentrism and centration

"An action is ... not combinable with others and incapable of being unfolded in two directions to the extent that it is 'centrated,' and it is that initial centration which explains simultaneously the fact of behavior, which is its irreversibility, and that illusion of the point of view, which is egocentrism or assimilation to the activity itself." L.P. 76. [La Th 279]

"Spatial egocentrism, which marks the beginning of representation of displacements, ... is, like intellectual and unconscious egocentrism, ... a system of illegitimate centrations which are opposed to grouping because of an irreversible source of assimilations." G.S. 38. [Co Ge 25]

"... it is that intellectual centration which characterizes which until now we called egocentrism." M.V. 167.

"Egocentrism consists only in taking as sole reality the one which appears to perception." D.Q. 277.

53

"Egocentrism is the coordination established according to the only proper perspective." D.Q. 242. (*See* **Centration of action**.)

2.2 **Egocentrism and irreversibility**

"Egocentrism is the opposite of 'grouping'." D.Q. 242.

"... is thus a system of relations impossible to be grouped and one can define it by its very irreversibility, thus by its non-grouping." (11) 250.

"It is the negation of the objective attitude, consequently of logical analysis. It leads on the contrary to subjective synthesis." L.P. 140. [La Th 140]

3.1 **Egocentrism, logical** produces autism

3.2 **Egocentrism, ontological** produces magic and pre-causality

"Just as logical egocentrism has given us the key to infantile judgment and reasoning [3.1], ontological egocentrism will give us the key to reality and causality in the child" [3.2]. R.M. 156. [Co Wo 168]

"... both falsify the perspectives of logical relationships and of things themselves, because both start from the postulate that others understand us and approve of us and that things revolve around us with the only aim to serve and resemble us." C.P. 339. [Co Ph Ca 302]

4. **Egocentrism and equilibrium**

"... egocentrism ought not to be defined only by the primacy of assimilation over accommodation, but by its disequilibrium of the two processes, with primacy alternating between one and the other." F.S. 307–308. [P1 Dr Im 290]

Element, intermediate, of comparison

"In any comparison ... as well as in any measurement, there always exists an intermediate element, which we should not qualify initially as a median term, but the function of which is to connect A and B or its inverse, or again to conserve A and B in this act of relating. Then, that intermediate element always originates from the activity itself before becoming detached in the form of a median independent term or of a common measurement." G.S. 65. [Co Ge 47]

1. **Encounter**

"Encounters, in the larger sense, [are] the points of junction between accommodation of schemas and objects." E.E.G. II 116.

2. **Encounter and coupling**

"The encounters are what is discovered of the objects during any action, and couplings the manner in which these discoveries are structured by the subject." E.E.G. II 116.

Enumeration, number, to
To enumerate is "to classify and seriate at the same time." Df. E.G. I 102.

1.   **Epistemology, genetic**
"The epistemological principle is ... to try to determine the role of the subject and of the object, not seeing them as such, but in the very process of growing knowledge. In this regard we can only hope to grasp the extent of the most advanced notions by connecting the extremes through laws of development." E.G. II 70.
"From the point of view of genetic epistemology ... which does not know the subject as such but only the successive objects recognized by the subject in the course of these steps, there is an evident relation between objectivity and its objects, but we have to determine this relation by development itself." E.G. II 71.
"... it is clear that the body of genetic epistemology largely surpasses that of child psychology." E.E.G. I 52.

1.1   **Epistemological (domain)**
"... we will call 'epistemological domain' that of the relations between knowledge and the different possible forms of realities (including eventuality of nonsensitive zones of existence)..." E.E.G. XIV 162.
"... epistemological problems [are] related to relations SF, SE, FE and to the system E" in the following three types: "system $S =$ activities of the subject; system $F =$ properties (forms, etc.) of the object; system $E =$ types of existence or of reality of the objects (zones of reality)." E.E.G. XIV 163.

2.   **Epistemology and logic**
This is "the study of knowledge as relation between the subject and the object and [we reserve] the term logic for the formal analysis of knowledge." T.L. 4.
"... Logic remains exclusively relative to activities of the subject and is not concerned with interactions between the subject and the object, which concern epistemology only." T.L. 5.

3.1   **Epistemology, restricted genetic**
"We shall call restricted genetic epistemology all psychogenetic research or historico-critical research about the methods of growth of knowledge, to the extent that it is based on a system of reference constituted by the state of knowledge existing at the moment of observation." E.G. I 45.

3.2   **Epistemology, generalized genetic**
"We shall call it on the other hand generalized genetic epistemology

when the reference system is itself included in the genetic or in the historical process which has to be studied." E.G. I 45.

4.1 **Epistemology, genetic (special form)**
"... is the study of successive stages of a science S as function of its development." E.E.G. I 13.

4.2 **Epistemology, genetic (general form)**
"Study of mechanisms of growth of knowledge." E.E.G. I 14.

Epistemology, normative
"... is the study of foundations by the methods of logical formalization." E.E.G. I 16.

"The principal fringe problem consists in determining from which level or from which structure logic, belonging to the subject, can be formalized from the normative point of view." E.E.G. I 25.

1. **Equality (Reciprocity)**
"For equality and authentic need of reciprocity there has to be a collective rule, produced *sui generis* by living in common: from actions and reactions of individuals upon each other, there has to grow the consciousness of necessary equilibrium, forcing and limiting at the same time the *other* and the *ego*." J.M. 254. [Mo Ju 318]

1.1 **Equality, moral**
"... it is not the result of a progression toward the homogeneous ... but of mobility which is the function of differentiation." J.M. 321. [Mo Ju 397]

1. **Equilibrium and reversibility**
"... the system is in equilibrium when the operations of which the subject is capable constitute a structure such that the operations can unfold in two directions (either by strict inversion or negation, or by reciprocity). It is therefore because the totality of possible operations constitutes a system of potential transformations which compensate each other—and which compensate each other as far as obeying the laws of reversibility—that the system is in equilibrium." L.E.A. 235–236. [Gr Lo Th 267]

"Equilibrium will thus be defined by reversibility." E.G. I 36.

"... equilibrium [is the] place of specific junction between the possible and the real..." E.G. I 36.

1.1 **Equilibrium, field of**
"(1) We shall call field of equilibrium the totality of objects or of properties of objects to which actions of a certain category are applied and which are susceptible to mutual equilibration." E.E.G. II 38.

56

1.2 **Equilibrium, the best**
"... the best equilibrated states, in the sense in which we understand this word, correspond to a maximum of activities and a maximum of opening up of exchanges." E.E.G. II 37.
"Of the two forms of equilibrium, the 'best' is the one which, according to an *optimum* dosage, which has to be determined in each special case, makes correspond to the widest field and to the greatest mobility (this is, the maximum of possible relations) the simplest and the best compensated transformations." E.E.G. II 43.

1.3 **Equilibrium, permanent**
"Df. We shall say that a structure has an equilibrium of permanent conditions, or simply a permanent equilibrium if, when the initial field C is modified to C', the substructure of the elements corresponding to C conserves the same equilibrium as before..." E.E.G. II 40.

1.4 **Equilibrium, displacement of**
"... we shall say on the other hand that there is a displacement of equilibrium if the new form of equilibrium corresponding to C' differs from the one which corresponded to C." E.E.G. II 40. (*See* **Displacement** 2.)

2. **Equilibrium, level of**
(1) *Permanent*: achieved grouping (V and VI) [operational].
(2) *Semi-permanent*: intuitive grouping (IV)—sensory-motor grouping (III).
(3) *Momentary*: perception and habit (II)—reflex (I) (11) 237.
"... a state of equilibrium is not a state of final rest, but constitutes a new point of departure." E.E.G. XV 20.

2.1 **Equilibrium, operational**
"... is present "when the *maximum* of possible distances (since intelligence tries to embrace the universe) and of paths of complexity (since the deduction is capable of the greatest 'detours')." P.I. 63–64. [Ps In 49–50]
Permanent equilibrium is "due to the fact that the intuitive regulations have achieved complete reversibility." M.V. 260. [Mo Sp 282] Cf. M.V. 166.
"The equilibrium finally reached between assimilation and accommodation explains then the reversibility of the operational grouping which is at the same time deduction or indefinite assimilation and continually accommodable to new situations." M.V. 172. [Mo Sp 185]

57

3.   **Equilibrium and structure**
      "Equilibrium and structure are the two complementary aspects of
      any organization of thought." L.E.A. 213. [Gr Lo Th 244]
      "... the structures can be interpreted as the product or the result of
      an autonomous process of equilibration." Just as "the structure
      (or organ) [is different from] the function (in the biological sense of
      the term): ... equilibration is a functional process different from
      structure..." E.E.G. II 43.

4.   **Equilibrium and learning**
      "... equilibrium would constitute a condition (necessary but not
      sufficient) of learning in the sense that all learning would presuppose
      the intervention of not learned reactions tending to its equilibra-
      tion..." E.E.G. X 183.
      "... these not learned coordinations ... constitute the specific domain
      of equilibration..." E.E.G. X 184.

5.   **Equilibrium** (explanations)
      We may "(a) conceive of equilibrium as characterized by *maximum*
      entropy, (b) or as due to the intervention of coordinations which
      introduce from outside an order diminishing the entropy, (c) or else
      as due to a sequence of 'strategies' of which each one will be oriented
      by the results of the preceding one up to the moment when the
      actions become reversible through the very coordination of these
      preceding strategies that would have been freed from the earlier
      historic process in order to reach equilibrium." E.E.G. I 37–38.

      Equity
      "... equity is an equality which takes into consideration the cir-
      cumstances of everyone in the particular case of age differences."
      J.M. 214. [Mo Ju 268–269]

1.   **Error of the standard**
      "The most attractive element is systematically overvalued." P.I.
      87. [Ps In 71]

2.1   **Error, elementary I, absolute overestimation** (perception)
      "... the elementary error I, or the error due to the centration on a
      single element independent of its relations of dimensional equality
      or inequality with others." M.P. 120. [Me Pe 87]

2.2   **Error, elementary II, relative overestimation** (perception)
      "... the difference between these elementary errors I creates a new
      source of error or elementary error II, consisting of relative over-
      estimations which measurement can verify." M.P. 121. [Me Pe
      87–88]

"... relative and no longer absolute overestimation of elements..." M.P. 123. [Me Pe 90]

3. **Error, composite, optico-geometrical illusions**
"... we now pass from the analysis of elementary errors I and II to analysis of 'composite errors,' that means of illusions related to a group figure or to a configuration in the ordinary sense of the term and not only to perception of a line L or to comparison of two lines L_1 and L_2..." M.P. 141. [Me Pe 104]

Ethics (*See* Morals)

1. **Evolution**
"Df. 33a. If a behavior can be characterized by a single quantifiable variable, we say that evolution presents to a subject a degree n of continuity if n refinements of measuring scales (from the most inaccurate measures which permit two distinguishing values only) always allow for observing the existence of intermediate values." E.E.G. IV 80.

"Df. 33b. If a behavior can be represented by a single quantifiable variable, we say that its evolution presents, in a homogeneous population at all ages considered, a degree n of continuity if we apply n refinements of measurement in comparable samples of this population (samples increasing in number with refinements of measurement), and we find an analogous number of subjects in all intermediate positions." E.E.G. IV 81–82.

2. **Evolution of child thought**
"... is characterized by the passage from general egocentrism ... to intellectual decentration..." P.I. 88. [Ps In 73]

1. **Experience**
"... experience does not necessarily mean abstraction originating from the object..." E.G. I 263.

"Experience is, therefore, not reception but action and progressive construction; this is a fundamental fact." N.I. 318. [Or In 365]

1.1 **Experience and deduction**
We have to refute "any radical dualism between experience and deduction and [we have to] consider the experience as a progressive structuration and not simply as reading, whereas deduction is a coordination of operations and not simply a speech..." M.P. 443. [Me Pe 358]

1.2 **Experience, immediate, and scientific experience**
"... the first contact of thought as such with the material universe constitutes what we can call immediate experience as opposed to

scientific experience or experience corrected through assimilation of things to the mind." C.R. 335. [Co Re 381]

"... experience such as the practice of sensory-motor groping is immediate in the sense that it considers things such as they appear instead of correcting them and elaborating them mentally." N.I. 283. [Or In 325]

2.1 **Experience, physical**

Physical experience includes the "differentiated actions as functions of the object." E.E.G. I 33.

"Consists in acting upon objects in a fashion so as to discover the properties which are abstracted from these objects as such; for example, to weigh an object in order to evaluate its weight." E.E.G. VII 24.

2.2 **Experience, logico-mathematical**

Logico-mathematical experience includes "general actions proceeding by abstraction from coordinations between the actions." E.E.G. I 33.

"Logico-mathematical experience consists in acting upon the objects, but in a fashion as to discover the properties which are ... abstracted from the very actions of the subject, in order that, at a certain level of abstraction, experience with objects becomes unnecessary, and coordination of the actions is sufficient to bring about an operational manipulation only symbolically and proceeding thus in a purely deductive manner..." E.E.G. VII 24–25.

"Logico-mathematical experience is not applied to action as individual process, but to the results of the actions as far as they are objectives and necessary." E.E.G. XIV 250. Cf. M.V. 31.

3.1 **Experience, initial mental**

At the "beginning of child thought," initial mental experience is the simple inner imitation "... but in this case the reasoning is not yet logical." P.I. 112. [Ps In 93]

"Epistemologically, certain mental experiences (I) consist simply in imagining a reality exterior to the subject..." E.G. I 59.

3.2 **Experience, achieved mental**

"At the achieved state, a mental experience is the reproduction in thought, not of reality, but of actions or operations which refer to it." P.I. 112. [Ps In 93]

"... mental experience does not at all consist of ready-made images which are evoked; it is an essentially constructed process of which representation is only a symbolic helping element, since there is true invention and it never has perceived reality identical to the one on which it is about to elaborate." N.I. 300. [Or In 344–345]

Certain mental experiences "(II) on the contrary come back to imagining, not simply the 'variations of facts' ... but the actions as such of the subject creating variations of the facts, which is not the same thing." We have to distinguish "... between the imagination of actions which are not well differentiated, insufficiently coordinated among themselves and consequently obliged to depend on the exterior reality in order to reach the prediction of its result (IIA) ... and the imagination of operations; that is, of actions which became reversible and sufficiently coordinated in order to create composition susceptible of precise anticipations (IIB)." E.G. I 60.

4.1   **Experience in the first sensory-motor stage**

"During the first stage there is naturally no direct contact with experience since activity is simply reflex. The accommodation to things is confused with reflex activity." N.I. 317. [Or In 364]

4.2   **Experience at the second stage**

"During the second stage, new associations are formed and that is how the pressure of experience starts. But those associations are limited, at the start, to relating two or more movements of the body itself, or else, a reaction of the subject to an external signal ... Only this 'experience' does not place mind in the presence of 'things' themselves; it places it exactly half way between the external environment and the body itself. Accommodation thus remains indissociated from repetitive activity, which acts simply upon the result acquired fortuitously instead of being due to the unfolding of reflexive activity." N.I. 317. [Or In 364]

4.3   **Experience at the third stage**

"During the third stage ... relations between things ... remain thus dependent upon action itself; that is, the subject does not yet experiment. His accommodation to things is a simple effort of repetition. Only the results produced are more complex than at the preceding stage." N.I. 318. [Or In 364]

4.4   **Experience at the fourth stage**

"... the experience comes still closer to the object. The coordinations between schemas allow the child to establish real relations between things." N.I. 318. [Or In 364–365]

4.5   **Experience at the fifth stage or experiment "in order to see"**

"... accommodation is definitely freed and gives way to true experiment, which is still developing in the course of the sixth stage." N.I. 318. [Or In 365]

"... if the child repeats movements which have led to an interesting result he does not repeat them as such but grades them and varies them so that he can discover fluctuations in the result. Experiment 'in order to see' has a general tendency to develop in order to master the external environment." N.I. 234. [Or In 267]

1. **Explanation**

"... if there has to be explanation, it is not sufficient to deduce laws in a formal manner; we have to apply this deduction on a real substrate on a concrete or abstract 'model' which permits to represent the relations involved and, in a more general manner, to coordinate the planes of reality or to introduce among the established laws a hierarchy from the point of view of their field of application (conscious estimates, reactions of behavior, physiological laws, etc.)." T.P. I 126.

"The explanation presupposes ... a system of laws such that one system may be constructed or reconstructed deductively from others and there is a first specific characteristic of the explanation as opposed to legality only..." T.P. I 127.

"... deduction of the law to be explained, starting from the system of laws which take them into account, does not remain simply ideal or 'logical' but it is applied to a real or model substrate which can lend itself to such a deduction and to 'represent' the diverse connections." T.P. I 127–128.

2. **Explanation, causal**

"Causal explanation consists in deducing the laws which connect the represented objects as functions of certain substrates of reality, and it presupposes therefore three conditions: (1) to be in possession of laws; (2) to choose a schema of deduction; and (3) to choose a substrate to which a deduction can be applied..." T.P. I 143.

"... Causal explanation will succeed to the degree in which during each transformation in relations between the objects there will correspond a transformation or operation in deduction, and this latter is by the same fact modeled on the real." "... the explanation presents the two characteristics which are classically attributed to causality, as opposed to simple lawfulness: (a) the necessity for relationships between causes and effects which come from their deducibility; (b) the reality of this causal connection underlying the measured phenomena (and which surpasses pure phenomenism), which is assured by the model used from the substrate to the deduction." T.P. I 128.

"If we admit that any causal explanation implies a part of deduction, whereas all deduction is not explanatory, the reason is without any doubt to be found in the opposition between deductions having to do simply with general relations and the structural deductions which end up in a system of interdependent transformations." E.E.G. I 65.

2.1 **Explanation, physical**

"Physical explanation consists in assimilating transformations of the real to the operations themselves..." E.E.G. II 116.

3. **Explanation, constructivist**

We may "consider as 'constructivist' the type of explanation which, being a neutral part of reductions (because it is then at least one aspect of any explanation), puts the principal emphasis on the process of construction ... [there are] three types of models ... theory of behavior ... models of a type more typically genetic ... and so called abstract models..." T.P. I 130.

"Any true explanation consists ... in reciprocal assimilation; that is, in the discovery or in the construction of a system of transformations which conserve simultaneously the qualities of the superior and those of the inferior and assure a passage from one to the other." E.G. III 78. (Without "simple reduction" of the superior to the inferior in psychological behavior.)

4. **Explanation of the virtual by the real**

Genetic analysis "must explain the virtual by the real every time an action opens, by its very execution, new possibilities and thus creates a system of virtual operations." E.G. I 35.

5. **Explanation in the language of the child**

"The word explain means to retrace through thought the causes of a phenomenon that these causes are efficient or final depending on the phenomena being natural or mechanical ... These 'why's of causal explanation' will be recognized from the fact that the expected answer implies the idea of cause or of final cause." L.P. 158. [La Th 166–167]

Exploration, perceptual opp. **Perceptual transport**

"The function of exploration is to coordinate the centrations on the same element in order to deduce a perceptual estimate. The function of transport is, on the other hand, to allow a comparison (which will by definition be a reciprocal transport) between L_1 and L_2." M.P. 226. [Me Pe 176]

63

1.   **Extension of a schema** opp. **Comprehension**
"Df. 8a. Extension of a schema is the union of the extensions of the actions of which it is the schema. Comprehension of a schema is the schema itself." E.E.G. IV 48.

2.   **Extension of an action**
"Df. 8b. Extension of an action is the totality of objects upon which they bear." E.E.G. IV 48.

F

Fabrication
"If a child, without reflecting, responds to the question by inventing a story in which he does not believe or which he believes by simple verbal training, we say it is a fabrication." R.M. XVI. [Co Wo 11]
"... consists in creating a reality through the word..." L.P. 21. [La Th 14]

Factors, hereditary (which condition the intellectual development)
Hereditary factors (1) "are of a structural order and are tied to the constitution of our nervous system and to our sense organs ... Now these structural data influence construction of the most fundamental notions." N.I. 8. [Or In 1–2]
"These characteristics of the first type, while furnishing the useful structures to intelligence, are essentially limiting, as opposed to the factors of the second group." N.I. 9. [Or In 2]
(2) "In the second type, we deal with heredity of functioning itself and not with transmission of such and such a structure." N.I. 9. [Or In 2]

1.   **Facts, psychological**
1.1   **Facts of consciousness and**
1.2   **Facts of behavior**
The psychological facts "... are on one hand, the facts of consciousness seen from the point of view of the subject and in a synchronic or static fashion, that is, at a given level of development independent of the latter [1.1]; there are on the other hand, the facts of behavior seen from the point of view of the observer in diachronic or genetic fashion, that is, as function of development" [1.2]. E.E.G. XIV 167.

2.   **Fact, normative, or Cognitive norm**
"We call 'normative fact' ... the kind of realities which are facts for the observer and norms for the subject..." E.E.G. XIV 167.

"They are obviously those normative facts of which Marbe was thinking when he spoke of 'logical factors'..." E.E.G. XIV 153.

"... normative facts [are] ... those norms [which] modify the behavior of the subject to the extent that the subject considers them valuable." E.E.G. XIV 156–157.

"'Normative facts' in order to designate exactly those facts of experience which permit one to observe that such a subject considers himself obliged by a norm (however valid from the observer's point of view)." E.E.G. I 30.

"... The geneticist considers the norms which he has not established himself as normative facts, that is, as facts observed in the activities of the knowing subject, but these facts present this particular characteristic to be conceived as norms by the knowing subject." E.E.G. I 24.

3. **Fact, individualized, or Object**

"... An individualized fact is necessarily either some special class resulting from the intersection of several subclasses or a center of relations constituting the intersection of multiple sections or of seriations which are more complex." T.L. 46.

"Psychologically and epistemologically, without logic having to take a position on this point, a fact or an individualized object is always related to the sectioning required by the action of the subject..." T.L. 48.

4. **Fact, general or Law**

Any experimental analysis arrives at generalizations or laws..." T.P. I 124.

1. **Feeling**

Feeling "directs behavior by attributing a value to its goals." P.I. 9. Feelings consist in: (a) regulation of internal energies: fundamental feelings (Janet), interest (Claparède); (b) regulations of exchanges of energy with the exterior: desirabilities (Lewin), valences (E. S. Russel). P.I. 10. [Ps In 5]

2. **Feeling, representative**

When "the feeling persists in the perceptual absence of the person loved or not loved." A.I. 73.

3.1 **Feeling of obligation**

"The feeling of obligation appears when the child accepts an instruction given by persons whom he respects." J.M. 33. [Mo Ju 53]

3.2 **Feeling of equity**

"Feeling of equity is a development of egalitarianism in the sense of relativity." J.M. 253. [Mo Ju 317]

4.1   **Feeling, semi-normative**
       Is tied to the morals of obedience and of unilateral respect. A.I. 106.

4.2   **Feeling, moral**
       Is tied to moral reciprocity. A.I. 106.

5.   **Feeling of the duration**
       "Depends upon affective regulations of the action." N.T. 259.

       Field of equilibrium (*See* **Equilibrium**)

       Figural
       It is "the semi-deductible or semi-irreducible character of the
       experiment which explains the ambiguous characteristics of the
       figural, which on one hand, tends toward organization of configura-
       tions to the extent they are states of deductible transformations, but
       which, on the other hand, furnish the only possible knowledge in
       the case where the states and their transformations are not yet
       deductible." M.P. 444. [Me Pe 359]
       "... (1) The figural furnishes indices which lead to preferring one
       deductible possible framework to others in the interpretation of the
       given fact; (2) the figural furnishes, on the other hand, a close and
       necessarily symbolic sketch (in the wider sense of imaginal symbols
       and indices for perception) of that given fact when its immediate
       mixed character or fortuitous contingency renders it impermeable to
       the deduction of detail." M.P. 445. [Me Pe 359]

1.   **Filiation**
       "Df. 32. We shall say that a behavior B is derived by filiation from a
       behavior A if there are between them certain common characteristics
       and if these characteristics which differentiate them appear accord-
       ing to a transformation of which one can serialize the steps at the
       same time from the point of view of increase or decrease of value of
       these characteristics (measurable or orderable) or from the point of
       view of the order of chronological succession (the said order has
       to be constant)." E.E.G. IV 76.

2.   **Filiation between analytic and synthetic**
       "... There is filiation between the analytic and synthetic, i.e., that
       the analytic coordinations ... derive genetically from the synthetic
       coordinations..." E.E.G. IV 141.

1.   **Finalism, integral or infantile**
       It includes animism, artificialism and moral causality. E.E.G. I 74.

2.   **Finalism and movement**
       "... It is through this finalism always more or less colored by anim-

ism [all movement tends toward a goal and presupposes a substantial active or creative force] by which we can explain the privileged importance which is accorded to infantile intuitions, at 'the point of arrival' of movement and therefore the 'overtaking' in the judgment of speeds." M.V. xi. [Mo Sp xi]

Finality (notion)

"If genetic epistemology has to have some meaning; in other words, if it is correct that the study of the real formation and development of a notion authorizes a judgment on the value of knowledge, the concept of finality has to serve as the touchstone for the validation of such a method." E.E.G. I 68.

"The notion of finality has first three meanings on which it seems that all the authors, finalists or anti-finalists, agree: they are, (1) functional utility, (2) adaptation, and (3) anticipation of anticipatory regulation. It has, on the other hand, a last meaning which is perhaps tied to the first three and on which the debate rests: (4) it is the one of the goal or pre-established plan. The whole problem of finality consists in knowing if the meanings (1) to (3) imply meaning (4) and divergencies start at this point." E.E.G. IV 69.

Flash of consciousness (*See*** Law of Conscious Realization)**

Force (notion)

The notion of force includes (1) an objective aspect (acceleration) and (2) a subjective aspect (effort). E.G. II 109.

Formalization

"... Formalization constitutes one of the superior forms of structurization of thought. As a matter of fact according to the rule of reflecting abstraction, formalization reconstructs with new structures (in this case, axiomatized structures) the structures of earlier stages (not axiomatized) and it reconstructs by abstracting the necessary elements, but also by combining them through renewed operations (procedure of demonstration)." E.E.G. XIV 271.

"... Formalization constitutes the most refined variety of 'reflecting abstraction.' One cannot consider it as radically foreign to natural thought." E.E.G. XIV 273.

"Formalization, on the other hand, puts an end to endless regressions by choosing undefinable and undemonstrable points of departure of its definitions and demonstrations and it breaks the circularity by instituting a linear order between the stages of demonstration which it artificially separates." E.E.G. XIV 299.

67

Formation of knowledge or cognitive development
1.   **Heredity** (maturation)
2.   **Acquisition**
2.1   **Immediate acquisition**
2.11 **Reading** (perception)
2.12 **Sensory-motor or notional interpretation** (not entirely deductive) (immediate preoperational comprehension)
2.2   **Mediate acquisition**
2.21 **As function of experience**
2.211 **Non-systematic control** (learning str.)
2.212 **Systematic control** (induction)
2.22 **Non-function of experience**
2.221 **Non-systematic control** (preoperational coherence – equilibration)
2.222 **Systematic control** (deduction and, at the limit, immediate operational comprehension)
     E.E.G. VII 38.

1.   **Form** opp. **content of thought**

"... There is a total complementarity between content and form of thought; the content consists of data of the world as it is perceived, and the form constitutes the only disposition which allows going back from state T of this world to state $T - 1$, i.e., to make reality reversible through thought." D.Q. 324.

"... Understanding by forms, not just any form (perceptive, etc.), but the ones which at a certain level may be detached from their content (deduction) or the ones which acquire sufficient generality to be applied to any kind of content (methods of proof in induction)." E.E.G. VII 40.

"The forms dissociate themselves only progressively from their contents." E.E.G. I 33, note 3.

"The same logical form is not ... before 11 to 12 years independent of its concrete content." P.I. 176. [Ps In 147]

"... in the first place, the forms are separated from their content as far as they are fabricated, i.e., according to their novelty; secondly, forms of intelligence do not originate from the forms of perception but do fold back on the contrary upon themselves by directing perceptual activities, because one can perceive better that which one can construct and reconstruct." M.P. 377. [Me Pe 303] Cf. M.P. 380, 447.

2.   **Forms, elementary logical**

"The most elementary forms, that is, the structures (definition 5), which are most individualized are the single classes or relations between a single term and another. But any singular class is solidary with other classes, therefore of a total class." T.L. 47.

Fraction

(1) "In order to have a fraction there must be a divisible totality, in other words, the whole composed of separable elements."

(2) "The notion of fraction represents a number of parts."

(3) "So that a piece cut out of a whole may be considered as a particular fraction of the whole it is necessary that the whole itself be used up by the fractioning." G.S. 392. [Co Ge 309]

(4) "The parcelling of a continuum ... presupposes a certain relation between the number of parts and the number of pieces..."

(5) "In order to have fractions and not only qualitative sectioning, the parts have to be equal..." G.S. 393. [Co Ge 310]

(6) "An operational sectioning leading to fractions in the proper sense of the word, i.e., solidary in a nesting system and not simply juxtaposed, presupposes that each fraction, even though it is a part of the whole, constitutes a whole in itself susceptible to new divisions."

(7) "It is clear that fractions of surface, as related to the totality from which they proceed by sectioning, leave that totality unchanged; in other words, the sum of the constructed fractions is equal to the total initial surface." G.S. 394. [Co Ge 310–311]

Foresight (*See* **Anticipation**)

Frames, mediate (schemas, conceptual frames and operational structures)

"... the properties of the object, even in its presence, are reached all the more 'objectively' as the subject has at his disposal the richer mediate frames and the immediacy is to the contrary a source of deformation as much as of information..." M.P. 368. [Me Pe 296]

1.   **Functions, cognitive**

1.1   **Functions, cognitive** (operative aspect)

1.2   **Functions, cognitive** (figurative aspect)

We can "distinguish at all levels of development cognitive functions, [1.1] an operative aspect (from motions to intellectual operations) and [1.2] a figurative aspect (perception, image, etc.)..." M.P. 353. [Me Pe 283]

2.   **Functionings, invariant, of thought**

The "... invariant functionings enter the picture of two very general biological functions: organization and adaptation." N.I. 11. [Or In 4–5]

"But what is invariant is not such and such a characteristic of

69

structure (if not, we could draw the primitive form as 'true' form); it is just function." J.M. 267. [Mo Ju 334]

3.1 Function, explicative

"It is the centrifugal moment during which thought tends toward the external world." L.P. 205. [La Th 235]

"... Two complementary aspects may be distinguished in any explication, one relative to the elaborative of *objects*, the other relative to *causality*, and these are at the same time the product of it and the condition of its development. Therefore, we have the circle object × space and causality × time in which the interdependence of functions becomes more complicated because of a reciprocal relation between matter and form." N.I. 17–18. [Or In 12]

3.2 Function, implicative

"It is the centripetal moment during which thought tends toward the analysis of intentions themselves and their connections." L.P. 205. [La Th 234]

"Implicative function contains, on the other hand, two functional invariants which we can find again at all the stages, the one corresponding to the synthesis of qualities which means of classes (concepts or schemas), the other to quantitative relations, or numbers." "... It deals with the totality of operations which make possible the deduction of reality, in other words, to confer a certain permanence while furnishing the reason for its transformations." N.I. 17. [Or In 12]

"Constitute two moments of any activity of thought much more than two closed frameworks." L.P. 205. [La Th 234]

3.3 Function, mixed

"Df. We propose to call mixed the function of explanation and psychological justification which participates in explanation as well as in implication." L.P. 206. [La Th 236]

4. Function, symbolic

"Df. We shall speak of symbolic function from the moment when the signifier and the signified are differentiated..." E.E.G. II 46.

"Representation starts from the union of signifiers permitting to evoke the absent objects with a system of meaning relating them to the elements present. This specific connection between the signifiers and the signified constitutes the characteristic of a new function going beyond sensory-motor activity and which we may call in a general way the symbolic function. It is this which makes possible the acquisition of language or of collective signs." F.S. 292. [P1 Dr Im 277–278]

"Starting from this moment when symbolic function appears, that is to say when the signifiers are differentiated, the form of symbols (images) or of signs (words) and the things signified, in the form of preconceptual or conceptual relationships..." R.E. 536. [Ch Co Sp 452]

4.1   **Function, general symbolic**
"... Which characterize ... the simultaneous appearance of representative imitation of symbolic play, of the imaged representation and of verbal thought." P.I. 151. [Ps In 126]

5.   **Function, propositional**
"A propositional function $\phi(x)$ is neither a true nor false statement but susceptible of acquiring a value of truth or of falsity according to the determination of the arguments substituted for the indetermined argument x." T.L. 50.
"... Propositional function (logical equivalent of that which psychologically is a schema of conceptual assimilation)." T.L. 51.

G

1.1   **Generalization, formal, generalization by inclusion**
"It is what proceeds from the individual fact to law..." E.G. II 292.
"Generality by simple inclusion and not by operational composition ... recognizes only the existence of inclusive or purely formal generality without perceiving the fruitfulness of the operational generalization..." E.G. II 296.
It is not explanatory and "is limited to enlarging the field of the laws involved because it consists only in a passage of 'some' to 'all' but to an 'all' of which the totality remains real and includes only the totality of observed or actually observable cases." E.G. II 346.

1.2   **Generalization by operational composition or constructivist generalization**
"Is accompanied then by explanatory power tied to the necessity of the compositions involved." E.G. II 292.
"... The general law is thus explanatory to the extent that it appears necessary and it becomes such to the extent that the generality is constructed and not observed and where the generalization of the construction emanates from its operational necessity." E.G. II 293.
"The generalization through composition ... going beyond the real through reversibility reaches all the possible, and attributes,

therefore, to actual relations, that is, to given laws, a character of necessity." E.G. II 346. Cf. E.E.G. VII 34.

2.1 **Generalization, simple** opp.

2.2 **Generalization, operational**

"As opposed to simple generalization [2.1] which includes a special law within a more general law, operational generalization [2.2] proceeds in the following manner. After having created a first system, it borrows certain elements from it in order to construct through new compositional means a second system which also goes beyond the first and includes it as a particular case; the reciprocal may be true, since through certain materials of the second system the operations of the first will in turn reconstruct the former." E.G. I 241.

3. **Generalization, empirical**

"... that is, a system of inductive analogies more or less plausible." D.Q. 311.

4. **Generalization and reasoning by recurrence**

4.1 **Generalization, initial**

4.2 **Generalization, true**

"It is therefore starting from simple repetition of the action which creates the generalization which will lead to reasoning by recurrence [4], but initially we are dealing with a global repetition which reproduces the most apparent characteristics of the initial action instead of conserving only it ... which has to make way for the generalization itself [4.1]..." "True generalization consists first in choosing the property which has to be generalized from the totality of aspects of the action which is susceptible of reproduction... [4.2]" G.S. 284. [Co Ge 219]

5. **Generalization, stimulus-response** (D. E. Berlyne)

"... the hierarchic family of habits, interpreted through adding transformational responses and 'stimulus-response' generalizations, may take the form of 'group'." E.E.G. XII 111.

6. **Generalization and symbolism**

"It is a sort of condensation." L.P. 152. [La Th 158] (*See* **Abstraction** 6.)

1.1 **Geometry, experimental, of real objects**

1.2 **Geometry of action itself**

"... the child constructs simultaneously experimental geometry from real objects, and the geometry of his own action (coordinations of actions whereas the latter is applied to objects) and these two geometries, first undifferentiated, are only very slowly separated into a mathematical geometry." E.G. II 50.

2.1 **Geometry of objects** opp.

2.2 **Geometry of viewpoints**

2.11 **Geometry, topological**

2.12 **Geometry, Euclidian**

2.1 "... studies [the object] as if the observer were coextensive with it, and able, for example, to touch it or to look at it continuously from all sides simultaneously." (2.11) R.E. 292. [Ch Co Sp 247]

"... passes from one object to the other or goes through one and the same object by means of a measure." (2.12) R.E. 292. [Ch Co Sp 247]

2.2 "... studies the object no more from the inside or on the immediate borders but from the outside and in its relations with the far away point of view ... The observer is ... located in a position from where he considers objects as they appear from this particular point of view." R.E. 293. [Ch Co Sp 247]

1. **Good form, perceptual**

"Perceptual restructuring ... is the discovery of final 'good form'..." D.Q. 270.

"... good forms are only ... appearances with numerous equivalences, where [the] ... compensations are more frequent or more probable than in the general case." M.P. 98. [Me Pe 68]

2. **Good form, logico-arithmetic**

"Logico-arithmetical 'good form' is that of groupings or group. All their operations are at the same time reversible and can be combined and associated." D.Q. 270.

1. **Groping in learning**

The intelligent gropings "constitute a true active experimentation." P.I. 128. [Ps In 105]

1.1 **Groping, nonsystematic**

In nonsystematic groping "successive attempts are relatively independent of each other and are not directed by experience acquired earlier. It is in this sense that groping is fortuitous, that discovery of the solution is thus due to chance. Only from the moment when nonsystematic gropings are always oriented by a felt need, thus by the schema assigning a goal to the action ... it is evident that earlier experience nevertheless plays a role and the system of schemas already elaborated is not foreign to the seemingly most disorganized behavior of the subject..." N.I. 350–351. [Or In 400–401]

73

1.2   **Groping, systematic**

"Systematic groping is characterized by the following: (1) that the successive attempts are mutually conditioned with cumulative effect, (2) that they are clarified by earlier schemas conferring a meaning to the fortuitous discoveries, and (3) that they are directed by the schemas serving as initial means and of the groping attempts which constitute the differentiations or gradual accommodations. Systematic groping is triply or quadruply directed, according to whether the initial end and means form a whole or are distinct." N.I. 350. [Or In 400]

1.   **Group of motor displacements**

"If you speak of 'groups' of displacements, you speak of the ordering of movements in time, and if you say 'permanence' of objects you necessarily understand causal connections between events..." C.R. 192.

There is determined by behavior: (1) return (or inverse operation), (2) conservation of the initial point (or identical operation) and (3) detour (or associative operation). E.E.G. I 45–46.

1.1   **Group and objects**

"... group presupposes the notion of object, and furthermore reciprocally, because to find an object again is to give the possibility of a return (by displacement of the object or of the body)." P.I. 137. [Ps In 113]

"... presupposes ... that complete decentration by which the body is located as an element among others in the system of displacements permits the distinction of the subject's movements from those of objects." P.I. 138. [Ps In 114]

1.2   **Group or practical grouping**

"... The sensory-motor group of displacements ... is a grouping only from the practical point of view: motor coordination of the means and the end as function of the end point and not coordination of the representative displacements." M.V. 265–266, note 1. [Mo Sp 288]

2.1   **Groups, practical heterogeneous**

There is an "initial state [in the child of 3–6 months] during which space consists of heterogeneous 'groups' (each perceptual cluster constitutes a space) and they are purely practical." C.R. 88. [Co Re 99]

There is "the gustative or 'buccal' space according to Stern, the visual space, the auditory space, the tactile space, and many others (postural space, kinesthetic space, etc.) ... they are nothing other than practical, unconscious of themselves, and not including the subject himself. In brief, action creates space, but it is not yet situated within him." C.R. 90. [Co Re 101–102]

2.2 **Group, subjective**
"Centered on action itself." P.I. 139. [Ps In 115]
"... the child begins to see himself act, begins to use the relationships of things among each other, in opposition to simple correspondence of things with the functioning of the organs ... The projection of the practical group into the perceptual field circumscribed by its own action thus defines what we call the 'subjective' group." C.R. 101. [Co Re 114]

2.3 **Group of simply reversible operations**
"At the fourth stage of the attainment of the notion of the object (active search for the disappeared object, but in a privileged position and without taking account of its successive displacements) there corresponds essentially a progress in the notion of group. The child becomes capable of hiding and finding, etc.; briefly, he elaborates the reversible operations which form the beginning of the objective group ... It is thus the stage of 'the group of simply reversible operations'." C.R. 88. [Co Re 100]

2.4 **Group, objective**
"... the formation of objective 'groups' of displacements presupposes time and memory, the same as time presupposes a spatially and objectively organized universe." C.R. 59. [Co Re 65]
"... objective groups: existence of substantial objects, differentiation of outside displacements and of movements themselves and the exteriorization of spatial relations so that the subject can locate himself 'in' space." C.R. 133. [Co Re 150]

3. **Group of quaternality**
Identity (I), Reciprocity (R), Negation (N), Correlative (C)
(a) $C^2 = N^2 = R^2 = I$
(b) $RN = C, RC = N, CN = R$ (commutative)
(c) $RNC = I$
E.E.G. XV 72.

3.1 **Commutative *INRC* group of 4 elements**
Definitions of the *INRC* operators (J. B. Grize):
(a) "Let us limit ourselves to the case of two propositions p and q. We know that each well-formed expression of the calculus of propositions could be expressed in the form of a function $f(\vee, \wedge, p, q, \bar{p}, \bar{q})$. It follows that the three functors '$\vee$' (nonexclusive

disjunction), '∧' (conjunction) and '−' (negation) play a privileged role. In particular, the four operations of Piaget's group can be defined as follows:

I, identity or the neutral element of the group:

$$If(\vee, \wedge, p, q, \bar{p}, \bar{q}) = f(\vee, \wedge, p, q, \bar{p}, \bar{q}).$$

N, inverse or negation:

$$Nf(\vee, \wedge, p, q, \bar{p}, \bar{q}) = f(\wedge, \vee, \bar{p}, \bar{q}, p, q).$$

R, reciprocity:

$$Rf(\vee, \wedge, p, q, \bar{p}, \bar{q}) = f(\vee, \wedge, \bar{p}, \bar{q}, p, q).$$

C, correlative:

$$Cf(\vee, \wedge, p, q, \bar{p}, \bar{q}) = f(\wedge, \vee, p, q, \bar{p}, \bar{q}).$$

E.E.G. XV 61. Cf. T.L. 285.

(b) Example (*See* **Combination**):

$$I(p \supset q) = p \supset q$$
$$N(p \supset q) = p \cdot \bar{q}.$$
$$R(p \supset q) = q \supset p$$
$$C(p \supset q) = \bar{p} \cdot q$$

(c) The group of transformations: identity (I), inverse (N), reciprocity (R) and correlative (C) constitute a commutative group.

I	R	N	C
R	I	C	N
N	C	I	R
C	N	R	I

3.2 **Group, *INRC*, and *Nh* of 8 elements**

If we consider the threefold operations of bivalent propositional logic we can form two *INRC* groups related to each other thanks to the heterological transformation *Nh* (which consists in denying the operations composed without modification of the composing operation).

Example:

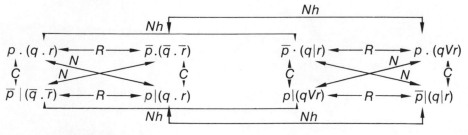

T.O.L. 38.

3.3 **Group, $INRC$, Nh, Ng, and Nd of 16 elements**

Nh, is the transformation of the operations constituting the left-hand side; Nd, is the transformation of the operations constituting the right, Cf. T.O.L. 40, Table 43.

3.4 **Group I, SN, SR, SC**

"There exist more elementary structures than the lattices, such as classifications or chains of asymmetrical relations which do not possess any further lower bounds than the elements themselves connected by each upper boundary $A \times B = A$ or $0(A \times A' = 0)$. Two of these semi-lattices multiplied among themselves already contain (other than the bigroup formed by the union of their disjoint parts, or by the operation of multiplication of their common parts) a group I, SN, SR, and SC which prestructure the $INRC$ group of inter-propositional logic." T.O.L. 207.

The biunivocal multiplication of classes or of relations is represented by the double entry table which already contains a primitive group I, SN, SR, SC. $SN =$ the semireciprocities, $SR =$ the semireversibilities, $SC =$ the semicorrelatives. Cf. T.O.L. (Appendix II).

3.5 **Group I Na Ra Ca of the upper and lower limits of the lattice of 256 ternary operations**

Transformation Rh of operations combined by their Reciprocals.

Transformation Ch of operations combined by their Correlatives (where $Nh = Rh$ Ch).

Transformation $Na = N$ of the operations combining their Inverses.

Transformation $Ra = R$ of the operations combining their Reciprocals.

Transformation $Ca = C$ of the operations combining their Correlatives.

T.O.L. 33–34 (where $Ch = Nh$ Rh, $Ca = Na$ Ra, Nh $Ra = I$, $Nh = Ra$, etc.) with $I = x . y$ (Lower Limit), $Na = x|y = \bar{x} \vee \bar{y}$, $Ra = x . \bar{y}$, $Ca = x \vee y$ (Upper Limit) and $I = x \vee y$, $Na = \bar{x} . \bar{y}$, $Ra = x|y = \bar{x} \vee \bar{y}$, $Ca = x . y$. We notice then: Na (Upper Limit) $= Ra$ (Lower Limit) and Na (Lower Limit) $= Ra$ (Upper Limit). T.O.L. 159.

3.6 **Group G of Arithmetic Additive operations** (P. Gréco)

"We have to wait for the formal level on which the subject knows how to coordinate the cardinal and ordinal operations (how much we have to add to M in order to have the same thing as K + 5)." E.E.G. XVII 16.

(1) System $\{\alpha\}$ of the additions (α) (or subtractions (α')) which are called cardinals.

(2) System $\{\delta\}$ the ordinal décalages (advances (δ) or retreats (δ') in the series)

where $\begin{cases} \alpha_i = \delta_i = (+_i) \\ \alpha_i' = \delta_i' = (-_i) \end{cases}$

$$N(\alpha_i) = \alpha_i' \qquad\qquad N(\alpha_i') = \alpha_i$$
$$R(\alpha_i) = \delta_i' \qquad\qquad R(\alpha_i') = \delta_i$$
$$N(\delta_i) = \delta_i' \qquad\qquad N(\delta_i') = \delta_i$$
$$R(\delta_i) = \alpha_i' \qquad\qquad R(\delta_i') = \alpha_i$$

$I = \pm0$; $NN = I$; $RR = C$; $NR = RN$; $NR = RN = I$. E.E.G. XVII 280.

1. **Grouping from the psychological point of view**

The logical and infralogical operations precede the numerical and metrical operations from the genetic point of view. These primitive operations contain the structure of 'grouping.' The psychological concrete operations present a structure of 'grouping,' whereas the formal operations present a structure of '*INRC* Group' (propositional combination).

The "final grouping results ... from the fact of assimilation, in ceasing to be deforming and has reached its point of equilibrium with accommodation." M.V. 172. [Mo Sp 185]

"It is assimilation freed from all experimental necessity." (9) 44.

"... the psychological criterion of the construction of a 'grouping' is the discovery of the conservation of the totalities, independent of the arrangement of the parts." E.G. I 85.

"There where there is a 'grouping' there is conservation of a whole and that conservation itself will not be simply presupposed by the subject through probable induction, but affirmed by him as certainty as the result of his own thought." P.I. 167. [Ps In 140]

1.1 **Grouping and intensive quantification**

"It is important then to see how the subject's activity allows him to progress from intensive operations, simple infralogical groupings ... to metric operations." E.G. II 39.

"The condition common to all groups [is] to define the transformations as functions of invariants and vice versa." D.Q. 74.

"... logical grouping (intensive quantification)" D.Q. 28.

"... a system of qualitative operations ('grouping')." M.V. 279. [Mo Sp 303 (note)]

1.2 **Grouping and reversibility**
"An operational reversible mechanism means ... logical groupings or ... arithmetic and geometric groups." D.Q. 322.
"Reversibility of operational grouping is at the same time deduction or assimilation undefined and perpetually accommodable to new situations." M.V. 172.
"That mobile equilibrium which consists in the mental life of the 'grouping' of direct and inverse operations." D.Q. 330.
"The grouping of operations is their reversible composition." D.Q. 51.

1.3 **Grouping and egocentrism**
"Decentration or the coordination of successively centered correspondences consequently form an operational 'grouping'." M.V. 171. [Mo Sp 183]
"In a general manner the logical grouping of a system of notions or of relations such as those of matter, of weight, or of substance, is thus a conquering of the corresponding forms of egocentrism." D.Q. 276.
"Grouping is the opposite of egocentrism." D.Q. 275.

1.4 **Grouping, practical**
"Or coordination of the means and ends which form in a general manner the qualitative valuations (totalizations of their values and the relations of means to ends) ... [That grouping] means the eight methods of [elementary] groupings (classes and additive and multiple relations)." (10) 201.

1.5 **Grouping and cooperation**
"Each grouping inside the individuals is a system of operations, and cooperation forms the system of operations carried out in common, i.e., in the proper sense of cooperation." P.I. 197. [Ps In 165–166]

2. **Grouping from the mathematical point of view** (J. B. Grize)
"Classes and relations on which the child depends in his development are not the abstract notions of the logician. They remain fundamentally qualitative even though structured, and it is that structure which Piaget has called grouping and which plays a role of the first magnitude in psychological explanation." E.E.G. XI 70–74.

2.1 *P*-**Grouping (naive)**

2.2 **Grouping (formal)**
"Let us suppose that we have classes nested into the following order: A, B, Γ, Δ ... which correspond to a zoological classification for example. Let us consider also the classes A', the complement of A under B, B' complement of B under Γ, etc. Let us write then our

classes in the form of a table having three lines, the class Λ being the null class:

$$A \quad B \quad \Gamma \quad \Delta \quad \dots$$
$$\Lambda \quad \downarrow \nearrow \downarrow \nearrow \downarrow \nearrow \downarrow$$
$$A' \quad B' \quad \Gamma' \quad \dots$$

These classes form a P-Grouping if the following conditions are satisfied:

(1) There exists an associative operation, let us call it 'o,' which permits the combinations: $A o A' = B, B o B' = \Gamma, \Gamma o \Gamma' = \Delta, \dots$

(2) There exists one operation, let us call it 'o'' which permits the combinations: $\Delta o' \Gamma' = \Gamma, \Gamma o' B' = B, B o' A' = A$. It is thus possible to advance closer and closer in the classification (in the direction of the arrows) and to return back to the starting point by the same route. These are the two primary conditions which assure the essential character of reversibility.

(3) There exists a neutral element, here Λ such that $A o' A = A' o' A' = B o' B = \dots = \Lambda$.

(4) Associativity of operations 'o' and 'o'' is limited. We could not have, for example:

$$(A' o B) o' A' = A' o (B o' A').$$

The left-hand member leads indeed to $B o' A'$ (by the 6th condition) or to A while the right-hand member will give $A' o A$ or B which is an absurdity.

(5) The compositions of operations are limited, which means that if X and Y are any two classes, $X o Y$ and $X o' Y$ cannot always be a class of the collection. In the usual zoological classification, one would not know how to form in effect the species 'brook trout' and the species 'gray fox' in order to find the genus belonging to that classification. Single ones are always composable by 'contiguous' terms like B, B' and Γ for example.

(6) The operation 'o' admits a principle of resorption: $A o B = B$, $B o \Gamma = \Gamma, \dots$

(7) Finally, the operation 'o' is tautological, in the sense that $A o A = A, A' o A' = A', \dots$

We will have to consider that a formal structure is a grouping if it possesses the analogues of the preceding seven properties." E.E.G. XI 71–72.

2.2   A grouping is a system $\langle M, \rightarrow, +, - \rangle$ where M is a non-null group, "$\rightarrow$" a relation (of partial order of which we can say "is contained in"), "$+$" and "$-$" two binary operations.

(1) If X is an element of $\mathbf{M}$, X is a term.

(2–3) If X and Y are elements of $\mathbf{M}$, $X + Y$ and $X - Y$ are terms.

(4) Nothing is a term except by (1)–(3).

We will not introduce the notion of a well-formed expression, since we have not incorporated logic within our system, but we have placed it in the metalanguage.

Let us pose now two definitions:

[$D1$: relation of equivalence; $D2$: relation of order where $D2$: $\rightarrow_i$ may be read as "is immediately contained in" if the following conditions are satisfied.]

($D1$) $X \leftrightarrow Y . = \mathrm{df.}\ X \rightarrow Y \wedge Y \rightarrow X$.

($D2$) $X \rightarrow_i Y . = \mathrm{df.}\ X \rightarrow Y \wedge \sim (X \leftrightarrow Y) \wedge (Z)(X \rightarrow Z \wedge Z \rightarrow Y . \supset . X \leftrightarrow Z \vee Y \leftrightarrow Z)$.

The system $\langle \mathbf{M}, \rightarrow, +, - \rangle$ is a grouping if the conditions here below defined are satisfied. $*$ = schemas of axioms

(Ref)* $X \rightarrow X$.

(Trans) $X \rightarrow Y \wedge Y \rightarrow Z . \supset . X \rightarrow Z$.

($G0$) If $Y \in \mathbf{M}$ and if $X \rightarrow Y$, then (a) $X \in \mathbf{M}$.

If $X \in \mathbf{M}$ and if $X \rightarrow_i Y$, then (b) $Y - X \in \mathbf{M}$, (c) $X + (Y - X) \in \mathbf{M}$.

($G1$)* $X + (Y + Z) \leftrightarrow (X + Y) + Z$ (associativity of $+$)

($G2$)* $X + Y \leftrightarrow Y + X$ (commutativity of $+$)

($G3$) $X \rightarrow Y . \supset . X + Z \rightarrow Y + Z$ (monotonic in the sum)

($G4$) $X \rightarrow Y . \equiv . X + Y \leftrightarrow Y$ (principle of resorption)

($G5$) $Y \rightarrow X + Z . \supset . Y - X \rightarrow Z$ (inverse operation $-$ of $+$)

($G6$)* $Y \rightarrow X + (Y - X)$

($G7$)* $X \rightarrow_i Y . \supset . X \rightarrow Y (Y - X)$ (limitation of the difference of the contiguous elements)

($G8$) There is an $0 \in \mathbf{M}$, such that $0 \rightarrow X$.

2.3 **Grouping, elementary**

The elementary groupings do not yet form combination and are not rejoined by all of the possible operations of Boolean algebra.

There are 8 elementary groupings (4 groupings of classes and 4 groupings of relations). T.L. §§11–21, (10) 200.

		Classes	Relations
Additive	asymmetric	I	V
	symmetric	II	VI
Multiplicative	biunivocal	III	VII
	co-univocal	IV	VIII

Examples: [I] That of the simple nestings: "Trout" included in

81

"Fish," included in "Animals," included in "Living beings." [II] Corresponds to "Vicariances": "the Americans plus all the foreigners to America = the Swiss plus all the foreigners to Switzerland." [III] That of tables with two or *n* entries: objects classified both as circles or squares and as reds or blues. [IV] classifications corresponding to a geneological tree: one of the dimensions is that of ancestry, of his sons, grandsons, etc., and the other dimension is brothers, first cousins, etc. [V] that of seriations (chaining of asymmetrical transitive relations) and [VI] that of compositions between symmetrical relations (transitive or aliotransitive). [VII] multiplications between two seriations bearing upon the same relation (serial correspondence between two distinct rows of objects arranged according to the same relation; example: larger and larger dolls corresponding to longer and longer walking sticks) or on two distinct relations (example: objects to be placed in order according to their weight and volume at the same time). [VIII] geneological relationships already treated under IV under classification of terms. E.E.G. XIV 188–189.

2.4 Groupings, lattices and groups

"... the grouping is a reversible lattice and at the same time closely related to the lattice by nestings of the parts within the whole, and of the group by its reversibility." T.L. 315. Cf. E.G.I. 84.

H

1. Heredity, general

"... the functional activity of reason (the *ipse intellectus* which does not come from experience) is evidently connected to general heredity of the vital organization itself: just as the organism does not know how to adapt itself to ambiant variations if it has not yet been organized, so the same intelligence is not able to understand any exterior datum without certain functions of coherence (thus the ultimate term is the principle of non-contradiction), of establishing relations, etc., which are common to all intellectual organization." N.I. 9. [Or In 2]

2. Heredity, special

"Special heredity of the human species ... comprise certain levels of intelligence superior to that of the apes, etc." N.I. 9. [Or In 2]

1. Hierarchy of behaviors

So-called "superior" behaviors are those which permit "... a progressive extension of the distances and progressive complications of the trajectories between the organism (subject) and the environment (objects)." P.I. 63. [Ps In 49]

2. **Hierarchy of values**

In intuitive and perceptual behavior the hierarchy of values, "determines the successive centrations of perceptual and imagined intuition of movement..." M.V. 53. [Mo Sp 55]

"... in the case of intuition as in that of perception, the point or the connection centered is overvalued ... and the others underestimated which means in our case that each of the relations successively focused on makes us immediately forget the others. This forgetting is manifest not by a phenomenon of simple memory (we do not forget within a few seconds what was just said) but by the sudden devaluing of reasons which motivated the preceding affirmation." M.V. 139. [Mo Sp 149-150]

"... intuitive thought does not achieve any more than perception does a permanent equilibrium: the present factors (the order of points of arrival, the order of points of departure, length, duration, etc.) are as though endowed with not logical, but causal, virtue. Thus it is sufficient that the attention is attached to one or the other according to the value of the exterior data and their modifications, in order to arrive directly at such and such an estimation or to have to reverse it and reengage in another direction such as in a sudden displacement of equilibrium." M.V. 153-154. [Mo Sp 165]

"... there is an absolute implication in each intuitive centration: the very fact of centering intuition on the relevant data results in valuing it exclusively and in hindering consequently the establishing of logical relationships with the others." M.V. 155. [Mo Sp 166]

"That centration consists on the other hand, of egocentric assimilation, since the value of order of the points of arrival is overestimated to the degree in which these points are involved in the activity itself as goals or aims of the movements or actions." M.V. 167. [Mo Sp 179] (*See* **Values**.)

Hyperregulations (hypercompensatory regulations)

The "... course of perceptual activities, which we cannot easily handle parsimoniously in this domain which is remarkable by the hyperregulations [estimations of size] naturally do not exclude at all crystalization in any way, automatization or sedimentation (whichever metaphor one would prefer) of such field activities..." M.P. 270. [Me Pe 212]

The "transformations with age [of perceptual constancies] ... tied to hypercompensatory regulations which witness growing super-constancies ... lead to the conclusion that the constancies originate in the perceptual activities and not only from automatic field effects." M.P. 277. [Me Pe 218]

1.   **Hypothesis, psychophysical, I**
"One can say, in certain regards, that relations between deduction and experience, as far as the connection between mathematics and physics is concerned, are of a comparable order to more general relations between consciousness and material causality in the domain of the connections between mind and body: in both cases we deal in effect with an isomorphism between a system of implications and a causal system." E.E.G. I 83.

2.   **Hypothesis, psychophysical, II [Interactionist opp. Unitarist]**
"In the sense where the operative structures of action need, in order to function, to be furnished with information (symbolically or not), by the figurative structures, and where those in return are constantly modified by the progression of the operational structures. The operational structures furnish knowledge of the transformations of a configuration to another and the figural structures furnish knowledge of the states themselves related by the transformations. There is thus a functional interaction, without prejudging the question of the respective role of transformations and states of knowledge, perceptual or general." M.P. 354, note 2.

I

Idea
"... ideas, that is to say, the conscious products of operational behaviors." E.G. III 136.

1.   **Ideal**
"We will call 'ideal' any system of values which constitutes a totality, thus all final goals of actions." N.I. 16. [Or In 16]

1.1   **Ideal and values**
"The correspondence between the ideals and the values are of the same order as those of the totality and of the relations, and it is self-evident that since the ideal is only the form not yet in equilibrium of the real totalities and that the values are nothing other than the relations of the means to the ends subordinated to this system." N.I. 16–17. [Or In 11]

1.2 **Ideal and desirability**

"... value is only the expression of desirability at all levels. Desirability, is, in effect, the index of a rupture in the equilibrium or of a totality not achieved which lacks some element of its formation and which strives for this element in order to realize its equilibrium." N.I. 16. [Or In 11]

Idealism and realism

"... the realistic direction [of scientific thought is] characterized by assimilation from above to below and by the primacy of notions centered on the object, such as those of substance and causality; and the idealistic direction [is] characterized by the postulate of irreducibility of the superior and by the primacy of deduction and of conscious implication." E.G. III 330.

1.1 **Identification, logical**

It is "qualitative equality." D.Q. 73.

For the logical grouping it is the logical tautology. P.I. 169. [Ps In 142]

1.2 **Identification, mathematical**

It is "quantitative equality." D.Q. 73.

For the arithmetic group it is numerical iteration. P.I. 169. [Ps In 142]

Identity

"Identity [is] a perceptual relation like equality or difference..." M.P. 314. [Me Pe 249]

Ideology opp. **Science and technology**

"... whereas technology and science constitute two kinds of objective relationships between men in society and the universe, ideology in all its forms is a representation of things centering the universe on human society, on its aspirations and on its conflicts." E.G. III 242.

"... from where the difficulty for science itself, of disassociating itself from ideology, and the absolute necessity of decentration of scientific thought in regard to sociocentric as well as egocentric thought." "... ideology is the symbolic conceptualization of the conflicts and aspirations born of [real] actions; science [on the contrary] prolongs the actions in intellectual operations permitting the explanation of nature and decentering the latter from himself for the reintegration within objective relationships which he elaborates thanks to his own activity." E.G. III 253.

1.1 **Illusions, primary perceptual**

"The two fundamental characteristics of primary illusions are that their qualitative properties (situations of the positive *maximum*, of negative *maximum* and of the null median error, in connection with the proportions of the figure) do not vary with age, but that their absolute quantitative value (force of the illusion) diminishes with development (or occasionally remains the same but does not increase with age)..." It is necessary "... to consider the primary illusions as the result of simple 'field effects'." M.P. 20–21. [Me Pe 3]

1.2   **Illusions, secondary perceptual**
The perceptual activities "... relate the elements up to now not related and new connections contain then certain deformations of the model of primary illusions. These new illusions, we will call 'secondary'..." M.P. 172. [Me Pe 133]

2.1   **Illusion of the implicit and**
2.2   **Illusion of the discontinuous**
"[2.1] illusion of the implicit consists in attributing the most complex notions to the elementary levels as if they had already been contained in the initial intuitions [2.2] and the illusion of the discontinuous leads to the admission of creations *ex nihilo* in the very course of development." I.H. 230.

1.   **Image, mental**
"The mental image is a product of interiorization of intellectual acts." N.I. 132. [Or In 147]
"... the image ... consists of a copy, not of the object itself, but of the accommodations appropriate to the actions which bear upon the object." R.E. 348. [Ch Co Sp 294]
"... the image while proceeding from a motor imitation never presents the states alone without the acts which become figures only through a succession of static images..." R.E. 349. [Ch Co Sp 295]
"The image could not by itself play an active role in the act of knowing: it is not an instrument of assimilation as such ... It plays only a role of signifier or of symbol, in relation to the act ... it is not the image which determines its meanings: it is the assimilatory action itself which constructs a relationship, of which the image is only the symbol." R.E. 540. [Ch Co Sp 455]
"The image is not the prolongation of the perception as such, but of the perceptual activity..." F.S. 79. [Pl Dr Im 77]
"The image is a sketch of the possible imitation." F.S. 72. [Pl Dr Im 70]
"... The image is only the symbol of an action, which consists either in forming a figure (by following the contours of an object, etc.) or in transforming it." E.E.G. XIV 232.

2.   **Image, mental (interiorized imitation)**

"It is an interiorized imitation, serving as simple symbolic signifier for the actions which bear upon the objects or to the latter as objectives of the actions." E.G. I 206.

"... it is not a first fact ... it is, like imitation itself, an accommodation of the sensory-motor schemas, that is to say, an active copy, and not a trace or sensory-residue of the perceived objects." P.I. 150. [Ps In 126]

"... the image, a kind of a schema or the summarizing copy of a perceived object and not the continuation of the sensory vividness." F.S. 80. [Pl Dr Im 77]

"The image is interiorized sensory-motor imitation as well as a sketch of representative imitations." F.S. 294. [Pl Dr Im 279]

3.   **Image (symbolic signifier)**

"... is a symbol of the object." (15) 53.

"The image is ... a previously accommodated schema, having been placed in the service of actual assimilations, also interiorized, as signifier in relation to these signs or meanings. The image is ... a differentiated signifier." F.S. 172. [Pl Dr Im 163]

It is "a type of signifier, that of symbolic images ... on the one hand, thanks to the progression of accommodations ... the indices always are molded more according to the characteristics of things and tend therefore to constitute themselves as 'images.' On the other hand, thanks to the progressive detachment of the indices in regard to the immediate action to the benefit of the mental combination, these images free themselves from direct perception in order to become 'symbolic'." N.I. 309. [Or In 355]

"... mental image is never a symbol only or knowledge in itself." E.E.G. XIV 231.

Images "are the representative symbols constructed at the same time as the correspondences of thought signified by it." R.E. 57. [Ch Co Sp 40]

4.   **Image (figurative structure)**

"... symbolic function and representation make possible the construction of other figurative structures such as images and imagined representations." M.P. 354. [Me Pe 284]

4.1   **Image, visual**

"... a visual image consists of an interior imitation or an imitation interiorized by the actions bearing upon the imagined objects." G.S. 22. [Co Ge 12]

"... the visual image corresponds largely to that which one would

draw of the object or the event when they are no longer perceived."
E.E.G. XIV 231, note 1.

Imagination, creative

"... creative imagination is the assimilatory activity at the state of
spontaneity..." F.S. 305. [Pl Dr Im 289]

1. **Imitation (reproduction)**

    "We call imitation the act by which a model is reproduced (which
    does not imply at all the representation of this model, because it may
    simply be perceived)..." F.S. 13. [Pl Dr Im 6–7]

    "... imitation begins with self-sufficient totalities (= with schemas
    already formed) only to be applied later to particular movements
    entering into these schemas as elements." F.S. 45. [Pl Dr Im 41]

    Imitation of reality "... is that fundamental tendency of the child's
    activity to reproduce, by gestures first, then simply by imagination,
    exterior movements to which the organism has to adapt, then in a
    general manner, the succession or the partial successions of events
    and phenomena; imitation is the desire of the self to retrace per-
    ceptually, for adaptation, the history of things. It is of little impor-
    tance whether that representation is physical or mental." J.R. 142.
    [Ju Re 173]

2. **Imitation (accommodation)**

    "Accommodation ... does not reach equilibrium except under the
    condition where a series of 'positives' is given, that is to say, stable
    copies or reproductions, indicating representation, strictly speaking.
    Imitation consists in that." F.S. 89. [Pl Dr Im 84]

    "It is only natural that pure and simple imitation of reality is not
    sufficient to produce at the outset reversible mental operations, if
    the imitation is not combined with an assimilation of the real to the
    self." "Thus imitation of reality could only lead to irreversibility,
    except if it is combined with assimilatory tendency." J.R. 142.
    [Ju Re 174]

2.1 **Imitation, deferred**

    "Deferred imitation, i.e., accommodation prolonging itself in imita-
    tive rough drafts, furnishes the signifiers that play or intelligence
    apply to the different things signified, according to the mode of
    assimilation, free or adapted, which characterize these behaviors."
    P.I. 150. [Ps In 126]

3.1 **Imitation, representative**

    "... the child begins to imitate new gestures by means of invisible
    parts of his own body (relative imitation of the movements of the

head, etc., which lead to representation of his own face) [and begins] the deferred imitations which prepare for symbolism..." N.I. 309. [Or In 355]

3.2 **Imitation, strictly representative**
"Starts only ... in the middle of symbolic play because like play it presupposes the image." P.I. 150. [Ps In 126]

4. **Imitation of the other**
"Imitation of the other, as shown by Baldwin, is the source of the *alter* and of the *ego*. One can truly go so far as to say that it represents one of the principal occasions of distinction between the exterior world and the self and consequently is a factor of substantiation and spatialization of the world." C.R. 278. [Co Re 318] Cf. L.P. 20.

5. **Imitation by training or pseudo-imitation**
"... imitation by training, with the differentiation of acquired schemas and without direct assimilation from the model or appropriate gesture ... is pseudo-imitation, ... pseudo-imitation is not in effect durable, except in the case of continuously renewed sanctions..." F.S. 25. [Pl Dr Im 18]

1.1 **Implication between propositions**
1.2 **Implication between operations**
There are "two kinds of implications: implication between propositions, which characterize in all cases formal thought, [1.1] and implications between operations which constitute either a particular case reducible to the preceding for as much as one expresses the properties of operations in the form of propositions or the general case itself (as much as one considers each proposition as expressing in its contents an operation of classes or of relations, and each formal connection between propositions as an operation of the second power as much as an interpropositional operation)." I.H. 206.
[1.2] We observe "the implicit connections especially between operations and indefinable notions. Or, instead of constituting simple implication between propositions, these connections would represent implications between operations ... these implications between operations constitute the correlate of what is genetically the abstraction *sui generis* starting from earlier actions or operations..." E.G. I 108.

2. **Implication, psychological forms of**
"... one can express the implications by three equivalent means: [2.1]: $p \supset q$; [2.2] $\bar{p} \vee q$ and [2.3] $p = p \cdot q$, expressions of which

the calculus produces the same product $p . q \vee \bar{p} . q \vee \bar{p} . \bar{q}$. For example, if p expresses the fact that a rod is slender and q the fact that it is flexible, that is the same as affirming "if it is slender, then it is flexible" $(p \supset q)$; "or else it is not slender, or it is flexible" $(\bar{p} \vee q)$, or again "to say that it is slender is equivalent to saying that it is slender and flexible $(p = p . q)$." L.E.A. 263. [Gr Lo Th 298]

"... the simplest psychological form of implication [is] $p = p . q$ for, before affirming 'if the rod is slender then it is flexible,' the subject ought to assert that slender is always equivalent to slender and flexible. Now $p = p . q$ and $q = p \vee q$ are the most direct translations of the product $A \times B = A$, and the sum $A + B = B$, form the basis of the inclusion $A < B$." L.E.A. 263–264. [Gr Lo Th 298]

"A relation of causality is diachronic, because connected to a succession in time, whereas the chain of implication is synchronic since it consists in a necessary and extemporaneous relationship." E.G. III 217.

3. **Implication, naive, between states of consciousness**
"... if the states of consciousness evolve in time, one could not say necessarily that they are 'causes' one of the others because they depend upon a mode of connection more noetic or inferential than causal. Their fundamental character consists of meanings from the cognitive point of view and of values from the affective point of view. Now one meaning is not 'cause' of another, nor the value of the other, but they get involved one with another by means of what we would call, for lack of anything better, a sort of naive implication, using the term in the popular sense of 'getting involved' and not in a technical sense." E.E.G. XIV 168.

4. **Implication by syncretism**
"Consists in a global fusion of two propositions." L.P. 138. [La Th 138]

1.1 **Index (in the larger sense)**
"It is the concrete signifier, related to direct perception and not to representation. In a general manner, we call an index every sensory impression or quality directly perceived of which the meaning (the 'signifier') is an object or a motor schema." N.I. 170. [Or In 191]

1.2 **Index (in the strict sense)**
"In the strict and limited sense of the word, an index is a sensory datum which indicates the presence of an object or the imminence

of an event (when the door opens it indicates a person coming.)"
N.I. 170. [Or In 191–192]

"... that is to say, an objective aspect given by outside reality..."
N.I. 172. [Or In 193]

Index and foresight

"The appropriate indices of secondary circular reactions [corresponding to a] third type of meaning ... encompass from the beginning an element of foresight relative to the things themselves..."
N.I. 172. [Or In 194]

"... only that foresight is still not independent from the action: the rope is thus signal, of which the meaning is the schema of "pulling to shake the hood'." N.I. 173. [Or In 194–195]

"The index strictly speaking belongs to the fourth stage [sensory-motor]. It permits the child to foresee not only an event connected with his action but even any event independently conceived and connected with the activity of the object itself." N.I. 218. [Or In 248]

1.1 **Indissociation, primary (nominal realism)**

"Realism consists in a primary indissociation, so to speak, an indissociation which consists simply in localizing characteristics in things belonging to the reality of the mind, but the mind does not yet know that they belong to it, (names, for example)." R.M. 237. [Co Wo 237]

1.2 **Indissociation, secondary (animism)**

"On the contrary, indissociation characterizing animism, is a secondary indissociation, which consists in lending to those things the characteristics analogous to the ones which the mind lends to itself: consciousness, will, etc." R.M. 237. [Co Wo 237]

Individual difference (*See* **Characteristics**)

1. **Induction and law**

"... induction will thus be the passage from deeds to laws, or if one prefers (for there does not exist any difference in nature between deeds and laws), the establishment of the deeds themselves, and their respective generalities." E.G. II 191.

"Induction is thus a group of proceedings of thought which tend to organize the data of observation or experience, that is to say, to classify them in form of concepts susceptible of nested hierarchies and placing them in logical or mathematical relationships susceptible of constituting entirely composable systems." E.G. II 193.

"[There are] two essential characteristics of induction ... organiza-

tion of the deductibility and the affirmation of its future value..."
E.G. II 200.

"Induction constitutes also a composition ... but a composition not achieved, that is to say, a 'grouping' or a group of operations not yet closed upon itself." D.Q. 324.

"Induction is a reasoning not yet grouped." D.Q. 338.

2. **Induction and probability**

"... the necessity for relying on induction always depends on the intervention of chance or of mixture ... induction is characterized ... by incomplete grouping of reasonings or operational transformations..." There is "intimate relationship between induction and irreversible chance, on the one hand, as well as between deduction and reversible mechanisms..." E.G. II 202.

"Induction ... affirms the highly probable character of deductability from reality." E.G. II 203.

"... between operational deduction and fortuitous transformation deductible induction is inserted, i.e., the totality of steps destined to draw, in the experiment, what is fortuitous and what is deductible, thus to prepare for later deduction." I.H. 225. Cf. I.H. 5.

3. **Induction and experiment**

"If we do not speak of induction as a specific reasoning, we create a method: a method which consists in using experimental data in order to remedy the shortcomings of deduction." E.G. II 192.

3.1 **Induction, empirical** opp.

3.2 **Induction, experimental**

"From phenomenism derive ... passive or empirical induction (as opposed to active or experimental) based on simple intuition of the frequent and the rare." I.H. 112–113.

4. **Induction and learning**

"... in induction as such the control is systemic and directed (the direction is applied to the totality of processes and not only to particular moments) whereas this is not the case in learning." E.E.G. VII 37.

1. **Inference**

"... there is always inference in the actions of a subject, when in the presence of physically given elements that subject calls upon elements which are not physically present in order to draw from this connection between physically given elements and those not physically present a knowledge which could not be obtained by means of the former only." E.E.G. VI 82.

"... inferences (or preinferences) as such contain always on these levels 4 aspects: (a) the physically given elements, i.e., those of which knowledge is assured by the intervention of sensory contact. (b) Elements which are used by the subject but which are not physically present. (c) Knowledge resulting from the composition of (a) and (b). (d) The method of composition assures the transition of (a + b) to (c)." E.E.G. VI 82–83.

"... is irreducible to perceptual contacts alone" but the observation, on the other hand, can include inferences. E.E.G. IV 65.

2. **Inference in the proper sense of the word**
    "Df. 2. We speak of ... inferences when, in the presence of elements a, the subject possesses a distinct knowledge of elements a, b, and c, and if he can dissociate them in a larger context by abstraction, and if the mode of composition allowing elements a and b together to pass to new knowledge c contains rules of which the subject has to be made conscious." E.E.G. VI 87.

3.1 **Inference, deductive**
3.2 **Inference, inductive**
    "... an inference may by deductive (= with conclusions considered as necessary) or inductive in the probabilistic sense (= with conclusions considered as having probability $p < 1$)." E.E.G. V 79.

Infinite
    "... from the operational point of view infinite beings are but the expression of operations susceptible of being repeated indefinitely." P.I. 29. [Ps In 20]

1. **Information, adapted**
    "... adapted information constitutes, with the majority of questions and their answers ... the only categories of the child's language with the function of communicating intellectual thought. This is in opposition to the diverse functions of egocentric categories." L.P. 29. [La Th 25]

2.1 **Information, primary**
2.2 **Information, secondary**
    "Primary information [applies to] observed events which do not depend on their prediction ... and secondary information depends on the action of the subject (prediction, hypotheses, etc.) and it must be decoded in order to furnish primary information. [Matalon] is led to think that perhaps there is never pure primary information, that means prior to secondary information and not resulting from it." E.E.G. X 164.

Secondary information would constitute primitive logic which co-ordinates the actions of the subject.

Infraclass, perceptual, or pre-infraclass

"... the prefix 'infra' does not have any meaning of genetic priority in our terminology but only that of an inferior scale from the point of view of the field of application, while the prefix 'pre' indicates something earlier or genetically inferior..." E.E.G. VI 62.

"On the other hand, if the comparison between perceptual aggregates is stripped of all meaning, it is legitimate to look for relations with 'infraclasses.' We call them thus continuous totalities (or those characterized by neighborhoods and topological separations between their elements) to which we could apply the infralogical partitive operations of addition and subtraction." E.E.G. VI 62.

Infralogic (concrete operation)

"The infralogical field ... is one where operations constitute space, time, movement and speed." M.V. 92. [Mo Sp 98]

Infralogical operations 'form the notion of the object; ... they are of the type 0 [the individual]. These operations apply no longer to the nesting of classes, but to the nesting of parts of the same object into the total object, replacing the notion of resemblance by that of proximity, the notion of difference in general by that of difference in order of placement (in particular that of displacement) and the notion of number by that of measure." R.E. 534. [Ch Co Sp 450]

Infrarelations

"We call infralogical relations or infrarelations, by analogy to infra-classes, the relations which are determined by elementary operations of 'placement' and 'displacement'." E.E.G. VI, note 1.

1. **Intelligence (adaptation)**

"Intelligence has both a biological and a logical nature." P.I. 8. [Ps In 3]

"Mental adaptations to new circumstances." (Df. Claparède) P.I. 15. [Ps In 9]

"Form of equilibrium to which tend ... [the] types of adaptation inferior to cognitive or motor adaptation." P.I. 12. [Ps In 6]

"This is just a generic term designating the superior forms of organization or of balance of cognitive structures." P.I. 12. [Ps In 7]

"It is an end result, and its origins blend with those of general sensory-motor adaptation, or, going further, they blend even with those of biological adaptation itself." P.I. 12. [Ps In 7]

"It is the farthest reaching mental adaptation, i.e., the indispensable instrument of exchanges between the subject and universe when the circuits go beyond immediate and momentary contacts so they attain far reaching and stable relations." P.I. 12. [Ps In 7]

"Intelligence is an adaptation ... it is essentially an organization and its function is to structure the universe just as the organism structures the immediate environment." N.I. 10. [Or In 3–4]

"... it has nothing to do with an independent absolute, but it is a relation, among others, between the organism and things." N.I. 24. [Or In 19]

2. **Intelligence (equilibrium)**

We must define intelligence "as progressive reversibility of mobile structures constructed by it." P.I. 17. [Ps In 11]

"... tends to total equilibrium trying to assimilate the whole of reality." P.I. 15. [Ps In 9]

"Intelligence is the same as making superior operations continuous with the whole of development, and the latter is conceived as evolution directed by internal requirements of equilibrium." P.I. 63. [Ps In 49]

3. **Intelligence and assimilation**

"... Intellectual adaptation contains an element of assimilation: i.e., of structuration by incorporating external reality to forms resulting from the subject's activity." N.I. 12. [Or In 6]

"... an act is the more intelligent the larger numbers of schemas it subsumes and the greater the difficulty of coordinating them." N.I. 279. [Or In 321]

"Intelligence consists ... in making a superior but weak tendency triumph (= the conclusion of reasoning) over an inferior and strong tendency (= perceptual appearances)." (12) 21.

"... behavior is the more 'intelligent' the more the trajectories between the subject and the objects of its action cease to be simple and demand an active composition." P.I. 16. [Ps In 10]

4. **Intelligence, systematic**

When "consciousness of relations is advanced enough to allow a reasoned prediction..." N.I. 289. [Or In 332]

"... implies deduction and representation..." N.I. 245. [Or In 280]

"Communicated intelligence is much more deductive and tries to explain connections between propositions, *therefore, if ... then*, etc. ... It insists more in proof ... It tends to eliminate the schemas of analogy by replacing them with deduction proper." L.P. 44. [La Th 47]

5.1 **Intelligence, elementary**
"... elementary intelligence, as all spontaneous activity, is essentially conservative; that which the child looks for ... is to grasp or to hold ... in short to do exactly that to which its circular reactions are accustomed." N.I. 202–203. [Or In 230]

5.2 **Intelligence, sensory-motor**
"Whereas habits and elementary perceptions are essentially one-way, sensory-motor intelligence (or pre-verbal) discovers the detour and return behaviors which forecast in part associativity and reversibility of operations." E.G. I 23.
This "mixture of assimilation to earlier schemas and accommodation to actual conditions defines motor intelligence." J.M. 63. [Mo Ju 87]

5.3 **Intelligence, practical**
Practical intelligence "prolongs sensory-motor intelligence ... with the progressive grouping of means and ends." (11) 260.

5.4 **Intelligence, perceptual, or Perceptual activity**
We observe "an activity located beyond perception and movements, but short of reflected thought. It is this activity which seems to prolong sensory-motor intelligence prior to language and which we shall call, after its appearance, perceptual intelligence or simply 'perceptual activity'." F.S. 78. [Pl Dr Im 75]

5.41 **Intelligence of perception**
It is "thought tied to an immediate observation which is or is not accompanied by language." L.P. 132. [La Th 128]

5.5 **Intelligence, pre-conceptual**
"... Characterized by pre-concepts or participations and on the level of early reasoning by 'transduction' or pre-conceptual reasoning." P.I. 152. [Ps In 127]

5.6 **Intelligence, reflexive gnostic or verbal**
"... limits itself to thinking of forms, or to construct them within in order to assimilate to them the content of experience..." N.I. 13. [Or In 6] Cf. E.G. II 74.
Verbal intelligence is "thought detached from immediate observation." L.P. 132. [La Th 128]
It is "the function of adaptation of the child not to the reality itself, but to words and expressions, heard from adults or other children, and by which the subject tries to imagine a reality." J.R. 96. [Ju Re 115]

Intension (*See* **Comprehension**)

1.1 **Intentionality and desire**

"Intentionality is defined as consciousness of desire, or of direction of the act, and this consciousness is itself a function of the number of intermediary actions required by the principal act." N.I. 133. [Or In 148] Cf. N.I. 199.

1.2 **Intentionality and means**

"... intentionality [is] the differentiation between means and ends..." N.I. 112. [Or In 122]

Interactionist (*See* **Hypothesis, psychophysical**)

Interest

"... is the regulation of forces necessary for a determined finality." A.I. 48.

"Interest would be a sort of mechanical connection between the forces at the disposal of the individual and the internal regulation resulting from it on the one hand and from values on the other..." A.I. 40. (*See* **Affective regulation**.)

Introjection

"... introjection is the tendency to locate in others or in things the reciprocal of emotions which we feel for them. The schema of introjection is very clear: all that resists or obeys the ego is conceived as having an identical activity to that of the ego which commands or tries to overcome the resistance ... the cause of introjection is simply egocentrism..." R.M. 242. [Co Wo 242]

"... introjection results from the egocentric tendency to believe that everything gravitates around us, and consists in ascribing to things powers to either obey or resist us." R.M. 244. [Co Wo 244]

Introspection

"Introspection is a variety of becoming conscious, or, more exactly, becoming conscious in the second degree ... it supposes not only that we take consciousness of relations woven by our thought but of the work of this thought itself." J.R. 119. [Ju Re 144]

1. **Intuition, imagined or perceptual**

The "intuited realities are essentially the 'signified' actions which are not replaced by the image." R.E. 541. [Ch Co Sp 455]

"Intuition [is nothing but] a representation constructed with interiorized and fixed perceptions and it does not yet reach the level of the operation. The latter consists of a composition freed from perception and relates all the successively perceived data in a

97

system that is at the same time coherent and mobile." G.N. 299.

"Intuition is ... action and ... irreversible perception." D.Q. 18.

"Intuition is an imagined thought ... it applies to total configurations and no longer to simple syncretic collections which are symbolized by examples..." P.I. 164–165. [Ps In 138]

"... remains phenomenistic because it imitates the outlines of the real without correcting them, and egocentric because it is constantly centered as a function of the action of the moment." P.I. 165. [Ps In 138]

"... we shall take the term intuition or intuitive thought in a limited sense, more limited than the mathematical one. This means for us that preoperational thought is thought which is not yet capable of 'groupings' and of 'groups' and relies only on perceptual configurations or on empirical gropings of action. We, therefore, must speak in this case of imagined intuition, or even 'perceptual' as opposed to rational intuition. We shall limit ourselves to speaking of intuition as such." M.V. VI. [Mo Sp x]

2. **Intuition and centration**

"... if the property of intuitive thought consists in evoking simply by imaginary representation and mental experience the process to be explained, it is sufficient that the latter contain several aspects or distinct relations in order for it to be sometimes one and sometimes the other which is 'centered,' just as when perception is fixed on one point or another of a total figure." M.V. 139. [Mo Sp 149]

3.1 **Intuition, simple**

"... simple intuition, if the subject succeeds in evoking through the image a static figure which imitates the one furnished by perception..." G.S. 340. [Co Ge 207]

"Immediate intuition of experience does not surpass the passive consciousness of immediate data." N.I. 316. [Or In 363]

"At stage I (6–7 years) intuition remains 'immediate' or 'amorphous,' i.e., it reproduces without perceptual relations the correct and inexact ones without being able to coordinate them into a coherent whole." N.T. 42.

3.2 **Intuition, articulated**

"... articulated intuition, while representation is applied to elementary transformations, surpassing perceptual data but without reaching mobility, reversibility and operational generality." G.S. 340. [Co Ge 267]

"... the subjects ... testify to a progress of temporal intuitions in the direction of articulated or relational intuition. This progress is effected due to a mechanism of representative decentration comparable to the one of perceptual decentration. This means that the privileged qualities given in initial egocentric intuition ... are little by little decentrated either by representative anticipation which prolongs the perceived movements or by representative reconstruction which by introspection restores a value to them which is different from the results of the action." N.T. 98.

"... is nothing but the product of successive regulations which finally articulate global relations and relations unanalyzable from the start, and not yet a grouping in the proper sense of the word." P.I. 158. [Ps In 132]

"... mental experience, or articulated intuitions..." M.V. 27. [Mo Sp 28]

"Articulated intuitions ... are ... the regulations or decentrations of the primitive sketchy intuitions." M.V. 22. [Mo Sp 22]

4.1   Intuition of space

"... intuition of space is not a noting of properties of the objects, but always an action applied to them..." R.E. 532. [Ch Co Sp 449] Cf. C.R. 190.

4.2   Intuition of duration

"... we may conclude, if we wish, that for an animated movement of uniform speed, there is an intuition of a whole duration such as $(B = A + A')$ is larger than one of its parts (A)." N.T. 41.

"There does not seem to exist at first a primitive intuition of duration, opposed to the order of succession which is easier to grasp as a function of the organization of the temporal content, i.e., of the events themselves." E.E.G. I 54.

4.3   Intuition of speed

Speed "is reduced to the intuition of overtaking." E.G. II 26.

4.31   Intuition, simple, of speed

"The simplest intuition of speed is based upon ... intuition of order; a moving thing is at any age conceived as faster than another if it overtakes it on a parallel trajectory, if after having been behind, in the sense of movement, or next to it, it is in front of it afterwards." M.V. 113. [Mo Sp 121]

"Intuition of speed could not consist of a relation between the traversed space and time, because of lack of general interest of the first and understanding of the second; it can therefore only be perception or representation of an active relation rather than an intellectual one, that of overtaking. This relation may be perceived or felt as direct function of the activity of the body itself, when a voluntary movement is stronger than another, in particular, when there is an effort (as Baldwin and Janet demonstrated), a feeling of acceleration or, inversely of putting on the brakes. But the overtaking may be perceived on two moving things of any type if they follow in the same sense two parallel paths and this is precisely the situation which is started by the intuition of exterior speeds." M.V. 117. [Mo Sp 125–126]

4.32 **Intuition, rational, of speed**
"Intuition of overtaking becomes rational when the two extreme order points of movements compared with each other or conceived as determining, at the same time, spatial intervals (displacements) and temporal (co-displacements). The first constitute the traversed way (length); the second constitute the duration; and, together the speeds." M.V. 123. [Mo Sp 132]

4.4 **Intuition, geometric**
"Geometric intuition in its beginnings is a totality of interiorized actions of which the image is only the symbol constituted by their imitating accommodation." E.G. I 207.
"... the image and the sensitive matter in geometric intuition play the same role as all thought: that of symbol or of signifier, as opposed to signified relations." R.E. 531. [Ch Co Sp 447]

Invariance
At the operational level of development "the child after having ignored or negated conservation of the most elementary forms of quantities, starts to consider as necessary the invariance of logical and numerical totalities, lengths, distances and continuous physical quantities, etc." E.E.G. I 46. (*See* **Conservation.**)

1. **Invention**
"An invention is the creation of a new and free combination not realized up to that point either in nature or in the mind of the subject, even if the elements, now combined in a new way, had been known earlier..." E.E.G. XIV 218–219.
"... invention by sensory-motor deduction is nothing other than spontaneous reorganization of previous schemas, which accommodate themselves to the new situation by reciprocal assimilation." N.I. 302. [Or In 347–348]
To invent "is to combine mental schemas." N.I. 296. [Or In 341]

100

2.   **Invention, sudden**
Sudden invention that is "instead of being controlled in each of its stages and *a posteriori* by the facts themselves, the research is controlled *a priori* by mental combination. The child foresees, before trying them, which maneuvers will not succeed and which will. The control of the experiment is therefore applied upon the totality of this deduction, and not as before upon the details of each particular step." N.I. 296. [Or In 340]

Inverse (N)
"The inverse of an operation (for example $p \lor q$) is the complement in relation to the complete affirmation $(p * q)$." T.L. 268. $N(p \lor q) = \bar{p} . \bar{q}$.

Inversion (action)
"We shall call an action an inversion, or else that there is empirical return to the point of departure, if the subject comes back to it without consciousness of the identity of the performed action in both senses." E.E.G. II 44.

Isomorphism (*See* Parallelism)
"... there is isomorphism, starting from a certain level of development, between logical operations of the subject and those which intervene necessarily in any intellectual cooperation at the point where, psychologically speaking, we have two separate aspects distinct from the reality of interactions in general." E.E.G. I 34.

J

1.   **Judgment**
"To judge does not necessarily mean to identify, as is sometimes said, but to assimilate. This means to incorporate new data into a previous schema, into a system already furnished with implications." N.I. 359. [Or In 410] Cf. N.I. 235.

2.   **Judgment, perceptual, opp. Intellectual construction**
"... in the choice which has to be made among the available designs, perception directs intelligence, even though the latter interprets the former according to free and not literal translation. We shall then say that there is perceptual judgment. On the other hand, in the case of design to be constructed using procedures of measurement or of comparison judged appropriate to conserve form in the course of

enlargement, it is intelligence which directs and uses perception as it sees fit. There is thus intellectual construction." R.E. 419. [Ch Co Sp 354]

1.1 **Justice, immanent**
The child believes in automatic sanctions which are produced by the things themselves.
"Belief in immanent justice comes from a transfer to things of feelings acquired under the influence of adult constraint." J.M. 208. [Mo Ju 261]

1.2 **Justice, retributive**
"Is defined by the proportionality between the act and the sanction." J.M. 158. [Mo Ju 198]

1.3 **Justice, distributive**
"Is defined by equality." J.M. 158. [Mo Ju 198]
"Because based on equality and on reciprocity, there could not be justice without free consent." J.M. 255. [Mo Ju 319]

Juxtaposition
"The phenomenon according to which the child is incapable of constructing a story or a wholly coherent explanation but has a tendency to break up the whole thing into a series of fragmentary and incoherent affirmations. These affirmations are 'juxtaposed' to the extent that there are between them neither causal and temporal nor logical relations." L.P. 123. [La Th 116] Cf. J.R. 21.

K

1. **Knowledge**
"... it is first an action upon the object and it implies in its very roots a permanent motor dimension still represented at the highest levels..." (16) 14.
"The starting point of knowledge is constructed from the actions of the subject applied upon reality." E.G. II 341.
"To know means to construct or reconstruct the object of knowledge, such as to grasp the mechanism of this construction; ... to know is to produce in thought, in order to reconstitute the 'mode of production of phenomena'." M.P. 441–442. [Me Pe 356]

2.1 **Knowledge (copy)**
There is "a model of knowledge (copy) according to which the operation would construct the image of simple exteriorly given or already realized transformations..." E.E.G. XII 113.

2.2 **Knowledge (assimilation)**

There is a "model of knowledge (assimilation), according to which the operation is an act which is acquired as function of the very co-ordination of the subject's actions, because that coordination in itself already implies some element of transformation in the logico-mathematical sense of the word." E.E.G. XII 113.

3. **Knowledge, physical**

"Physical knowledge is due neither to exterior experience alone nor to internal experience alone but to a necessary union between the logico-mathematical structures initiated in the coordination of these actions and the experimental data assimilated to them." E.E.G. II 16. Cf. E.G. II 14.

4. **Knowledge, unconscious**

"The reflexes and the morphology of organs to which they are connected form a sort of anticipated knowledge of the exterior environment, unconscious knowledge and all material knowledge, clearly indispensable to the ultimate development of effective knowledge." N.I. 19. [Or In 14]

5. **Knowledge and conservation**

"All knowledge, either of the scientific order or arising from simple common sense, presumes a system, explicit or implicit, of principles of survival." G.N. 6. [Co Nu 3]

L

Language of the child

1.1 **Language, egocentric**

"... the child speaks only of himself ... and does not try to place himself at the point of view of the interviewer." L.P. 18.

(a) Repetition (ecolalia). (b) Monologue. (c) Monologue between two or collective monologue. L.P. 18. [La Th 9]

"If egocentricism is an absorption of the self in things and in people without differentiating between his own and other points of view, it is indeed clear that verbal behavior of the child, in what we call egocentric language, is a particular case of this general phenomenon and may in this respect be used as an index in the analysis of his development as a function of age." L.P. 64. [La Th 262]

1.2 **Language, social**

(a) Adapted information... (b) Criticism... (c) Orders, petitions and threats... (d) Questions... (e) Responses. L.P. 18–19. [La Th 9–10]

103

2. **Language, spontaneous**
It is the totality of all categories of language (1.1 and 1.2) except for responses. L.P. 36. [La Th 35]

3. **Language, magical**
"... consists in acting through the word only, without contact with things or people." L.P. 21. [La Th 14]

Lattice (*See* **Net**)

1. **Law of conscious realization (Claparède) or Law of the Décalages**
"... the 'law of conscious realization of Claparède specifies that becoming conscious of a relation occurs later than when its usage in action is more primitive and automatic..." E.E.G. XIV 203–204. Cf. E.E.G. I 47, J.M. 43.
"The appearance of a new type of rules, at the practice stage, does not automatically lead to new consciousness of the rule. Each psychological operation [must] be relearned on different levels of action and thought." J.M. 61. [Mo Ju 85] (*See* **Décalage**.)
"... the law of 'décalages': when an operation moves from one level of consciousness or action to another, it has to be relearned on this new level." C.R. 69. [Co Re 77] (*See* **Conscious realization**.)

2.1 **Law of perceptual equilibrium** opp.

2.2 **Law of operational composition**
"... the laws of perceptual equilibrium are of statistical and ir-reversible order, and those of operational composition are necessary and reversible." N.T. 175.

3. **Law of relative centrations**
"... any contrast is exaggerated by perception." P.I. 90.
$P = L_2(L_1 - L_2)/S \times nL/L$max; [where P = illusion]. Cf. M.P. 24–27 [Me Pe 7], 140–147. (*See* **Coupling** and **Composed error**.)

4. **Law, infantile notion**
"... any 'law' for a long time appears to the child as physical and moral at the same time." J.M. 63. [Mo Ju 88]

1. **Learning (Circular reaction)**
"... learning is nothing more ... than a circular reaction leading to reproductive assimilation, recognitive and generalizable." N.I. 259. [Or In 296]
"... that is to say the cumulative element of groping..." N.I. 258. [Or In 296]

2. **Learning**
"... (a) all learning presumes the use of coordinations not learned (or not entirely learned) which constitutes a logic or prelogic of the

104

subject; (b) learning of logical structures presumes the use of other logical or prelogical structures not previously learned (or not entirely learned)." E.E.G. X 184.

3.1 **Learning in the strict sense**
"In the strict sense we speak of learning only to the extent that a result (understood or performed) is acquired as a function of experience. That experience could otherwise be of a physical type or logico-mathematical type or both..." E.E.G. VII 36.

"In contrast to perception and immediate understanding it is necessary then to reserve the term learning to an acquisition as a function of experience but unfolding in time, that is mediate and not immediate like instantaneous perception or understanding." E.E.G. VII 37.

3.2 **Learning in the broad sense** or **Development**
"... we call 'learning in the broad sense (s. lat.)' the combination of learning in the strict sense (s. str.) and [of the] processes of equilibrium." E.E.G. VII 38. ("or development") E.E.G. VII 41.

Legality opp. **Causality**
"... 'legality' means regular succession and not yet 'causality,' which means understanding of this connection." C.R. 257. [Co Re 294]

1. **Line, straight**
"... a straight line is not only conceived at its [operational] level *IIIA* as the result of the aim, as the only line conserving its form in perspective or as the product of the conservation of the same direction ... but also as the only line conserving its form in the course of a rotation of itself and taking itself for its own axis of rotation." G.S. 324. [Co Ge 252]

1.1 **Line, projected straight** opp.

1.2 **Line, topological**
"... contrary to a topological line forming an object in itself, the projected line appears when the elements of this line are related with a subject by considering them as 'the edge' and perceiving them as masking each other." (Directed Behavior.) R.E. 226. [Ch Co Sp 190–191]

Logicism
"... logicism is the tendency to interject into the context of causal explanations, which psychology tries to base on experience alone, considerations taken from logic; i.e., from a discipline where the object is based on deductive validity and not on questions of fact." E.E.G. XIV 151. (*See* **Psychologism.**)

1. **Logic and psychology**

"If logic is a formal theory of operations of thought, psychology and sociology, or at least certain parts of these disciplines, form a real theory of the same operations: of operations effected by the individual or exchanged through language and effected in common." T.L. 11.

"Formally, operations are transformations permitting to establish certain propositions or relations originating from other propositions or relations, and of transformations of which the validity is regulated by accepting (or rejecting) certain axioms. In reality, the operations are equilibrated actions." T.L. 12.

Logic is the axiomatic of operational structures and psychology and sociology of thought study its function. T.L. 16.

"Logic is an axiomatic of reason of which psychology of intelligence is the corresponding experimental science." P.I. 37. [Ps In 27]

Logic is "the mirror of thought and not the inverse." P.I. 37. [Ps In 27]

"Logic is not co-extensive with intelligence, but consists in the totality of rules of control which intelligence uses in order to give itself direction." J.M. 323. [Mo Ju 398]

"Formal logic or logistic constitutes simply the axiomatic of states of equilibrium of thought." P.I. 7. [Ps In 3]

"Logic is the morality of thought, as morality is the logic of action." J.M. 322. [Mo Ju 398]

"Logico-mathematical structures originate from coordination of actions..." E.G. II 16.

"The logical universe constitutes the domain of the possible." E.G. I 35.

2. **Logic and genesis**

2.1 **Logic of action**

"... there is a logic of action which characterizes intelligent co-ordinations from the preverbal level and is prolonged to the verbal level effecting a progressive junction with logic. It develops subsequently through language behavior in the sense of communication." E.E.G. I 35.

2.2 **Logic, egocentric**

"Is more intuitive, more syncretic, than deductive; that means that its arguments are not made explicit. Judgment moves in a single jump from premises to conclusions, omitting steps." L.P. 44. [La Th 46–47]

106

2.3 **Logic of concrete operations** (from 7–8 to 11–12 years)

"Logistic schematization [of grouping] furnishes the rules of logic of entities." P.I. 53. [Ps In 40] Logic of concrete operations applies to objects and not at this point to propositions, and they do not at this point show complete disassociation between form and content. E.E.G. I 27.

2.4 **Logic of formal or propositional operations** (11–12 to 14–15 years)

Logic of formal or propositional operations with a sort of hypothetico-deductive reasoning based on interpropositional operations ($p \supset q$, etc.). E.E.G. I 28.

"The property of logic of propositions ... [has] to be a verbal logic; it is especially a logic of all possible combinations of thought. These combinations may originate in experimental problems or in purely verbal questions." L.E.A. 222. [Gr Lo Th 253]

"... the interpropositional operations apply to statements. Their intrapropositional content consists of operations of classes and of relations." L.E.A. 223. [Gr Lo Th 254]

3. **Logic and logical theories**

3.1 **Logic, formal**

"... the 'formal' which characterizes logic is not a given quality which characterizes a state, but the expression of a process or of movement of formalization. The definition of logic which we just accepted means in reality only an ideal; logic is in fact theory but not formal (in an achieved state) but formalizing or formalizable from deductive operations." T.L. 23.

"... the role of logic is not only the foundation of mathematics but also the duplication of it. That means it has to disengage all elementary structures, in particular those which precede mathematization." T.L. 99.

3.2 **Logic, natural**

"... a logistic construction is more or less natural or artificial according to the degree of correspondence with the psychological (mental operations of the subject or systems of communications, etc.) or mathematical systems." T.L. 27.

3.3 **Logic, static,** opp. **Operational logic**

There is "... a static conception which sees any or all operations as an impoverishment of 'complete affirmation' [normal disjunctive form of tautology in bivalent propositional logic; $pq \lor \bar{p}q \lor p\bar{q} \lor \bar{p}\bar{q}$] and an operational conception which sees this 'tautology' as a formal matter upon which the subject acts and which reserves the

107

quality of 'total truth' to designate the system of all the operations as mobile and reversible transformations." T.L. 267.

M

Magic
"We shall call magic the use that the individual thinks he can make of relations of participation in order to modify reality. Any magic presupposes participation, but not the reverse." R.M. 117. [Co Wo 132]

(a) by participation of gestures and things

(b) by participation of thought and things

(c) by participation of substances

(d) by participation of intentions (magic by commandment) [Co Wo 132–134]

"... if all magic tends toward symbolism ... magic is thus the pre-symbolic stage of thought." R.M. 149. [Co Wo 161]

"... it constitutes the first form of representative causality (as opposed to partially sensory-motor causality, which remains immanent to elementary techniques) and is nothing else but the unfolding of beliefs in the efficacy of acts, i.e., of gestures, and even words." E.G. II 282.

Matter opp. Form
We shall call matter or content of infantile knowledge all that which experience and direct observation impose on him. We designate as form of knowledge that which the child adds to matter, i.e., all the prerelations and prenotions from which we, the adults, are already freed. C.P. 262. [Co Ph Ca 282]

1. ### Maximum, spatial
    "We shall call spatial *maximum* of an optico-geometrical illusion the *maximum* of illusion which corresponds to certain spatial proportions of the figure, for equal times of presentation." M.P. 23 note 1. [Me Pe 6 note 1]

2. ### Maximum, temporal
    We shall call "temporal *maximum* the *maximum* of illusion which corresponds to a certain optimal duration of presentation, for spatial proportions which are held constant." M.P. 23 note 1. [Me Pe 6 note 1]

108

1.   **Meanings** (System)

"If language consists indeed of the most perfected system of meanings (because of the inherent mobility of 'arbitrary' signifiers which
are verbal signs), we find meanings at all levels of the hierarchy of
behaviors. (The indices and perceptual or sensory-motor signals,
representative imagined symbols and verbal signs, are as many
signifiers relative to the things signified distributed over all stages
of development.)" E.E.G. I 32.

The system of meaning consists of: (a) the sensory-motor signals,
(b) the perceptual indices, (c) the imagined symbols, and (d) the
linguistic signs. E.E.G. I 81.

2.1   **Meaning of perceptual data**

"Any perceptual datum carries a meaning, without leaving the
borders of perception, but the 'signifiers' and the 'signified' belonging to these perceptual meanings do not go beyond the framework
of 'indices' and remain thus relatively indifferentiated and inter-
changeable..." M.P 357. [Me Pe 286]

"The signified of a perception [is] the object itself; [it is] thus an
essentially intellectual being ... for perceiving the individual realities
as real objects. We absolutely have to complete what we see by
what we know." N.I. 169. [Or In 190]

2.2   **Meaning of an action**

"Df. 9. From the point of view of the observer, the meaning of an
action is the totality of actions which it makes possible and of those
which it makes impossible."

"Df. 10. From the point of view of the subject S, the meaning of an
action is the totality of sub-actions of which the subject S composes
it and the totality of actions of which the same subject makes it sub-
action (the words 'action' and 'sub-action' could be replaced respectively by 'coordination of actions' and 'partial or coordinated
actions')." E.E.G. IV 48.

2.3   **Meaning of an object**

"Df. 11 (1). The meaning of an object A for a subject S in a situation
T is the totality of actions of S which are applicable to it in T."

"Df. 11 (2). In the larger sense, the meaning of an object for a
subject in a given situation is the union or intersection or the structure of schemas of actions which are applied to that object in that
situation."

"Df. 11 (3). In the absolute sense, the meaning of an object is the union, the intersection, or the structure of meanings of that object for different subjects in different situations." E.E.G. IV 50.

2.4 **Meaning of a statement**
"Df. 12. The meaning of a statement in a given situation for a given subject is the totality of the actions which his emission or his reception makes possible or not." E.E.G. IV 50.

2.5 **Meaning of a term**
"Df. 13. The meaning of a term is the totality of the modifications produced, in the meaning of the statements where he would figure, by the substitution of this term for another." E.E.G. IV 51.

2.51 **Meanings, abstract**
Are "those which imply representation." N.I. 169. [Or In 191]

1. **Measure**
"Measure consists ... in displacing a conceived element as a unit by relating it to other parts of the total to which it belongs; the measure constitutes, therefore, a synthesis of partition and displacement. G.S. 12. [Co Ge 3] Cf. G.S. 76, 163, 497, E.G. I 116, D.Q. 272.
"... implies three conditions at least: (1) a partition cutting from the center of the whole a part chosen as a unit; (2) a displacement permitting the carrying of a unit part upon other parts of the same whole or of a second one; (3) a relation of transitivity permitting the conclusion that if $A = B$ and $B = C$, then $A = C$." M.V. 65–66. [Mo Sp 68–69]
"To measure is to compose units which are conserved and to introduce a system of equivalence between these compositions." G.N. 285. [Co Nu 230]

2.1 **Measure, common intuitive**
"... The common intuitive measure [originates] through representative delegation of the imitating gesture ... The first of these facts is that this common measure or *tertium comparationis* plays first of all an essentially symbolic role and makes way for behavior which we might properly call imitative. This is still rather far removed from operational transitivity..." G.S. 70–71. [Co Ge 51]

2.2 **Measure, common operational**
"Common operational measure proceeds from the average imagined or imitative term ... as soon as perceptive and intuitive transpositions are freed from their felt or imagined dependencies, that is, symbolic dependencies, and become reversible, thereby reaching complete transitivity." G.S. 81. [Co Ge 58]

110

3. **Measure, spatial**
"... Spatial measure is essentially a movement which consists in applying the measure upon what is to be measured and applying it as the part which was chosen as unit enters into the whole to be measured." G.S. 40. [Co Ge 27]

"... unidimensional measure depends on logical additive groupings ... while the measures of two or three dimensions depend on the multiplicative logical groupings (double or triple partitions and placements)..." G.S. 220. [Co Ge 170] Cf. G.S. 223.

4. **Measure, perceptive**
"Perceptive estimation [for example, perception of the 'middle' of a straight line] implies a partition with displacement which almost constitutes a measure. Only a perceptual measure is in general inexact or approximate..." G.S. 43. [Co Ge 29]

1. **Measurement**
"Euclidean measurement rests on the notion of displacement, and the displacements constitute, mathematically speaking, a group which may be represented in a three dimensional space structured by a system of coordinates." G.S. 11. [Co Ge 3]

2. **Measurement of time**
"Measurement of time appears as operational synthesis of the nesting of durations assuring the synchronizing with equalization of successive durations consequently assuring isochronism." N.T. 203.

"... Temporal measurement presupposes a new postulate unknown in the usual spatial measurement, that of conservation of movement and of movement and its speed." N.T. 71.

1. **Membership, inclusive**
"Df. 8. Inclusive membership (symbol epsilon $= \epsilon$) [is the] relation between an individual x and a class A of which it is a member, or $(x) \epsilon (A)$." G.S.L. 16. [Ea Gr Lo 8]

2. **Membership, partitive**
When "an element x is not a spatial part or a 'piece' of a whole object (like the relation of the nose to the face)." G.S.L. 16. [Ea Gr Lo 8]

3. **Membership, schematic**
"'Schematic membership,' or identification of an element x by recognitive assimilation to a perceptual or sensory-motor schema." G.S.L. 16. [Ea Gr Lo 8]

"... schematic membership permits only to qualify objects in com-

111

prehension, but without binding them to the collections in extension..." G.S.L. 19. [Ea Gr Lo 10]

"... partitive membership assures that ... connection [of binding the collection in extension] but independently of the resemblances involved in the schematic membership." G.S.L. 19. [Ea Gr Lo 10]

1. **Memory**

"... memory depends on the activity, and true activity presupposes interest." J.M. 31. [Mo Ju 50]

"Active memory is interiorized recitation." N.T. 261.

"... memory is a reconstitution of the past, 'recitation' as P. Janet says. That is true on higher and verbal levels of activity, or a sensory-motor reconstruction on lower levels. Necessarily it appeals to causality..." N.T. 5.

2. **Memory of evocation (representative series)**

"The representative [temporal] series is nothing but objective series spread out because of intellectual operations belonging to the sixth [sensory-motor] stage, and these operations as far as they entail representations related to time are nothing else but memory of evocation. The latter does not constitute in any way a special faculty; it is only the psychic assimilation and in particular reproductive assimilation as far as it reconstitutes mentally and no longer in reality a more and more extended past." C.R. 304. [Co Re 346]

3. **Memory, affective**

There is decentration "of affective order ... which consists in reliving earlier values or in anticipating earlier values, however by experiencing them as well. This is therefore where [an] affective memory comes in..." A.I. 130.

Mentalization, progressive

"The fundamental law which seems to regulate progressive mentalization of action is in effect that of passing from irreversibility to reversibility, in other words, the advancement toward definite progressive equilibrium." E.G. I 23.

Meter

"... a constructed meter is a condensation of operations which have already been performed..." G.S. 40. [Co Ge 27]

1. **Method, scientific**

Presents two functions: "(1) to establish laws (= description); (2) to deduce them as far as they are deductible and to confer on them thereby a certain amount of necessity (= explanation)." M.P. 9-10. [Me Pe xxii]

2.   **Method, genetic**
      "Genetic method [in epistemology] means to study knowledge as function of its real or psychological construction and to consider all knowledge as relative at a certain level of the mechanism of this construction." E.G. I 13.

3.   **Method, relational**
      "... relational method [in psychology] considers, with Gestalt psychology, that the elements are not given in advance; hence they do not exist independently of relations which unite them, but instead of directly invoking a whole of which the elements would be only the reflection, it tries to compose the whole starting with these relations." M.P. 15. [Me Pe xxvi]

1.1   **Mobility, retroactive mental**
      It is necessary for the behavior of classification (operational stage) "that retroactive mobility be [explained] by handling and changing (shifting) of criteria of which the child is capable during the intervention of the newly noticed property or of new elements to be joined to the previous collections..." G.S.L. 199. [Ea Gr Lo 196]

1.2   **Mobility, anticipatory mental**
      "Anticipatory mobility [manifests itself] in the form of interior plans of classification, preceding the effective manipulation, especially in the form of choice among several possible plans in order to find the most adequate one without exterior gropings." G.S.L. 199. [Ea Gr Lo 196]

2.   **Mobility of equilibrium**
      "Df. This mobility may be defined through spatio-temporal distances between the elements of the field [of equilibrium] as these distances are traversed at supposedly equal speeds by (effective or interiorized) actions of the subject." E.E.G. II 39.

1.   **Monologues**
      "The general character of monologues is the absence of social function of words. Speech is used to accompany, to reinforce or to supplant action." L.P. 23. [La Th 16]

1.1   **Monologue in the proper sense of the word**
      "The child simply accompanies his action with sentences pronounced out loud." L.P. 22. [La Th 14]

1.2   **Monologue and magic**
      "Speech is not so much used to accompany or to accelerate the action as to replace it by an illusory satisfaction." L.P. 23. [La Th 16]

2.   **Monologues, collective**
      "... pseudo-conversations of children from 2 to 6 years during which

the children speak only for themselves while having the desire to be faced with a partner who stimulates them." J.M. 24. [Mo Ju 41] Cf. L.P. 18.

1.   **Morals**
"All morals consist of a system of rules, and the essence of all morals is to be found in the respect which the individual acquires for these rules." J.M. 1. [Mo Ju 13]

2.   **Morals, common**
"When several mountaineers climb the same mountain ... you may say that their individual points of view are always inadequate ... the common morals will be defined by the system of laws of perspectives which make it possible to pass from one point of view to the other which then would permit the drawing of a map or objective representation of the mountain or the country..." "... consists not in a thing given from the outside to individuals, but in a totality of relations among these individuals." J.M. 282. [Mo Ju 350–351]

3.1   **Morals of authority or of duty**
"... are morals of duty and obedience [and] lead in the field of justice to confusion of what is just with the content of the established law and to recognition of the expiatory sanction." J.M. 259. [Mo Ju 324]

3.2   **Morals of mutual respect or of right**
"... it is that of the good (as opposed to duty) and of autonomy [and] leads in the domain of justice to the development of equality constituting the notion of distributive justice and of reciprocity." J.M. 259. [Mo Ju 324]
The morals of good are elaborated progressively and constitute, in respect to society, a kind of ideal form of equilibrium dominating the false, real and unstable equilibria arising from constraint." J.M. 284. [Mo Ju 353]

Motivation
"... motivation does not play an independent role in respect to cognitive schematism, but the two factors are always inseparable (motivation corresponding to energetic and cognitive aspect of the structures of the same sequences)..." E.E.G. XII 117.

1.   **Movement**
"A movement is a change of position (displacement) in respect to a system of fixed positions (placement)." M.V. 275. [Mo Sp 298] Cf. M.V. 264, 150, 89, 69, 66.

2.1   **Movement, real,** opp.

2.2   **Movement, ideal**
"We say movements, i.e., real movements, as opposed to 'displace-

ments' or ideal movements of geometry. These are simple changes of position or of 'placement' without taking speed into account. That is why displacement is still a spatial notion, whereas time appears with the movement as such, that is with speeds." N.T. 269. (2.1) "... if the said movement is real and not fictional, that is if it contains a finite speed..." N.T. 77.

N

Narcissism
"Narcissism is only affectivity corresponding to indifferentiation between the self and the non-self." A.I. 35.
We can only speak of narcissism provided we deal with a "narcissism without Narcissus" since the self is still not differentiated from the non-self.

1. **Necessity, logical**
"... logical necessity does not come from a question of fact, but from the conscious obligation inherent in implications." T.P. I 151.
"Logical necessity constitutes a form of obligation comparable to moral obligation in the sense that the subject feels obligated by this necessity only as far as his reasoning is 'honest'..." M.P. 360. [Me Pe 289]

2. **Necessary, the, and the probable**
"... just as the [operationally] 'necessary' in comprehension corresponds to 'always' or to 'all' in extension, the different degrees of the 'probable' in comprehension correspond biunivocally to the different values of the 'frequent' in extension." I.H. 261.

1. **Need and assimilation**
"Need is the total act of assimilation..." N.I. 130. [Or In 142]
"... need is ... the expression of a momentarily incomplete whole and leads to reconstructing itself, that is precisely what we call a cycle or a schema of assimilation. Need manifests the necessity which the organism feels or any organ which uses some exterior data for its own functioning." N.I. 45. [Or In 45]

1.1 **Need and satisfaction**
"All need is ... the expression of a relationship of fitness between an exterior object and a schema of assimilation and all satisfaction the expression of an equilibrium between assimilation and accommodation." E.G. III 167.
"Need ... is essentially the conscious realization of a momentary

disequilibrium, and satisfaction of the need is the conscious realization of reequilibration." A.I. 44.

1.2 **Need and repetition**

"... the need to repeat is only one aspect of a more general process, which we can qualify as assimilation. The tendency of reflexes is to reproduce themselves. It incorporates into itself any object which can excite." N.I. 35. [Or In 33]

"... need which serves as motor does not consist in repetition only, but in adaptation: i.e., in assimilating a new situation to old schemas and in accommodating these schemas to new circumstances." N.I. 162. [Or In 182]

2. **Need for survival**

"From the psychological point of view, the need to survive consists then in a sort of *a priori* function of thought; that is, in the course of his development or of the historical interaction which establishes itself between internal factors of maturation and external conditions of experience, this need becomes necessary." G.N. 7. [Co Nu 4]

3. **Need and interest**

"... need is nothing other than the cognitive or affective aspect of a schema in as much as they demand its normal aliment, i.e., objects which it can assimilate; and interest (as Claparède has said) is only the affective relation between need and the object which can satisfy it." E.E.G. VII 46–47.

Net of logic of propositions (= Lattice)

"Is constituted psychologically as far as generalization of operations of classifications is concerned." E.E.G. I 28.

"Conjunction (common part or 'lower limit') of any two elements of a propositional net, for example p and q, is to one of them as the other is to their disjunction (sum or 'upper limit')

$$\frac{p \cdot q}{p} = \frac{q}{p \vee q}$$

the complete form of which is:

$$\frac{p \cdot q}{p[q]} = \frac{q[p]}{p \vee q}. \text{ L.E.A. 279. [Gr Lo Th 315]}$$

Non-contradiction, arithmetic and logical

"... every numerical equation in which the direct and inverse operations do not cancel one another [is contradictory]: such as $+n -n \gtrless 0$. It results that the arithmetic non-contradiction contains

116

another criterion, and much finer than simply logical or intensive non-contradiction stemming from complementarity only." E.G. I 322.

1. **Norms, F, or logical**

    Let "F be the norm of formalized logic (for example the axioms of the logic of propositions, or the functions of the first order, etc.). We are dealing thus with the hypothesis of norms in which only the logician is competent, without the intervention of any psychological data." E.E.G. I 28.

    F: norms of logic consisting in a body of verbalized doctrines.

    F': norms considered by professional logicians as the canon of correct deduction. E.E.G. I 29.

2. **Norms, S, of normative facts**

    Let "S be the cognitive norms of both external and internal origin to which the subject conforms and which the observer describes as 'normative facts.' For example, the child at level II remains insensitive to transitivity of equality of length and of weight, while at level III he is forced by logical necessity to admit, from 7–8 years on for length and 9–10 years on for weight, that if $A = B$ and $B = C$ (by successive observations, A being hidden after comparison) $A = C$ 'necessarily'." E.E.G. I 28–29.

    S: individual norm; S': collective norm.

3. **Norms, M, of mental, social and psychological mechanisms**

    Let "M be the mental, social or physiological (language, coordination of action, nerve coordination, etc.) susceptible of explaining the formation of norms S." E.E.G. I 28–29.

    M: individual; M': collective.

4. **Norm, moral**

    "We will say that there is a moral norm, feeling of a norm as such, when three conditions are met: [1] when the feeling of obligation lasts beyond the perceptual or representative configuration of the situation ... in which the norm has been created by an instruction. [2] It has ... to be applicable to multiple situations, in other words, generalizable in all analogous situations, by a sort of generalization of the norm ... [3] when there is feeling of autonomy, that is to say, when the feeling of that which has to be done becomes independent of a simple obedience..." A.I. 107–108.

    "... rational norms, and, in particular, this norm so important that reciprocity, source of the logic of relations, can only be developed in and through cooperation." J.M. 79–80. [Mo Ju 107]

Notion, concrete
"... the 'groupings' remain relative to the type of concrete notions (i.e., of mentalized actions)." P.I. 175. [Ps In 146] (*See* **Interiorized Action**.)

1. **Number**
"Is ... a collection of objects conceived as both equivalent and orderable." P.I. 172. [Ps In 144]
Number consists "in transforming elements into units." E.G. I 100.
"... number is but a collection of elements all made equivalent by generalized resemblance, and yet kept distinct due to a vicariant order or a generalized difference. Each of these elements constitutes, in effect, a unit which is both cardinal (since $A = 1, A + A' = 2A, A + A' + B = 3A$, etc.) and ordinal (since there is always a first element independent of whatever order is chosen)..." E.G. I 101.
"Number is at one and the same time classes and asymmetrical relations." E.G. I 102.
"Number is ... a system of units." D.Q. 251.
"... number is organized, stage upon stage, in close connection with gradual elaboration of systems of inclusions (hierarchy of logical classes) and of asymmetrical relations (qualitative seriations). The succession of numbers thus constitutes an operational synthesis of classification and of seriation." G.N. II [Co Nu viii] Cf. D.Q. 337, D.Q. 272.
"The finite numbers are thus necessarily both cardinal and ordinal..." G.N. 195. [Co Nu 157]
But in the preoperational stages of thought (before 7–8 years) the child does not necessarily coordinate the cardinality and the order of numbers. "It is the equalization of the differences which is the source of the unit, and therefore of number." G.N. 120. [Co Nu 94] (*See* **Vicariant order**.)

2.1 **Number, cardinal**
"... is a class of which the elements are conceived as 'units' equivalent one to the others and thus as distinct. Their differences consist of the fact that one can seriate them, thus order them." G.N. 195. [Co Nu 157]

2.2 **Numbers, ordinal**
"... are a series of which the terms, while succeeding each other according to the relations of order which give them their respective ranks, are equal units and consequently susceptible of being reunited cardinally." G.N. 195. [Co Nu 157]

3.   **Number as operator**
"... all numbers can be considered either as the static result of an operation, or as the operator itself in its formative dynamism." E.E.G. I 125.

4.   **Number, intuitive or figurative**
Are those which compose the collections of less than 5 elements. Cf. I.H. 150.

O

1.   **Objectivity**
"... (1) objectivity is constructed as a function of as well as gradually from the subject's activities; (2) the initial state of each process does not furnish the properties of the object, but an undifferentiated collection of the properties common to both the subject and object; (3) it is in his decentering by correspondence to the initial states that the subject gradually succeeds in both regulating his activities by coordinating them and attaining the specific characteristics of an object by correcting the deformations due to the initial centrations." N.P. 451.
"... objectivity is constructed thanks to the coordination of actions or operations instead of resulting simply from the play of perceptions and their associations." E.E.G. V 58.
"Objectivity does not mean thus the independence in relation to assimilatory activity of intelligence, but simply the dissociation from the self and its egocentric subjectivity." N.I. 320. [Or In 367]

2.   **Objectivity** opp. **realism**
"But there are two ways of being realistic. Or rather, we must distinguish objectivity and realism. Objectivity consists in knowing so well the thousand intrusions which derive from it—illusions of the senses, of language, of points of view, of values, etc.—that in order to dare to judge, we start by disengaging ourselves from the hindrances of the self. Realism, on the contrary, consists in ignoring the existence of the self, and then in taking the perspective itself as objective and absolute." R.M. 4. [Co Wo 34]

1.   **Object**
"It is a polysensory complex which continues to exist outside of all perceptual contact. We recognize this presence in infantile thought from the double characteristic of solidity ... and of localization..." A.I. 35.

In order that "... the picture recognized become an object, it has to be dissociated from the action itself and be situated in the context of spatial and causal relations independent of the immediate activity." C.R. 12. [Co Re 6]

"All objects are simultaneously affective and cognitive." A.I. 66.

2. **Object and assimilation**

"... the notion of object is far from being innate and requires a construction by both assimilation and accommodation." N.I. 13. [Or In 7]

"The object is 'schematic abstract' before being 'schematic' and it is the very coordination of actions having schematized reality as objects which we have to invoke in the first place..." E.G. I 253.

"... the object becomes exteriorized and objective the more it is assimilated to general coordinations of action or of thought, and no longer to the momentary activity as such." E.G. II 17.

At the level of development of the tertiary circular reaction "the object becomes definitely independent of action: it is the source of entirely autonomous activities, which the child studies from the outside now oriented toward novelty." N.I. 228. [Or In 260]

"The object is at first only a prolongation of movements of accommodation (prediction). Then it is the point of intersection, i.e., of reciprocal assimilation of the multiple schemas which represent the different modalities of the action (concordance of experiences)." C.R. 78. [Co Re 88]

3. **Object, permanent, and group of displacements**

"The construction of the schema of a permanent object, i.e., of the notion of a possible return to the point of departure of each modification of reality." M.V. 261. [Mo Sp 283–284]

"Without conservation of objects it will not be possible to have a group since everything appears to change state. The object and the group of displacements are thus indissociable, the one consisting of the static aspect and the other of a dynamic aspect of the same reality." P.I. 138. [Ps In 113]

The object "is so to speak the invariant of the group of displacements." A.I. 61. Cf. P.I. 137.

4. **Object and categories**

"... in the domain of the phenomena on our scale, the object is at the same time the point of departure for logico-arithmetic operations (a class is a group of objects) and the point of arrival of spatio-temporal operations (which belong to the composition of the object itself). I.H. 252.

120

The *total object* consists of *partial objects* separated by the activity of the subject. Cf. R.E. 544.

Observable

"In the first place, the observable is far from constituting a simple sensory datum, passively registered. It is the result, observed without presupposition, of an experimental action exercised upon reality ... In the second place, the observable is directly translated into operational symbols, of a mathematical character but entirely free in respect to geometrical representation." E.G. II 229.

Observation of experience opp. **Understanding**

"In the course of the first stage, (5–6 years to 6–7 years) experience is observed only without being understood and without giving way to any prediction whatsoever beyond the simple reproduction of that static and limited observation. Thus, the activity of a subject, without being therefore null, is reduced to a simple centration of intuition about the given fact, to which is attributed a privileged value precisely because of the circumstance that it is not related to any other previous or subsequent fact." M.V. 29. [Mo Sp 30]

1. **Operation and reversibility**

"Df. We shall call operations [the] interiorized actions or interiorizable actions, reversible and coordinated in total structures..." E.E.G. II 45.

"... every system of intellectual operations psychologically has two parallel aspects: environmentally it is concerned with coordinated actions (effective or mentalized actions); whereas interiorally, i.e., in consciousness, we deal with correspondences implying each other." T.L. 14.

"... psychologically the operation is an interiorized action and becomes reversible by coordination with other interiorized actions in the same structure of a group containing certain laws of the whole." E.E.G. I 35.

"Df. 10. We will call 'operation' a reversible transformation of one structure into another, either by modification of the 'form,' or by substitution relating to 'content'." T.L. 58.

"... the property of operations is that of constituting systems." P.I. 46. [Ps In 35]

"An operation is a reversible action." D.Q. 277. Cf. D.Q. 17, 24, 42, 140, 270, 271.

"... the operation is both a possible modification of reality and an assimilatory action whose reversibility demonstrates the ability as such." F.S. 300. [Pl Dr Im 284]

"Operation ... is nothing but an articulated intuition rendered mobile and entirely reversible, because it was emptied of its representative content and subsists as simple 'intention'..." M.V. 26. [Mo Sp 27]

"... the criterion of an operation is composition or 'calculation'." M.V. 26. [Mo Sp 27] Cf. M.V. 27, 52, 168.

"Operations are reversible because they contain everything possible, whereas reality is irreversible to the degree that it is drawing only a sample from among these possibilities." E.G. II 185.

"Construction of time is a beautiful example of collaboration between reversible operations of the subjects and the irreversible processes of the object." E.G. II 43.

2. **Operation and grouping**

"The criterion for the existence of operations will be their grouping..." M.V. 20. [Mo Sp 21]

"The direct operation is formed by any action as long as two of these actions combined reproduce an action of the same type and as the inverse action is a part of the same system." D.Q. 329.

"If we have actions–operations, sometimes called 'manipulations,' or thought–operations, they are the concern of the psychologist: from the logistical point of view, we deal with formalizable operations and that is sufficient for characterizing a logically coherent theory." T.L. 10.

"... the difference between operations and articulated intuition is that the first are indefinitely combinable while the second is limited to the narrow field within which the articulation was produced, without generalization to other questions." M.V. 18. [Mo Sp 19]

"... the grouped operations appear as the terminal form of equilibrium of reasoning." M.V. 260. [Mo Sp 282]

Operations are grouped (1) by the "coordination of the successive points of view of the subject (with possible return in time and in anticipation of their sequence)" and (2) by the "coordination of the perceptible and representable modifications of objects (previously, actually, or by later unfolding)." P.I. 170. [Ps In 143]

3. **Operations, genetic level of**

"... in their elementary stages, all operations are both logical and physical." D.Q. 279.

"It is ... experience alone which furnishes the content of operations, i.e., it decides which ought to be brought about and in what sense." D.Q. 320.

3.1 **Operations, infralogical, physical, or spatio-temporal**

Are "the operations which do not belong to the class of objects, of relations between invariant objects, or of numbers, but only to positions, states, etc. They thus express the transformations of the object instead of leaving them constant." N.T. 35.

They "... have for their upper limit an individual object continuous or of a single piece which may for instance be a segment of a straight line, or an organism, or the entire universe considered as a total object, and for lower limit the parts of the object on the usually chosen scale (the point for a mathematician, the cell for an histologist)." E.E.G. VI 60. Cf. D.Q. 332.

"Physical operations ... unfold in time and in space and thus transform correspondences of classes into sections, the asymmetrical relations into displacements, and number into measures, permitting the quantification of the first two." D.Q. 216.

In the notion of infralogical operation "*infra* does not mean prior to logic, but refers to elements of a 'type' inferior to the individual object, which is type 0 in the hierarchy of types from the point of view of classes." G.S.L. 45. [Ea Gr Lo 38]

"... the line of separation between operations or logico-arithmetic correspondences and the operations or spatial correspondences is situated precisely between notions of resemblance (or of difference), the source of logico-arithmetic relation, and of the neighborhood (or the difference in position), the source of spatial relation..." R.E. 511. [Ch Co Sp 430–431]

3.2 **Operations, logical or logico-arithmetic**
"... belong to the union of elements or of individual objects considered inseparable (such as type 0 in the hierarchy of Russell's types) and they have as upper limit the total class of the system considered (or the universe of discourse)." E.E.G. VI 60.

"The logico-arithmetic operations consist of groupings of classes and of relations or in groups of numbers combining the preceding two together." D.Q. 216.

"... logico-arithmetic operations are those of classes (or unions of equivalent terms), of asymmetrical relations (or series) and of numbers." D.Q. 271.

3.21 **Operations, concrete**
"The operations of the first degree to which belong the formal operations are themselves concrete operations." [concrete manipulation of objects] M.V. 90. [Mo Sp 96]

3.22 **Operations, formal or hypothetico-deductive**
The formal operations "... constitute exclusively the structure of final equilibrium, toward which tend the concrete operations, when

they are reflected in more general systems combining the propositions they express." P.I. 179. [Ps In 150]

"... formal or hypothetico-deductive operations. Now, those formal operations are, in their structure, nothing but concrete operations, but transposed into terms of propositions, i.e., integrating concrete classes and relations into a system of implications and of incompatibilities expressed by propositions." M.V. 192. [Mo Sp 206]

3.3   **Operation, practical**
Practical operations "... coordinate simply the means and ends (values, value scales, law of the least effort, etc.)." (11) 258.

4.1   **Operation, interpropositional**
"Df. 2 ... every transformation permits the construction, by means of any proposition, p, q, r, of which we know only their truth value, of other well-determined propositions, and characterized respectively by the different possible combinations of these positive or negative values." T.L. 36.

4.2   **Operation, intrapropositional**
"Df. 3 ... those operations permitting to decompose a proposition into its elements (that decomposition could reach various degrees) and to construct new propositions determined by the transformations of its elements; those truth values thus result in the combinations of their elements." T.L. 37.

5.   **Operation, complementary**
"... means that they can be deduced from each other, but both cannot be simultaneously achieved in the same grouping..." N.T. 287.

Operational opp. **operative**
"We distinguish ... the terms of operation (= relative to operations in the strict sense) and of operative (= relative to the actions at all levels and to operations)." M.P. 353, note 1. [Me Pe 283]

Order, vicariant
"The As ordered in the form $A \rightarrow A \rightarrow A$ conserve the same order if one permutes the elements, i.e., there will always be a first element, a second, etc., even if they change place: such generalized order would be called a 'vicariant order'." E.E.G. XIV 285. (*See* **Number.**)

1.   **Organization and adaptation**
"From the biological [and psychological] point of view organization is inseparable from adaptation: they are the two complementary processes of a unique mechanism. The first of these is the internal

aspect of the cycle of which adaptation constitutes the exterior aspect." N.I. 13. [Or In 7]

2. **Organization, collective**

It "... acts on the elaboration of space indirectly, by imprinting on any spatial construction a form permitting the formation of groups. The latter are not predetermined through ready-made structures ... [it] could be conceived as dependent upon general common heredity of all living organization." C.R. 189–190. [Co Re 217]

Overdetermination

Is "a simple particular case of syncretism, and, consequently, of deforming assimilations ... the diverse components are not assimilated completely, but remain partially estranged..." J.R. 143. [Ju Re 176]

"The image is not, from the point of view of psychology ... only one but a great number of contents. It is in this sense that an image or symbol is called 'overdetermined.' Now here is a phenomenon which we find in all primitive and little directed thought." J.R. 130. [Ju Re 158]

"Overdetermination is, for lack of being globally conscious, a system in unstable equilibrium." J.R. 131. [Ju Rc 159]

1. **Overestimation, absolute**

"Absolute overestimation varies according as B is compared to A or is isolated." M.P. 131. [Me Pe 96]

2. **Overestimation, relative**

Relative overestimation is the "relation or correspondence between absolute overestimation = coupling between encounters." M.P. 131. [Me Pe 96]

1. **Overtaking**

Is "the interversion of order of respective positions of two moving things in the course of displacement." M.V. 271. [Mo Sp 293]

"... intuition of overtaking constitutes — only a particular case of ... judgments of order." M.V. 152. [Mo Sp 163]

"The schema of overtaking has to be interpreted as a function of the action of advancing, i.e., a global intuition of order, relative only to the points of arrival." M.V. 165. [Mo Sp 177]

"Overtaking is the intuitive figure in which compensations are the most easily completed (by relative decentration) and consequently the easiest to use for representing all the differences of speed (by absolute decentration)." M.V. 171–172. [Mo Sp 184]

1.1 **Overtaking, virtual**
"The child limits himself to generalization of the idea of overtaking by bringing back in thought one of the trajectories compared to the other or by prolonging in thought the perceived movements." E.G. II 57.

P

1. **Parallelism, psychophysical**
"The concrete correspondences uniting the objects of the exterior world are [constructed] at the same time as formal relations of the schemas..." N.I. 187. [Or In 211]

2. **Parallelism, psychophysiological**
"... if the parallelism between the facts of consciousness and the physiological processes lead to an isomorphism between the systems which imply meaning and the material systems of causal order, it is then evident that this parallelism is not only complementary, but finally a hope motivated by the isomorphism between the organistic and the logico-mathematical schemas used by abstract models." T.P. I 152.

1. **Participation**
"We will call 'participation,' according to the definition given by Mr. Lévy-Bruhl, that relation which primitive thought seems to perceive between two beings or two phenomena which it considers either as partially identical, or as directly influencing each other, even without having any spatial contact, nor intelligible causal connection." R.M. 117. [Co Wo 132]

The child at the preoperational stage "does not handle general classes, because of the lack of distinction between 'all' and 'some' ... if the notion of the individual permanent object is achieved in the field of close action, does not yet exist for distant spaces or in reappearances of spaced durations ... from which come true 'participations' between distant and remote objects." P.I. 152–153. [Ps In 127–128]

2.1 **Participation, dynamic** opp.

2.2 **Participation, substantial**

2.1 "Things have intentions which take part in our own, and our desires force them thus to obey and to act according to certain moral rules." C.P. 296. [Co Ph Ca 261–262]

2.2 "Two things which uphold correspondences either of resemblance, or of general affinity, are conceived as having something in common, which permits them to act at a distance upon each other ... like the one being a source of emanations and the other the emanation of the first." C.P. 295. [Co Ph Ca 260–261]

Partition, arithmetic

"There is an arithmetic partition as soon as elements of the whole can be equalled while remaining distinct when a relation of a group of a class is decomposed into subrelations or its subclasses. Their unions imply no equality but only their inclusion in the whole." G.N. 30. [Co Nu 23]

"Numerical partition is essentially an equalization of differences like proportion itself." G.N. 31. [Co Nu 23]

Passage and blocking

In the firing of the nervous impulse we can consider two operators (+ and −). The passage consists in opening the circuit A' and transforming A into B; $A + A' = B$. The blocking consists in excluding A' from circuit B; $B - A' = A$; $B - A = A'$. (14) 250.

Path traversed (*See* **Road traversed**)

1. **Perception**

"... perceptions are not the first and independent elements of intelligence; they are the result of intellectual activity..." C.R. 185. [Co Re 212]

"All perception which goes beyond the most primitive contact with the object contains the virtual correspondence completing the actual or real correspondences." "Perception is thus a perception of schemas and not only of objects. These schemas constitute precisely the group of virtual correspondences which perceptual activity could recover in the perceived object or actualize in connection with it." E.G. I 182.

"To perceive is to construct intellectually." J.M. 148. [Mo Ju 188]

"... in all domains perception starts with a clear advantage over representation and is afterwards more and more surpassed by it." M.P. 436. [Me Pe 352]

"All perception appears to us as an elaboration or an application of a schema, i.e., as a more or less rapid organization of the sensory data as function of a group of acts and of movements, explicit or simply outlined ... all perception is an accommodation (with or without regrouping) of schemas which require for their construction systematic work of assimilation and organization..." N.I. 341. [Or In 390]

127

2.   **Perception and system of relations**
"All perception is a system of relationships, and no element is ever perceived in isolation..." E.G. I 174.
Perception "always constitutes a system of a group of relationships, and may be conceived as the momentary form of equilibrium of a multitude of elementary sensory rhythms which are united or interfered with in two different ways." P.I. 203. [Ps In 170]

3.1   **Perceptions, primary (Gestalt)**
Primary perceptions are "those which can be obtained by means of a single act bearing upon the elements given simultaneously (a single centration of regard, etc.) ... Structures of primary perceptions could be called *Gestalt* in the sense that they are irreversible and non-associative." E.E.G. II 45. (*See* **Field effects**.)

3.2   **Perceptions, secondary**
Secondary perceptions are "those which stem from perceptual activities, i.e., from comparison of spatio-temporal distances which go beyond the same field." E.E.G. II 45.

1.   **Permanence of the object**
"The first principle of conservation [is] the faith in permanence of a solid object, of its form and of its dimensions." D.Q. 6.
"It is action which confers a momentary conservation to the object, and it ceases to possess it when the action ends." P.I. 133. [Ps In 109]
"Permanence of the object constitutes the first [of the] fundamental notions of conservation." P.I. 131. [Ps In 108]

2.1   **Permanence, perceptual**
2.2   **Permanence, substantial**
Perceptual permanence is "distinct from substantial permanence which subsists beyond the perceptual field and which is manifest, around 8–10 months, by the search for an object which has disappeared..." E.E.G. V 72.

Permutation
"If the change of order is within itself, an elementary (or 'concrete') operation, a multiplication of changes of order is on the other hand only a simple operation, since we have then an operation influencing other operations, i.e., an operation to the second power." I.H. 206.

Personality
"... if the self is naturally egocentric, the personality is the decentered self. The more powerful it is, the more hateful the self is now, whereas a strong personality is that which can discipline itself.

Personality, in other words, is the submission of the self to an ideal which it embodies but which surpasses and dominates it..." L.E.A. 311. [Gr Lo Th 349]

"... personality is the decentered self, the individual as far as he enters into a social group, as far as it submits to the collective discipline, as far as it embodies an idea belonging to a certain work, and with the work to a scale of values, to a program of life, and to the adoption of a social role. In brief, it is in certain respects contrary to the self." A.I. 151.

Phenomenism

Phenomenism expresses "the surface of reality as it appears to the subject, egocentrism [expresses] the more immediate or the most local aspect, thus also the most superficial of activity." E.G. II 103.

"The child conceives things as being always as they appear and endowed with qualities similar to his own." L.P. 70. [La Th 271]

"It is the appearance of things, it is the immediate experience of perception..." D.Q. 276.

Picture, perceptual (*See* Universe of presentations)

"In the totality of impressions which assail his consciousness, the child distinguishes and recognizes very quickly certain stable groups which we will name 'pictures'." C.R. 10. [Co Re 4]

Examples: "ball-under-the-armchair," "doll-hanging-from-the-trapeze," "watch-under-a-pillow," "papa-by-the-window," etc.... C.R. 57. [Co Re 63]

Placement-displacement

"Placements and displacements are the infralogical operations engendering the relations which can later be seriated." D.Q. 332.

"Operations of placement (or of displacement) determine the asymmetrical relations of order ... The two kinds of operations are distinct but complementary..." G.S. 196. [Co Ge 148]

Is "a system of simultanieties." M.V. 272. [Mo Sp 295]

Is "a system of fixed positions." M.V. 275. [Mo Sp 298]

"The operations of placement constitute a first type of qualitative grouping." M.V. 257. [Mo Sp 279]

1. **Play (assimilation)**

"Play is, at first, simple functional or reproductive assimilation."

"Utilization of things by an activity having its end in itself, primitive play starts, therefore, to be mixed up with the totality of sensory-motor behaviors of which it constitutes only one pole: that of behaviors which do not require any new accommodations and which

129

are reproduced by pure 'functional pleasure'..." F.S. 92. [Pl Dr Im 87]

"... play proceeds ... by relinquishing the adaptive effort and by sustaining or exercising activities for pleasure only, to dominate them and to draw from them a feeling of skill or power." F.S. 94. [Pl Dr Im 89]

1.1   Play of exercise

"... simple exercises start a varied collection of behaviors, but without modifying their structure so that it appears at the stage of actual adaptation. Only function differentiates these kinds of play. They exercise those structures so to speak in a vacuum without any other goal than the mere pleasure of functioning." F.S. 117. [Pl Dr Im 110]

2.1   Play, egocentric

"... in which to 'win' means not to win over others but to play for oneself." J.M. 22. [Mo Ju 39]

2.2   Play, social, or play with rules

"From now on we are confronted not simply with play with companions but with regulating the game by systematic laws which assure the greatest receprocity." J.M. 27. [Mo Ju 45–46]

"The rule is a regularity imposed by the group and, therefore, its violation represents a mistake." F.S. 120. [Pl Dr Im 112–113]

3.   Play, symbolic, or play of imagination

"The purest form of egocentric and symbolic thought." P.I. 152. [Ps In 127]

"... the symbol implies a representation of an absent object since it is the comparison between a given and an imagined element, and fictitious representation as this comparison consists of a deforming assimilation." F.S. 118. [Pl Dr Im 111]

"Symbolic play contains its own belief which is subjective truth." F.S. 178. [Pl Dr Im 168]

"... play of imagination constitutes ... a symbolic transposition which submits things to activity as such without rules or limitations." F.S. 92. [Pl Dr Im 87]

1.   Pleasure, motor, opp.

2.   Pleasure, social

"The child quickly persuaded that his play is 'suitable' ... does not dream of using his acquisitions only for himself; his pleasure simply consists still in developing his own skill and in succeeding in the trials which he makes. Pleasure is essentially motor ... and not social." J.M. 24. [Mo Ju 41]

130

1. **Poles, subject–object**
    "The lesson of this decentration is that there exist two poles or two opposing orientations in what we call the subject, and two poles consequently in what we call the object. These two pairs of poles correspond to the initial and final phases of development." E.E.G. X 188.

1.1 **Pole, initial, of the subject**
    "... the initial pole of the subject is not that of transforming operations eliminating all individual subjectivity to the benefit of the impersonal norm, but that of an assimilation to the actions and consequently deforming." E.E.G. X 188.

1.2 **Pole, initial, of the object**
    "... the initial pole of the object is not characterized by the effects leading to an 'objective' knowledge, but rather by phenomenism indissociable from subjective attachments..." E.E.G. X 188.

2.1 **Pole, final, of the object and**
2.2 **Pole, final, of the subject**
    "... the final poles of the object and subject are characterized, but in solidarity and resulting from their equilibrating interactions, through objectivity, on the one hand, and, reciprocally, through the structures constituting the transformatory operations." E.E.G. X 188.

Possibility of an event
    "Df. 27a. A subject in a given situation thinks an event *e* is possible if, given his goals, he chooses the behaviors which maximize the probability of reaching them, for a class of events containing this *e*. A subject thinks an event *e* impossible if, given his goals, he chooses those behaviors which will give only a slight chance of reaching them if *e* occurs." "Df. 27b. A subject thinks an inference is necessary if he thinks the truth of the premises and the falsity of the conclusion are impossible." E.E.G. IV 66.

1. **Possible, the, in concrete operations**
    (According to form) "The possible is reduced to a simple potential prolongation of actions or operations applied to the given content (for example, when, after having seriated some objects, the subject knows that it could continue with others, and this according to the same anticipatory schema of seriation which permitted him to bring about its real seriation)." L.E.A. 218–219. [Gr Lo Th 249]
    (According to content) "From the point of view of content concrete thought presents this limiting particularity of not being immediately generalizable to all content, but to proceed field by field, with a décalage extending often to several years between the structuration

131

of a content (for example, length) and that of the following (for example, weight)." L.E.A. 219. [Gr Lo Th 249]

2.   **Possible, the, in formal operations**
"... reality is subordinated to the possible: facts are henceforth conceived as the sector of effective realizations at the heart of a universe of possible transformations, for they are not explained, nor even admitted as facts before a verification bearing on the totality of possible hypotheses compatible with the given situation." L.E.A. 220. [Gr Lo Th 251]

2.1   **Possible, the formal (physical subjective meaning)**
"... to equilibrate his successive affirmations (which is the same as avoiding being contradicted by later facts) the subject tends to insert on his own at first supposedly real connections in the totality of those which he recognizes as possible. In this manner he chooses subsequently the true ones by examination of certain transformations effected at the heart of these possible connections." L.E.A. 225. [Gr Lo Th 256]

2.2   **Possible, the formal** (physical objective meaning)
"... to understand the possible, formal thought is forced to dispose, in each particular situation, from the extended matrix of potential operations, surpassing the domain of momentarily utilized operations. These potential operations constitute a necessary condition for equilibrium..." L.E.A. 226. [Gr Lo Th 257]

3.1   **Possible, the materially**
The operations and relations which the subject himself considers possible: "those which he can effect or even construct without really doing it." L.E.A. 228. [Gr Lo Th 260]

3.2   **Possible, the structurally**
One can "attribute the qualification of possible to the operations and relations which the subject would be capable of carrying out or of constructing, but without his thinking about doing it, i.e., without becoming conscious of this eventuality or even of his proper capacity in this respect: it is what we call structurally possible, which is the possible, from the point of view of the observer." L.E.A. 228. [Gr Lo Th 260]

Precausality
"... precausality presupposes indifferentiation between the psychic and the physical such that the true cause of a phenomenon is never to be found in the 'how' of its physical realization but in the intention which starts it." R.M. 379. [Co Wo 359] Cf. L.P. 168, 172, 190.

Preconcepts

"Are the notions attached by the child to the first verbal signs which he uses. The proper character of these schemas is to remain midway between the generality of the concept and the individuality of the elements which compose it." P.I. 152. [Ps In 127]

"It is a schema already representative and which succeeds in particular in evoking a large number of objects by means of privileged elements believed to be exemplary types of the preconceptual collection." P.I. 153. [Ps In 128]

"Remaining thus midway between the individual and the general, the infantile preconcept constitutes a sort of 'participation' in the sense of Lévy-Bruhl, if one agrees to give to this kind of correspondence the following criterion: absence of inclusion of the elements in a whole and direct identification of partial elements among themselves without the intermediary of the whole..." F.S. 241. [Pl Dr Im 226–227]

Predicate in comprehension

"... any predicate in comprehension is reduced to a relation..." T.L. 62.

"... to write $\phi(x)$ to designate $\phi(x_1)$; $\phi(x_2)$; $\phi(x_3)$ etc., is to establish between the terms in extension x_1; x_2; x_3; ... a relationship of equivalence ϕ definable by the co-possession of the same quality." T.L. 63.

1.   **Preinferences**

"Df. 3. We say that there is a preinference when the subject understands only the result c of an inferential process, without distinct consciousness of the elements a (data) or b (superaddents), which remain in this case indifferentiated in c, and without the intervention of necessarily imposed abstractions or of rules of composition." E.E.G. VI 88.

2.1   **Preinference of the first level**

"Df. 4. We say that there is a preinference of the first level when the elements a are infraperceptual in nature and the elements c are situated at the level of the threshold." E.E.G. VI 88.

2.2   **Preinference of the second level**

"Df. 5 ... when the elements a and c are both situated at the level of the field effects (field determined by a single centration)." E.E.G. VI 88.

2.3   **Preinference of the third level**

If "... the physically given elements a are two kinds a_1 and a_2, the

133

a_1s may be perceived independently of the perceptual activities considered and the a_2s on the contrary are being perceived as a function of such actual activities." E.E.G. VI 103.

1. **Probability**

"... probability constitutes a sort of matching of the operations, i.e., a sort of assimilation of chance to the combinatory operations. Because we are unable to deduct each interference, it is the collection as such and in its totality, which the operatory mechanism reconstitutes. That's why we have reduction afterwards of the real cases to the totality of possible combinations." I.H. 12.

"... Judgment of probability would consist in separating all the possible combinations (additive disjunction), i.e., element by element or multiplicatively, i.e., associations of two, three, and n elements, and to determine the correspondence between the combinations considered and the totality of possible encounters." I.H. 174.

2. **Probability of elementary perceptual recognition**

"... between the parts of a perceived object and those of the sensory organs..." M.P. 99. [Me Pe 69]

Projection or **Adualism** (between the self and things)

"Because it is simply an undifferentiation between the self and the outer world, it is the absence of consciousness of self."

1.1 "In other cases, there is projection when we attribute to things the characteristics of the self or of thought. When the child who localizes in the sun the 'name of the sun,' 'projects' an internal reality into the exterior world."

1.2 There is also "the case in which we lend to things not our own characteristics but the reciprocal of our states of consciousness: thus the child who is afraid of fire will presume there are threatening intentions in the fire." R.M. 5. [Co Wo 35]

1. **Properties of an object**

"From the point of view of behavior (perceptual comparisons and schematizations of actions), the properties of an object are always relations." E.E.G. IV 45.

2. **Property introduced by the action**

"Df. 15. A property is said to be introduced by an action in an object if this action is a necessary condition of the fact that this object has this property." E.E.G. IV 52.

2.1 **Property of type I**

"Df. 16. We shall say that a property of type I is introduced by an

134

action in an object (singular or collective) if that property does not modify the previous properties of that object." E.E.G. IV 53.

For example, to count a collection of tokens, this collection has from then on a new property: "to have a number."

"... a property of type I is recognized in the fact that it could not be subject to a primary perceptual reading." E.E.G. IV 54.

2.2 **Property of type II**

"Df. 17. We shall say that the property of type II is introduced in the object by an action (singular or collective) when this property modifies the previous properties of this object." E.E.G. IV 55.

For example, to add or to take away some tokens from the collection.

Proportions, logical

1. **Simple**

"We will call (simple) logical proportions any system of 4 operations $\alpha, \beta, \gamma, \delta$, set out under the form $\alpha/\beta = \gamma/\delta$ and such that they have:
(1) $\alpha . \delta = \beta . \gamma$ \qquad (2) $\alpha \vee \delta = \beta \vee \gamma$.

Such a system derives from an *INRC* group since we can write:

(I) $\quad \dfrac{\alpha = I}{\beta = C} = \dfrac{\gamma = R}{\delta = N}$ \quad for example $\quad \dfrac{p . q}{p \vee q} = \dfrac{\bar{p} . \bar{q}}{p | q}$.

In effect (1) $\alpha . \delta = \gamma . \beta$ because $I . N = R . C$ and (2) $\alpha \vee \delta = \gamma \vee \beta$ because $I \vee N = R \vee C$." T.O.L. 223.

2. **Reciprocal**

"We could equally draw out of the *INRC* group a proportionality which we will call reciprocal whose form and properties are the following:

(IV) $\quad \dfrac{\alpha = I}{\beta = N} = R \dfrac{\gamma = R}{\delta = C}$ \quad for example $\quad \dfrac{p . q}{p | q} = R \dfrac{\bar{p} . \bar{q}}{p \vee q}$.

T.O.L. 225.

"The proportions which we will name RR, when $\gamma = R\alpha$ and $\delta = R\beta$ but not $\delta = C\alpha$ nor $\gamma = C\beta$:

(VI) $\quad \dfrac{\alpha}{\beta} = RR \dfrac{\beta = R\alpha}{\delta = R\beta}$ \quad for example $\quad \dfrac{p}{q} = RR \dfrac{\bar{p}}{\bar{q}}$

or

$$\frac{p . q}{p . \bar{q}} = RR \frac{\bar{p} . \bar{q}}{\bar{p} . q}. \quad \text{T.O.L. 225.}$$

135

3. **Correlative**

(VII) $\quad \dfrac{\alpha = I}{\beta = N} = C\dfrac{\gamma = C}{\delta = R}\quad$ for example $\quad \dfrac{p \cdot q}{p|q} = C\dfrac{p \vee q}{\bar{p} \cdot \bar{q}}.$

T.O.L. 226.

"The proportions which we will name CC, in which we have $\gamma = C\alpha$ and $\delta = C\beta$ but not $\alpha = R\delta$ nor $\beta = R\gamma$:

(IX) $\quad \dfrac{\alpha}{\beta} = CC\dfrac{\gamma = C\alpha}{\delta = C\beta}\quad$ for example $\quad \dfrac{p \cdot q}{\bar{p} \cdot q} = CC\dfrac{p \vee q}{p \supset q}$

T.O.L. 226.

4. **Negation**

"There exists a negative form of proportion which does not exist in the parts common between α, β, γ and δ and when one has $\alpha \vee \beta \vee \gamma \vee \delta = {}^*$. When the two conditions are replaced, thus:

(X) $\quad \dfrac{\alpha}{\beta} = N\dfrac{\gamma}{\delta}\quad$ for example $\quad \dfrac{(p \cdot q \cdot r) \vee (p \cdot q \cdot \bar{r})}{(p \cdot \bar{q} \cdot r) \vee (p \cdot \bar{q} \cdot \bar{r}) \vee (\bar{p} \cdot q \cdot r)}$

$$= \dfrac{(\bar{p} \cdot \bar{q} \cdot r) \vee (\bar{p} \cdot \bar{q} \cdot \bar{r})}{\bar{p} \cdot q \cdot \bar{r}}.$$

T.O.L. 226, 227. Cf. T.O.L. Appendix I and II. T.L. 8, 9, 31.

1. **Proposition, psychological**

Df. 22. "Is a proposition for a subject whatever is held by the subject as susceptible of being true or false." E.E.G. VI 60.

"... psychologically any proposition constitutes a coordinable and reversible action but purely symbolic and hypothetical." E.G. I 66.

2. **Proposition, logical**

"We shall call 'propositions' p, q, r, etc., categorical statements, true or false and affirmative (positive) or negative." T.L. 36. (df. 1)

Pseudo-constancy of form

It is a "current mechanism according to which the unconscious creates from the subjective point of view (ignorance or ignorance due to egocentrism) absolute falsity." R.E. 212. [Ch Co Sp 178]

Psychologism

"... is the tendency to ask questions of validity by considerations of fact, in other words, the tendency to substitute the purely deductive methods of logic by methods in which psychological data intervene." E.E.G. XIV 151. (*See* **Logicism**.)

Psychology, operational

"Essentially a theory of forms of equilibrium and transitions from one form to another ... realizing an always more mobile and stable equilibrium..." E.E.G. III 164.

"Studies the ways in which factual equilibrium is formed from actions and operations." P.I. 26. [Ps In 18]

Punishment (*See* **Sanction**)

Q

Quality

"... two actions distinct in their intensity are different qualities ... but the relationship of these qualities is precisely a quantity!"

"... the most elementary forms of quality and of quantity are confused with logical comprehension and extension." E.G. I 75.

"... There is a common quality in two elements as soon as they are related by action..." G.S.L. 285. [Ea Gr Lo 286]

1. **Quantification, intensive**

"... applies to relations of part or totality only." D.Q. 25.

"With this quantification the only possible statement is: if $A + A' = B$, then $A \leqslant B$ and $A' \leqslant B$. It belongs to the logic of classes which do not contain the four quantifiers: *one*, *all*, *some*, and *none*." E.G. I 78.

2. **Quantification, extensive**

"There is extensive quantification as soon as we compare the parts among themselves quantitatively." D.Q. 26. Cf. G.S. 420.

2.1 **Quantification, extensive non-metric**

Given a class B composed of $A + A'$, as soon as we affirm, for instance, that A contains "almost all" the elements of B, this non-metric quantification already determines $A > A'$. This inequality among the complementary classes cannot be decided with intensive quantifiers alone.

2.2 **Quantification, extensive metric**

"... appears when the parts (or differences) being equalized among themselves, and a notion of unit may be introduced." (Iterable) D.Q. 26.

"If in a totality B, the complementary parts A and A' may be reduced to a common unit. If $A = A'$, then $B = 2A$ or $B = 2A'$." E.G. I 80.

1. **Quantity**
   "... quantity is given at the same time as quality; it is formed by the asymmetrical relationships which necessarily connect the qualities among themselves." G.N. 15. [Co Nu 10–11]

2.1 **Quantities, intensive**
   Are "the quantities formed by intensive relationships..." T.L. 72.
   Example: "conceived as a simple passing, speed becomes a qualitative value (or intensive quantity)." E.E.G. I 56.

2.2 **Quantities, any**
   Are "the quantities formed by indifferently intensive or extensive relations." T.L. 72.

3. **Quantity, measured**
   "Measured quantity is a synthesis of partitioning and of placement (or displacement) by equalization of the unit parts and of generalization of the idea of order (any rows which may be constructed by joining the same units having the same value)." D.Q. 337.
   "A continuous quantity (such as weight) constitutes a system of units applied to the variations of a given quality." D.Q. 251.

4. **Quantities, raw**
   "Are ... the relationships expressed in 'more,' in 'equal,' or in 'less,' which are immediately perceived between the given qualities, but not yet combined among them." G.N. 91. [Co Nu 76]

   Quasi-structures, numerical (P. Gréco)
   "There is no preoperational arithmetic forming a structure of a coherent totality ..." but we may speak of a "... specificity of numerical quasi-structures, which cannot be reduced to preclasses or to prerelations only, but which testify without doubt to a beginning of synthesis between the two (without attaining the stage which will be characterized by complete synthesis between groupings of classes and relations, leading to the first numerical structures in the proper sense of the word)." E.E.G. XI 23.

R

1.1 **Reaction, circular** (J. M. Baldwin)
   "Active reproduction of a result obtained first by chance." P.I. 122. [Ps In 101]
   "This conservation of interesting results obtained by chance is therefore that which Baldwin has called circular reaction." N.I. 126. [Or In 138]

"The repetition of the cycle acquired in reality or in the process of being acquired." N.I. 50. [Or In 49]

"... repetition of behavior which has been acquired or which is in the process of being acquired and of behavior directed by the object toward which it is aimed." N.I. 35. [Or In 33]

1.2   **Reaction, circular** (in the restricted sense)

"... functional exercise aimed at maintaining or rediscovering a new interesting result..." N.I. 55. [Or In 55]

2.   **Reaction, circular, and adaptation**

"Circular reaction is a required functional exercise which prolongs reflex exercise and has for its effect to fortify or to keep up not only an already established mechanism but a sensory-motor totality with new results which are obtained for their own sake. As far as adaptation is concerned, circular reaction implies according to the rule a pole of accommodation and a pole of assimilation." N.I. 64. [Or In 66]

"Circular reaction is to be conceived as an active synthesis of assimilation and accommodation. It is assimilation as far as it constitutes a functional exercise which prolongs the assimilation reflex: to suck the thumb or the tongue means to assimilate these objects to the activity of sucking. But circular reaction is accommodation as far as it realizes a new coordination not given in the hereditary reflex mechanism." N.I. 60. [Or In 61]

"... the essence of circular reaction or reproductory assimilation [is] an effort of conservation." C.R. 41. [Co Re 43]

It is a "typical example of reproductive assimilation." P.I. 122. [Ps In 104]

3.   **Reaction, simple circular**

"... The simple circular reactions either primary, secondary or tertiary are judgments..." N.I. 235. [Or In 267–268]

3.1   **Reaction, primary circular (RC I)**

Is characteristic of the second sensory-motor stage (after the stage of simple reflex exercise). The lower limit of RC I is non-hereditary adaptation and the upper limit of RC I is intentional movement (RC II). N.I. 48. [Or In 47]

It "implies the discovery and conservation of the new and in this it differs from pure reflex, but it is prior to intentionality and in this it precedes intelligence." N.I. 126–127. [Or In 138]

3.2   **Reaction, secondary circular (RC II)**

"... the movements are centered upon a result which is produced in the outer environment and the action has as its only goal to maintain this result; it is also more complex and the means start to be differentiated from the goal, at least after doing it." N.I. 141. [Or In 157]

"... behavior consists in finding the gestures which have by chance performed an interesting action on things." N.I. 135. [Or In 151]

It is "activity constructing and using relations with things among themselves and not only the relations of things with the functioning of the organs..." C.R. 115. [Co Re 131]

"The only difference between this secondary and primary reaction is [for RC II] that the interest is centered on the external result and not only on the activity as such." N.I. 158. [Or In 178]

3.3 **Reaction, tertiary circular (RC III)**

"... tertiary circular reaction is an 'experience in order to see' which does not consist in reproducing simply an interesting result, but in varying it in the course of repetition." N.I. 228. [Or In 260]

It is a "reproductory assimilation with differentiated and intentional accommodation." P.I. 126. [Ps In 104]

From the functional point of view they constitute "the functional and also the sensory-motor starting point for experimental judgment..." N.I. 235. [Or In 268]

4. **Reaction, deferred circular**

Deferred circular reaction is the first form of localization of memory. "We deal with interrupted action which the subject takes up again as soon as the interruption stops and without the intervening of a new habitual excitement." C.R. 291. [Co Re 331]

1. **Realism**

"It is taking immediate possession of the object but so immediate that the subject, ignoring himself, is not able to come out of it in order to locate himself in a universe where relations are disengaged from subjective attachments." L.P. 70. [La Th 272]

"The child is realistic, which means that in almost all domains he tends to consider as things (as external objects) to 'make real' the contents of his consciousness." J.M. 147. [Mo Ju 187]

It is an illegitimate exteriorization of intellectual processes and an illegitimate fixation of each moment of the constructed movement. J.M. 148. [Mo Ju 188]

Realistic thought is "entirely projected into things and blended with them as far as the consciousness of the thinker is concerned." J.R. 122. [Ju Re 148]

140

1.1 **Realism** opp. **Objectivity**
"If the subject attributes to the external reality objects or characteristics which are really subjective." C.P. 274. [Co Ph Ca 241]

1.2 **Realism** opp. **Reciprocity**
"If the subject considers his point of view as absolute." C.P. 274. [Co Ph Ca 247]

1.3 **Realism** opp. **Relativity**
"If the subject considers that there exists in himself an object or a characteristic which really depends on other objects or characteristics or on the perspective under which he sees the perception." C.P. 274. [Co Ph Ca 247]

2. **Realism, evolution of**

2.1 **Realism, absolute**
"A phase during which the instruments of thought are not at all distinguishable and where only things seem to exist." R.M. 110–111. [Co Wo 126]

2.2 **Realism, immediate**
"A phase during which the instruments of thought are distinguishable from things but are located in the things..." R.M. 110–111. [Co Wo 126]

2.3 **Realism, mediate**
"A phase during which the instruments of thought are still conceived as a kind of thing or are located at the same time in the body and in the environment." R.M. 110–111. [Co Wo 126]

3. **Realism, nominal**

3.1 **Realism, ontological nominal**
The child considers names as being "in" the object and "generated" by the object (rather than produced by the subject). R.M. 38.

3.2 **Realism, logical nominal**
The child considers names as being endowed with intrinsic values (instead of giving them conventional meaning). R.M. 38.

3.1 "From 9–10 years on ontological nominal realism is abandoned

3.2 [but] it is only toward 11–12 years that logical nominal realism disappears." R.M. 66.

4. **Realism, moral**
Is the "tendency of the child to consider his duties and the values which are attached to them as existing by themselves independently of consciousness and as being imposed in a compulsory fashion." J.M. 82. [Mo Ju 111]

141

"Moral realism originates from the encounter of constraint with egocentricism." J.M. 127. [Mo Ju 163]

5. **Realism, naive**

"... is by definition ignorance of all relativity." J.R. 77. [Ju Re 90]

"Realism is a sort of immediate and illegitimate generalization; relativism is mediate and legitimate generalization." J.R. 109. [Ju Re 133]

6. **Realism, optical**

Is a phase during which the child "substitutes for the physical relationship of the body the visual relations which correspond to the apparent data of perception ... it constitutes a residue of intermediary behaviors between the primitive egocentric stages and the stages of objectification..." C.R. 314. [Co Re 358]

7. **Realism, dynamic**

"Dynamic realism is the residue of the assimilation of things to actions..." C.R. 314. [Co Re 358]

8. **Realism, epistemic**

"... knowledge could not be a copy, since it is always an establishing of relations between object and subject, an incorporation of the object to the schemas, due to activity, and accommodating themselves simply to the subject while rendering the object comprehensible to him. In other words, the object does not exist for our knowledge except in relations with the subject, and if the mind advances further to conquer things it means that it organizes experience always more actively instead of mimicing from outside a ready-made reality. The object is not a 'datum' but the result of a construction." N.I. 327. [Or In 375]

9. **Realism and operationalism**

"The realistic [psychologist] will affirm that the object is distinct from the totality of its meanings. The pure operationalist will identify, on the other hand, the object with the totality of its meanings." E.E.G. IV 55.

1.1 **Reality, true**

"True reality is that which locates the data in the totality of realizable possibilities, but which are not realized simultaneously." E.G. II 350.

1.2 **Reality, apparent**

"Apparent reality is reduced to actual, as opposed to possible, reality." E.G. II 350.

142

Realization, conscious (*See* **Décalage** and **Law of Conscious Realization**)
"Conscious realization is a reconstruction and yet an original construction superimposed on the constructions due to action; it is slower than the activity as such." J.M. 138. [Mo Ju 177] Cf. (6) 107.
"Conscious realization would be centripetal: the feeling of duration of action would enter through consciousness of the obtained result." N.T. 244.

Reason
"Reason in its double aspect, both logical and moral, is a collective product." J.M. 324. [Mo Ju 400] Cf. N.I. 24.

1. **Reasoning, infantile or primitive**
"... is neither deductive nor inductive. It consists in 'mental experiences' which are not reversible; i.e., not entirely logical, not subject to the principle of contradiction." J.R. 120. [Ju Re 146] Cf. J.R. 159–178.
"It will consist in a series of discontinuous judgments which are determined by each other in an extrinsic and not in an intrinsic manner, or, if you prefer, which train each other mutually as in unconscious acts and not as conscious judgments." J.R. 170. [Ju Re 212]

2. **Reasoning, logical**
"... is a discussion with ourselves which reproduces internally the aspect of a real discussion." J.R. 165. [Ju Re 204]

3. **Reasoning, hypothetico-deductive**
"Upon simple assumptions without necessary relations with reality nor with the beliefs of the subject and trusting in the necessity of reasoning itself (*vi formae*) as opposed to the agreement with conclusions from experience." P.I. 177. [Ps In 148]

4. **Reasoning by recurrence**
"... if the numbers are constructed as functions of total structures, and if these structures are different from classifications and seriations, it is probable that there are forms of inference specific to number, which is the same as to say that reasoning by recurrence is not reducible to any serial inference..." E.E.G. XI 11–12.
"In the elementary form, reasoning by recurrence is simply, in the case of the circle ... or the straight line ... to deduce at the point where the totality has the said property and if the following has it equally, all of them will have it." G.S. 286. [Co Ge 221]
"... proceeds directly from iteration of operations, and this iteration

is specific to mathematical operations contrary to simply logical operations (of which pure repetition creates only a tautology). But it is also the proof ... that an iterable operation differs in nature, and not only in degree, from empirical or inductive intuition, even if it constitutes a state of reversible equilibrium marking the final point of the development of this intuition." G.S. 290. [Co Ge 225]

"One may presuppose that recurrence expresses the dynamism of which any number is instantaneously static and that between numbers and recurrence there exists as between concepts and judgments an analogous relation to that of states and transformations for one and the same structure." E.E.G. XI 51–52.

Recentration opp. **Decentration** (*See* **Decentration**)

"There is much more than one 'recentration' (Umzentrierung) in a system of reasoning: there is a general decentration, which supposes a sort of dissolution or melting of the static perceptual forms in order to achieve more operational mobility, and, consequently, there is a possibility of indefinite building of new structures which are perceptible or pass the limits of any real perception." P.I. 80. [Ps In 65]

1. **Reciprocity, logical**
1.1 **Reciprocity of relations**
The reciprocity of relations. Example: the reciprocity of $A = B$ is $B = A$. E.E.G. I.

1.2 **Reciprocity of propositions**
"Df. 33. The reciprocity of an operation (such as $p \lor q$) is the same operation, but bearing upon the propositions of inverse signs: ($\bar{p} \lor \bar{q}$ in the case of $p \lor q$)." T.L. 269.

2. **Reciprocity, topological**
"... reciprocity of [spatial] neighborhoods (which may be applied naturally also to separations) constitutes the infralogical equivalent of groupings of 'vicariances' on the logical level." R.E. 551. [Ch Co Sp 464]

3. **Reciprocity, social**
"Reciprocity is the mutual coordination of attitudes and of affective as well as cognitive points of view..." A.I. 71.

3.1 **Reciprocity, negative** opp.
3.2 **Reciprocity, positive**
"If we define mutual respect and if we explain its mechanism by substitution of points of view, then this substitution of points of view includes only one possibility: it is what I like to call positive reciprocity as opposed to negative reciprocity." A.I. 133.

Recitation
Is "the behavior which consists in reconstructing the course of events when this chain cannot be the object of direct perception." N.T. 260–261.

Recognition
"... what [the child of less than 5 months] recognizes as object is his own reaction from before..." C.R. 11. [Co Re 6]

1. **Reduction of the higher to the lower**
1.1 **Reduction by correspondence** (by isomorphism)
The reduction by correspondence is of interest to the relation between purely deductive and experimental knowledge, between mathematics and physics, and between psychology and mathematics. E.G. III 323.

1.2 **Reduction by interdependence**
Reduction by interdependence is of interest, on the contrary, to relations between two sections of experimental knowledge, between physics and biology, between biology and psychology. E.G. III 323.

2.1 **Reductions of the object to the subject**
2.2 **Reductions of the subject to the object**
Scientific thought proceeds by "a sort of spiral or cyclic process, in which one of the directions is characterized by gradual reduction of the object to the subject [mathematics and psychology] and the other by inverse or complementary reduction [biology and physics]." E.G. I 47. (*See* **Fundamental Epistemological Circle**.)

1. **Reductionism, organistic**
"Organistic explanations, in general, insist on reductions from the psychological to the physiological." T.P. I 130.

2. **Reductionism, physicalistic**
"Physicalistic explanations [start from] isomorphism between mental and organic structures according to field models, [they] are based definitely on the latter as far as physical considerations are concerned (for example, the Gestalists inspired by Koehler)." T.P. I 130.

3. **Reductionism, psychological**
"... consists in finding an explanation for a certain number of reactions or for various behaviors in the deduction to a same causal principle remaining unchanged during the transformations. We shall find an example of this kind of explanation by identification in the recent experimental works of psychoanalysis of the Freudian school about the development of 'object' relations." T.P. I 130.

145

4. **Reductionism, sociological**
"Sociological explanations in psychology, or psychosocial explanations in general, tend to interpret individual reactions as function of interactions between individuals or structures of social groups at different levels." T.P. I 130.

Reflection
"Reflection is the act by which we unify our different tendencies and beliefs, in the way in which conversation and social exchange unify individual opinions, making a part of each one and drawing from all of them the median opinion." J.R. 164–165. [Ju Re 204]
It is the "tendency to unify beliefs and opinions, to systematize them in order to avoid contradictions among them." L.P. 94. [La Th 74]

1.1 **Registration, synchronous (perception)**
1.2 **Registration, diachronic (learning)**
"... synchronous registration is the perception (thus the result is, on the other hand, the figurative characteristic) [1.1] ... temporal or diachronic registration is learning (and thus the result is a series of movements or of actions)" [1.2]. E.E.G. VII 2.
"... the immediate acquisition which constitutes perception, but on the progressive and mediate acquisition which characterizes learning." E.E.G. VII 15.

1. **Regulation and intelligence**
1.1 **Regulation, energetic external**
Is determined by the value of the sought-for solutions and the objects of research. P.I. 11. [Ps In 6]

1.2 **Regulation, energetic internal**
Is determined by interest, effort, and ability, etc. P.I. 11. [Ps In 6]

2. **Regulation and rhythm**
"When the elements of the action are no longer creating simple repetitions, they constitute static systems of totalities which are defined as certain conditions of equilibrium. The movements oriented in an inverse sense from each other and of which the alternation constituted successive phases at a level of 'rhythm' then become simultaneous and represent the components of this equilibrium. (12) 12–13.
Regulation is "the product of a rhythm of totalities of which the components $(A \rightarrow B$ and $B \rightarrow A)$ would have become simultaneous." P.I. 206. [Ps In 172]

3. **Regulation and equilibrium**
Regulations are "partial compensations which have the effect to

146

moderate deformations (= non-compensated transformations), by retroaction or by anticipation." E.E.G. II 46.

"In case of modification of external conditions the equilibrium is 'displaced' by accentuation of one of the tendencies involved, but this accentuation is sooner or later limited by one of the opposite tendency (regulation)." (12) 12–13.

Is "an operator of moderation diminishing the non-compensated transformation in the sense of a closer reversibility." E.E.G. VI 80.

"... it anticipates, perhaps, the superior logical connections." E.E.G. I 36.

4. **Regulation and decentration**

"There is regulation to the extent that there is decentration, automatic or by active comparisons." P.I. 88. [Ps In 72]

"Regulations are partial compensations due to decentrations which tend to moderate the deformations which are inherent in each centration. Regulation is, therefore, on the way to reversibility and constitutes the intermediary between deforming assimilation (centration) and operational assimilation." M.V. 170. [Mo Sp 182]

5. **Regulation, perceptual**

Is independent "in [its] source of judgment as such but influences it in the sense of a progressive equalization" of the terms to be compared. G.S. 135. [Co Ge 100]

"Perceptual composition could not pass the level of what we call the 'subjective' group." P.I. 140. [Ps In 115]

6. **Regulation, intuitive**

"Consists like perceptual regulation in surpassing the movements which are initially centered by a game of representative anticipations and reconstitutions..." N.T. 101.

Bear "on decentrations of attention more than of perception." G.S. 135. [Co Ge 100]

7. **Regulation, affective**

"Outside of energetic or 'economic' regulations which mark the transition between the psycho-organic rhythms and regulations which we properly call affective, there exists a regulation of 'values' which characterize the latter. Interest would constitute the point of junction between these two kinds of regulations." (12) 18. (*See* **Interest**.)

Reinforcement, internal

"We shall speak of internal reinforcement [of learning] to the degree that satisfaction of desire or need is not due to an empirical success,

but to a success connected to the deductive activity of the subject."
E.E.G. VII 32.

1.   **Relation, logical**
Df. 9. "A relation is what characterizes one term by the intermediary
of another." T.L. 57.
The criterion of psychological existence of relations "is the possibility of their composition, or, in other words, construction of their
logical transitivity (or the justification of their non-transitivity if
they cannot become transitive)." G.N. 16. [Co Nu 11]
"... a relation does not exist as logical relation before the moment
when it could be 'multiplied' by others, and at the level of 'prerelations' the child is content with relations of two terms which can be
coordinated." G.S. 19. [Co Ge 9–10]

1.1   **Relation, symmetric**
"Are those which connect the elements of the same class and may
be called relations of classes." G.N. 262, note 1. [Co Nu 203, note 2]

1.2   **Relation, asymmetric**
May be translated into more or less and is the expression of a
difference. G.N. 121. [Co Nu 94]

1.3   **Relation, co-univocal**
Df. 29. Is "any asymmetric relation uniting one term to several."
T.L. 159.

1.4   **Relation of resemblance**
Df. 2. Are "the qualities common to the members of one class when
this quality is formulated as predicate and not relative. For example,
'all herbs (A) are green (a)' means that they resemble each other
as far as they are green and present the relation of 'co-green'."
G.S.L. 16. [Ea Gr Lo 7]

1.5   **Relation of positive equivalence**
Df. 25. Are "the symmetrical relations which are transitive and
reflexive $\underset{\longrightarrow}{a}$; $\underset{\longrightarrow}{b}$; etc., which express co-possession of the distinctive characteristics which are properties of classes A, B, etc.,
as having as limit the identity $\underset{\longrightarrow}{o}$ relative to the singular classes
(x_1), etc." T.L. 150.

1.6   **Relation, positive of complementarity**
Df. 26. "$\underset{\longleftrightarrow}{o'}$; $\underset{\longrightarrow}{a'}$; $\underset{\longrightarrow}{b'}$; etc., [are] the symmetrical relations which
are intransitive and irreflexive, expressing co-possession of the
specific characteristics of classes A (for $\underset{\longrightarrow}{o'}$); B (for $\underset{\longrightarrow}{a'}$); C (for
$\underset{\longrightarrow}{b'}$), etc. and the non-common possession of characteristics
belonging to the classes of inferior rank (x_1) for $\underset{\longrightarrow}{o'}$; A for $\underset{\longrightarrow}{a'}$;
A and B for $\underset{\longrightarrow}{b'}$; A, B, and C for $\underset{\longrightarrow}{c'}$; etc." T.L. 150.

1.7 **Relation of negative equivalence**
Df. 27. Are "$\underleftrightarrow{\bar{o}}$; $\underleftrightarrow{\bar{a}}$; $\underleftrightarrow{\bar{b}}$; the symmetric intransitive and ir-reflexive relations expressing non-common possession of distinctive characteristics belonging to classes of corresponding rank: (x_1) for $\underleftrightarrow{\bar{o}}$; A for $\underleftrightarrow{\bar{a}}$; etc." T.L. 150.

1.8 **Relation of negative complementarity**
Are "the so called negative complementarities, $\underleftrightarrow{\bar{o}'}$; $\underleftrightarrow{\bar{a}'}$; $\underleftrightarrow{\bar{b}'}$; etc. the symmetric, intransitive and reflexive relations, negating corresponding complementarity." T.L. 150.

2. **Relation, spatial**

2.1 **Relation, projective**
By differentiation of points of view. E.E.G. I 48.

2.2 **Relation, Euclidian**
By the introduction of invariance of distance. E.E.G. I 48.

2.3 **Relation of affinity**
By conservation of parallels. E.E.G. I 48.

2.4 **Relation of similarity**
By conservation of parallels and angles. E.E.G. I 48.

1. **Relationship, logical**
Is "a relationship which the explainer would use in order to anchor his propositions to a point of view of clear deduction or of demonstration." L.P. 118. [La Th 108]

2.1 **Relationship of constriction**
"... which characteristic it is to impose from outside on the individual a system of rules with compulsory content." J.M. 320. [Mo Ju 395]

2.2 **Relationship of cooperation**
"Of which the essence is to bring about in the mind the consciousness of ideal norms regulating all the rules." J.M. 320. [Mo Ju 395]

3.1 **Relationship, intensive**
3.2 **Relationship, extensive** Cf. T.L. 72 (*See* **Quantities**)

4. **Relationship, spatial**
They are worked out according to mechanisms "but starting from their construction and especially once they are constructed they are, thanks to the 'signifiers,' 'signified' consisting exactly in sensory indices." R.E. 536. [Ch Co Sp 451–452]

Relativity
"The 'relative' [is] the totality of co-variations inherent in the systems of reference..." E.G. II 106.
"Relativity is the measure of decentration..." E.G. II 85.

"If you consider every object or every characteristic as existing only as function of other objects, and other characteristics, or even as existing as function of the point of view of the perceiving subject." C.P. 274. [Co Ph Ca 241]

2.1   **Relativity, perceptual and intuitive,** opp.

2.2   **Relativity, operational or intelligent**

(2.1) "Relativity belonging to perceptions attributes, for example, qualities of bitter or of sweet to a sensory impression according to that which has preceded it and which conditions it (mechanism of Weber's illusions)." It prevents any objectivity ('everything is relative')." "Perceptual or intuitive relativity is a mutual deformation of the related terms."

(2.2) "Relativity of judgment conceives of notions which have left and right, up and down, etc., as relations and not as absolute predicates." It constitutes the necessary condition for objectivity. "Operational relativity conserves the absolute value of the elements which are connected." N.T. 190. Cf. P.I. 91.

1.   **Representation**

"Df. We shall speak of representation and of thought from the moment when the solution of problems (intelligence) uses the symbolic function and adds a system of conceptual schemas to the sensory-motor schemas." E.E.G. II 47.

It is "the capacity to evoke through a sign or a symbolic image the absent object or the action which is not yet completed." N.I. 214. [Or In 243]

"True representation starts at the moment when no perceptual index demands belief in permanence, i.e., from the moment when the object disappeared and is displaced according to an itinerary which the subject can deduce but not perceive." C.R. 75. [Co Re 85]

"Representation starts when there is simultaneously differentiation and coordination between the 'signifier' and the 'signified' or meanings." F.S. 7. [Pl Dr Im 3]

"There is representation when we imitate an absent model." F.S. 8. [Pl Dr Im 3]

"Representation consists ... either in evoking objects in their absence, or when it parallels perception in their presence to complete their perceptual image by referring to other objects which are not actually perceived. It introduces also a new element which is irreducible to it: a system of meanings..." R.E. 30. [Ch Co Sp 17]

"Representations as such [are those] which are momentarily detached from the action..." G.S. 17. [Co Ge 8]

150

"Representation supposes intuition of possible modifications." R.E. 358. [Ch Co Sp 304]

"Spatial representation is an interiorized action and not simply the imagination of any exterior data, even if it would be the result of an action." R.E. 539. [Ch Co Sp 454]

1.1 **Representation, conceptual**

1.2 **Representation, symbolic, symbol or image**

The term representation has two meanings: "In the larger sense, representation is mixed up with thought. In the narrower sense, it is reduced to the mental image or to the memory image, and this means to the symbolic evocation of absent realities ... it is possible that all thought is accompanied by images, because, if to think is connecting meanings, the image would be a 'signifier' and a concept a 'signified.' [1.1] Let us call 'conceptual representation' the representation in the larger sense and [1.2] 'symbolic or imagined representation' or 'symbols' and 'images,' simply representation in the narrow sense." F.S. 68. [Pl Dr Im 67–68]

2. **Representation, preoperational**

The period "during which sensory-motor acquisitions are re-elaborated on the level of representation but without being extended into more complex situations containing transformations as opposed to configurations." E.E.G. I 27.

3. **Representation, rational, and ludic representation**

"Spatial representation is an interiorized action (like any rational representation), while ludic representation is a substitute for action." R.E. 539. [Ch Co Sp 454]

Repression

"Repression and its effects remain an essential element of the functioning of schemas: the schemas tend to assimilate each other as a whole or in part. From these the total or partial transfers occur which constitute the equivalent of implications in the domain of intelligence, and if that is impossible they tend to exclude each other, which is the equivalent of incompatibilities in the intellectual domain. Repression of one affective schema by another is the very condition for the organization of a number of schemas." F.S. 224. [Pl Dr Im 208–209]

Research, philosophical

"Philosophical research is nothing else than the act of aggressive incorporation into consciousness of the currents of thought which traverse the social states while supporting them." J.M. 321. [Mo Ju 396]

1.   **Respect, mystical, for moral rule**
     "The rules are eternal, due to paternal authority ... It is forbidden to change them, even if the entire opinion would support this change, the opinion will still be wrong." J.M. 40. [Mo Ju 61]

2.   **Respect, mutual moral**
     "If you say 'respect' you say admiration for a personality as far as this personality submits to rules." J.M. 71. [Mo Ju 97–98]

     "Mutual respect seems to us a neccssary condition for autonomy in its double intellectual and moral aspect." J.M. 80. [Mo Ju 107]

     "Mutual respect is in some way a form of equilibrium toward which unilateral respect tends, when the differences are eliminated between the child and the adult, the younger and the older, as cooperation constitutes a form of equilibrium toward which force or constraint tend under the same circumstances ... These are not only limited but ideal forms of equilibrium." J.M. 70. [Mo Ju 96]

1.1 **Responses, copy**
     "Copy responses [are] to be considered direct responses to a stimulus situation..." E.E.G. XII 110.

1.2 **Responses, transformation**
     We have to consider "transformation responses as sort of indirect responses or, more precisely, responses in the second degree, which have as their effect to connect one copy response to the following by the intermediary of a non-copy transformation, but effected (in real or interiorized action) and modifying consequently the said copy responses." E.E.G. XII 110.

2.   **Response, verbal**
     It is "the adapted speech given by the interviewer after having heard and understood the question ... We connect the refusals and ac-ceptances to the responses, which are no longer given to questions of an observing nature but to orders and petitions..." L.P. 31. [La Th 28–29]

1.   **Responsibility, primitive**
     "Primitive responsibility is first of all objective and communicable; ours is subjective and strictly individual." J.M. 263. [Mo Ju 329]

2.   **Responsibility, objective**
     "The objective notion of responsibility appears as a product of moral constraint exercised by the adult." J.M. 101. [Mo Ju 133]

1.   **Reversibility**
     "Df. We shall call reversibility the capacity to execute the same action in both directions but being conscious that we are dealing with the same action." E.E.G. II 44.

"This reversibility which contains a causal aspect (from this point of view characterizes the very existence of a state of equilibrium), contains also an implying or logical aspect: a reversible operation is one which has the possibility of an inverse." T.L. 15.

"It is nothing other than the criterion of equilibrium." P.I. 17. [Ps In 11]

"True reversibility is the discovery of the inverse operation as operation." D.Q. 17.

Complete reversibility is the one which contains the inverse operation (N); $N(A) = -A$ and the operation of reciprocity (R); $R(A = B) = (B = A)$. E.E.G. I 27.

2. **Reversibility, perceptual**

"At the perceptual level already (even though we have not yet complete reversibility) the inversions correspond to additions or eliminations of elements, and the reciprocities correspond to symmetries and similarities." L.E.A. 240. [Gr Lo Th 273]

3. **Reversibility, operational**

"To operational reversibility, which is the inversion of a direct operation (or thetic) in inverse operation, corresponds the operational identity which is the product of direct operation and of the inverse operation combined (for example, $+1 - 1 = 0$). But beforehand some intuitions of (empirical) possible return to the point of departure may exist, and to these preoperational intuitions determining an incomplete reversibility may correspond some equally preoperational identification, characterizing a sort of generation." G.S. 419. [Co Ge 330]

"Operational reversibility is ... only the final state of mobile equilibrium which has been attained by perceptual and then intuitive regulations, or also by reciprocal adjustment of representative assimilation and accommodation." G.S. 81. [Co Ge 58]

"In order to have reversibility, there must be operations in the proper sense of the word, i.e., constructions or decompositions, either manual or mental, which aim at foreseeing or reconstituting the phenomena. A simple succession of images without other direction than the one which is given by an unconscious desire will not be sufficient for creation of a reversible process." J.R. 141.

"As soon as intelligence reaches a certain relativity, i.e., as soon as it removes itself from naive realism, tied to primitive mental experiences, the problem of reversibility appears in a new light: i.e., it means to find no longer directly the reciprocal of a relation given between two phenomena, but a reciprocal of a general point of view. Or if you prefer, it means to find the key which allows to pass from one personal or momentary point of view to another without contradiction." J.R. 156. [Ju Re 192–193]

4. **Reversibility and action**

"Reversibility of phenomena is in part relative to the scale of our action which may be applied to them, whereas irreversibility, solidary with the simply probable characteristic of statistical laws, is in part related to the limits of our action." E.G. II 222.

Rhythm

Is a "system of alternating reuniting regulations in a unique totality of succession." P.I. 206. [Ps In 172]

"Alternation of two antagonistic processes functioning one in the direction $A \to B$ and the other in the inverse direction $B \to A$." P.I. 202. [Ps In 169]

It is "the biological antecedent of grouping which replaces composition by its periodic repetition and conservation by its procedures appropriate to propagation (oscillations around a point of equilibrium)." (11) 239.

It is a double alternating regulation and the regulation is the product of rhythm of which the two phases would come together simultaneously. (12) 14.

(1) Elementary action consists in movements which are repeated as such. Whether they are relatively simple or coordinated into complex sequences is of little importance. In the latter case there is an indissociable block constituted by those which give way to repetition.

(2) Movements which combine actions are characterized by two alternating phases: an ascending or positive phase (for example, opening the mouth or moving a limb) and a descending or antagonistic phase (for example, closing the mouth or replacing the limb in the initial position).

(3) This periodicity is at intervals more and more regular, according to whether it depends on internal or external factors. (12) 10.

The antagonistic phase of rhythm is certainly the starting point of regulation. (12) 14.

Rituals

"The assimilation of any new object to the motor schemas which already exist may be conceived as the starting point of rituals and of symbols, at least from the moment when assimilation is stronger than accommodation." J.M. 16. [Mo Ju 31]

Road traversed

"The spatial interval between two successive placements of the same element (thus interval between two extreme positions of the same displacement) constitutes a traversed road." M.V. 272. [Mo Sp 295] Cf. M.V. 66, 69, 93.

Romancing (*See* **Fabrication**)

1. **Rule, moral**

"The essential function of the rule is to conserve values, and the only social way to conserve them is to make them compulsory and enforce them. Any value tending to conserve itself in time becomes normative..." E.G. III 206.

"Submission to something superior to the self characterizes the appearance of any rule." J.M. 20. [Mo Ju 35]

1.1 **Rule and regularity**

"We have to distinguish these behaviors in which pleasure of regularity only enters and behaviors in which an element of obligation is present. It is this consciousness of the obligation (and here we agree with Durkheim and Bovet) which distinguishes a rule as such from regularity." J.M. 18. [Mo Ju 33]

2.1 **Rule, motor**

"At its origins the motor rule is confused with habit. The motor rule results from a sort of feeling of repetition, starting where there is ritualization of schemas of motor adaptation." J.M. 62. [Mo Ju 87]

"Motor rule is at the same time a sort of experimental legality or rational regularity and a playful ritual. It is directed in one of these two directions according to the circumstances." J.M. 72. [Mo Ju 99]

2.2 **Rule, rational**

"Rational rule is the primitive motor rule but taken away from individual whim and subjected to the control of reciprocity." J.M. 63. [Mo Ju 88]

3. **Rule, collective**

"Appears as the product of reciprocal approbation of two individuals as well as the authority of one individual over another." J.M. 34. [Mo Ju 53]

"A collective rule is first something outside of the individual, and therefore sacred; then it is slowly interiorized and appears in this measure as the free product of mutual consent and of autonomous conscience." J.M. 14. [Mo Ju 28]

4.1 **Rules of constitution or constituting rules**

"Rules of constitution make it possible to have cooperation." J.M. 71. [Mo Ju 98]

155

"Constituting norms define the very laws of reciprocity." J.M. 310. [Mo Ju 384]

4.2 **Rules, constituted**

"Constituted rules result from the same exercise" (exercise of co-operation). J.M. 71. [Mo Ju 98]

"Constituted rules result from reciprocal agreements." J.M. 310. [Mo Ju 384]

S

1. **Sanction by reciprocity**

"It accompanies cooperation and the rules of equality." J.M. 163. [Mo Ju 205]

"Sanctions by reciprocity are necessarily 'motivated' when there is correspondence between contents and nature, between crime and punishment." J.M. 164. [Mo Ju 206]

2. **Sanction, expiatory**

Seems "to pair up with constraint and with the rules of authority ... Expiatory sanction presents thus the characteristics of being 'arbitrary'; that means there is no relationship between the content of the sanction and the nature of the sanctioned act." J.M. 163. [Mo Ju 205]

1. **Schema**

"A schema is a mode of reactions susceptible of reproducing themselves and susceptible above all of being generalized." A.I. 95.

"Schema of an action is, by definition, the group structured by the generalizable characteristics of that action, and that means of those which allow repetition of the same action or application to new contents. Now the schema of an action is neither perceptible (one perceives a particular action, but not its schema) nor directly introspectible, and one becomes conscious of its implications only in repeating the action and in comparing the successive results." E.E.G. XIV 251.

"It is why such schemas have the entirely general content and do not characterize simply one or the other of the actions of a single individual. But it is also why they remain unconscious as long as a 'reflective abstraction' does not transform them into operations." E.E.G. XIV 252.

Schemas "represent actions susceptible of being applied to objects." N.I. 187. [Or In 211]

"A schema is applied to the diversity of the exterior environment and generalizes itself thus to the function of the contents which it subsumes, while a *Gestalt* cannot be generalized and even is less applied to than imposed on the perceived situation in immediate and interior fashion." N.I. 336.[Or In 384]

"Schemas have a history; there is a mutual reaction between former experience and the present act of intelligence." P.I. 81. [Ps In 66]

"Schemas of action constitute the principal source of concepts." M.P. 385. [Me Pe 309] Cf. M.P. 400. [Me Pe 321]

1.1 **Schema, final**
It is the schema which assigns "a goal to the action." N.I. 202. [Or In 229]

1.2 **Schema, negative**
The "tendency to repeated application and the generalization of the schema presents the limits, because of an inhibitory factor, which is the source of the negation of this application and source of that which we may call the complementarity of schemas or negative schemas." E.E.G. VII 43.

1.31 **Schema, particular**
"Has special or singular content..." N.I. 209. [Or In 238]

1.32 **Schema, generic**
"Has multiple content..." N.I. 209. [Or In 238]

1.33 **Schema, unique**
"If the movements and sensory elements are associated, and do not yet present themselves in an isolated state, we say that there is a unique schema." N.I. 119. [Or In 129]
Example: "placing the thumb in the mouth [is a unique schema] because, at the age when the child learns to suck his thumb, he knows how to suck other things than his thumb, but he does not know how to accomplish in other circumstances, by means of his hand, the action which he executed in putting it in his mouth..." N.I. 119.[Or In 129]

1.34 **Schemas, mobile**
They are schemas "appropriate to coordinations and new syntheses..." N.I. 209. [Or In 238]
"Subject to multiple combinations." N.I. 221. [Or In 251]

2. **Schema of the permanent object**
It is "due to one sensory-motor assimilation, provoking the search for an object, once having left the field of perception, and attributing to it thus a conservation issuing from the continuation of the actions, then projected onto exterior properties." P.I. 135. [Ps In 111]

"To have the notion of an object is to attribute the perceived figure to a substantial support, such that the figure and the substance of which it is thus the index continue to exist beyond the perceptual field." P.I. 130–131. [Ps In 107–108]

3. **Schemas (evolution of)**
3.10 Schema, sensory motor
    3.11 Schema, perceptual
    3.12 Schema, practical or habitual
    3.2   Schema, symbolic
    3.3   Schema, intuitive
    3.41 Schema, concrete operational
    3.42 Schema, formal operational
    P.I. 181.

3.10 **Schema, sensory-motor**
"Df. We call sensory-motor schemas the sensory-motor organizations capable of being applied to a group of analogous situations and thus giving evidence of reproductory assimilations (repetition of the same activities), recognitive (to recognize objects by attributing meaning to them as function of a schema) and generalizable (with differentiations as function of new situations)." E.E.G. II 46.

It is "a definite and closed system of movements and perceptions; the schema presents, in effect, the double characteristics of being structured (thus structuring itself the field of perception or of understanding) and of constituting itself beforehand as totality without resulting from an association or from a synthesis between the previously isolated elements." N.I. 330. [Or In 378]

The "sensory-motor schemas are not simply what we sometimes call *'patterns'*; that is to say that they have further power to generalize and further power to assimilate." A.I. 95–96.

3.11 **Schema, perceptual**
"The perceptual schema is only a temporal schema with successive assimilations and without the possibilities of being united into a simultaneous whole which would characterize the class." M.P. 362. [Me Pe 291]

The perceptual forms for example "exist in themselves whereas the schemas are only the systems of relations. The further developments remain always dependent on each other." N.I. 344. [Or In 393]

3.12 **Schema, practical or habitual**
The child coordinates "the actions among themselves in the form of

158

practical 'schemas,' a sort of sensory-motor preconcept, characterized by the possibility of repeating the same action in the presence
of the same objects or of generalizing it in the presence of analogous
others." E.G. I 97.

3.2   **Schema, symbolic (verbal)**
The "first verbal schemas are only sensory-motor schemas on their
way to conceptualization." They imply (1) "generalizable modes of
actions being applied to always more numerous objects," (2) "a
semi-detachment in respect to the activity itself," and (3) they an-
nounce communication. F.S. 234. [Pl Dr Im 219–220]

3.3   **Schema, intuitive (representative or mental)**
"In order to become mental [or representative] the sensory-motor
schemas ought to be able to be combined in all kinds of ways." N.I.
296. [Or In 341]

3.4   **Schema, operational**
"An operational schema is a method of reversible composition."
D.Q. 133.
"An anticipatory schema could not arise from thought alone, because
representation cannot predict anything without being guided by the
action. It is only at the level where coordinated actions constitute a
grouping of reversible operations that the system of compositions
inherent in that grouping can be translated into psychological terms
under the form of an anticipatory schema of an operational nature."
G.S. 423. [Co Ge 334]
Anticipatory schema is "nothing but the grouping of operations."
R.E. 162. [Ch Co Sp 134]

4.   **Schema relative to persons**
"The schemas relative to persons are cognitive and affective simultaneously. The affective element is perhaps more important in the
domain of persons and the cognitive element in the domain of things,
but it is only a question of degree." A.I. 95.
Schemas of reaction constitute "the general element and that common to cognitive and affective reactions." A.I. 97.

4.1   **Schemas, affective**
"Means simply: the affective aspect of schemas which are otherwise
also intellectual." F.S. 222. [Pl Dr Im 207]

4.2   **Schemas, moral**
"The affective schemas do not reach exactly the degree of generalization and abstraction of the logical schemas, except in the exclusive
case where they are found regulated by reversible and reciprocal

159

operations, etc.; that is, where they become therefore moral schemas." F.S. 226. [Pl Dr Im 211]

5.   **Schema, transitive**

It is "the schema used as means..." N.I. 202. [Or In 229]

6.   **Schema, stimulus-response**

"The stimulus-response schema is to be conceived, not as a linear process leading from S to R, but as a circular process of initial assimilation of S to the schema R and accommodation of R to S thus qualified." E.E.G. X 188.

Semi-isomorphism between the norms F and S

Cf. E.E.G. I 30.

Semi-net (Semi-lattice)

Cf. E.E.G. I 29 (*See* **Grouping, Elementary.**)

Semi-overtaking

"... the action of catching up is – a semi-overtaking." M.V. 165.

Semi-reversibility or relative irreversibility

Cf. E.E.G. I 36–37. (*See* **Regulation.**)

Sensation

Sensation is "the index of a mental assimilation of an object to a schema of action." E.G. I·21.

Sentiment (*See* **Feeling**)

Seriation

Seriation is "an addition of differences by opposition to addition of classes which is an addition of equivalent elements to the given point of view." G.N. 226. [Co Nu 183]

1.   **Series, temporal practical**

"The practical series, however ordered in time from the point of view of the observer, remains global and undifferentiated from the point of view of the subject." C.R. 284. [Co Re 324]

2.   **Series, temporal subjective**

Consists in "an application of time itself to things, but to the degree that the succession of events which are produced at the heart of the thing is regulated by the subject himself." C.R. 287. [Co Re 327]

3.   **Series, temporal objective**

Orders "in time the exterior events themselves and not only the appropriate actions or their prolongations." C.R. 300. [Co Re 342]

Shares (P. Gréco)

We observe "... the existence of numerical equalities (shares) before the conservation of quantity. This last notion is without any doubt solidary through the extension of classes and of their nestings. The fact that it may appear as numerical, but not quantitative, equalities between the collections where the optical correspondence, term for term, is destroyed, seems to indicate that it is especially the serial aspect of the chain of totalities which brings about this equality, without complete synthesis with the aspect of inclusion between classes." E.E.G. XI 29

"... This discordance between numerical and quantitative equality appears between a level where the first does not exist and a level where the two are united in a stable synthesis..." E.E.G. XI 29–30.

1. **Sign (symbol)**

"The sign is a collective and arbitrary symbol. It appears during the second year with the beginning of language and without doubt in synchronism with the constitution of the symbol." N.I. 170. [Or In 191]

2. **Sign (index)**

"The 'signal' (in the sense of conditioned behaviors) is incorporated into a schema in a rigid or indissociable fashion and triggers its use more or less automatically, whereas the index is a mobile sign detached from the ongoing action and permitting the prediction of a near future or reconstruction of a recent past." F.S. 46. [Pl Dr Im 42]

The mobile signs or indices "give way to predictions relative to an activity of the objects themselves independently of the actions of the subject." N.I. 174. [Or In 196]

3. **Sign and signal**

"The signal is a more elementary index: it consists in a sensory impression simply associated to the reaction and to the perceptual pictures characteristic of all schemas; it announces from then on these pictures and triggers the reactions to the extent that it is assimilated to the schema in question." N.I. 171. [Or In 193]

"Signals intervening in the conditioning are only indices." N.P. 374.

The total practical meaning of a signal "has no other effect than of triggering the action of a schema of assimilation to which it is tied by a constant and necessary bond." N.I. 220. [Or In 250–251]

Signifiers appropriate to the early sensory-motor habits are signals. N.I. 171. [Or In 193]

Simultaneity

"Simultaneity is a limited case of the relations of succession, that where the succession tends toward being null." N.T. 114.

Socialization of individual intelligence

Socialization of individual intelligence is generated "by the triple intermediary of language (signs), of content of exchanges (intellectual values) and of rules imposed on thought (collective logical or prelogical norms)." P.I. 186. [Ps In 156]

1. **Society**

"Society is the totality of social relationships." J.M. 320. [Mo Ju 395] Cf. P.I. 186.

"Society begins with two individuals, as soon as the connection of these individuals modifies the nature of their behaviors." J.M. 306. [Mo Ju 379]

"Society is nothing other than a series (or rather an intersection of series) of generations pressing each upon the following." J.M. 268. [Mo Ju 336]

"In all societies a constraint is exercised by the whole social group upon individuals. This constraint takes the form of cooperative solidarity in our civilizations while remaining limited to obligatory conformity in primitive societies." J.M. 278. [Mo Ju 346–347]

2. **Society, child**

"It is the society in which the individual and social life are not differentiated." L.P. 40. [La Th 41]

Solopsism

The baby takes the totality of his universe for his self, in the manner of a solipsist who identifies the world with his own representation." (5) 100.

The true solipsist is really alone in the world; that means that he has no idea ever of anything which could be outside himself; he does not have a self; he is in the world. (5) 102.

Sophism, the psychologist's

It is "the attributing to the subject a structure surpassing his level and related to that of the observer." E.E.G. IV 47.

1. **Space, coordinations of movements**

"... from the genetic point of view ... space is the coordination of movements and time the coordination of speeds." E.G. II 93.

"... space and time result in operations like concepts (classes and logical relations) and numbers, but they are operations interior to the object and finally bear by nesting the partial objects into each other on the transformations of this unique object which is a spatio-temporal universe." N.T. 35.

1.1 **Space and contents**
"Space is not at all perception of a container, but of the contents, which means the things themselves, and if space becomes in a sense a container, it is to the extent that the relations constitute the very objectivation of these things and succeed in coordinating themselves up to the point where they form a coherent whole." C.R. 87. [Co Re 98]

"Space is an organization of movements such as to imprint always more coherent forms on perception." C.R. 189. [Co Re 217]

"But space itself is not a simple 'container.' It is the totality of relations which is established between the things which we perceive or conceive or, to say it better, the totality of relations which we use in order to structure these things so that we may perceive them and conceive them. It is, properly speaking, the logic of the perceptible world or of at least one of the two essential aspects of the logic of objects (the second being time)..." N.T. 1.

1.2 **Space, container** (Euclidian, usual)
Usual space "is a system of coordinates in relation to which the objects would be 'placed' whereas unoccupied spaces would be at the state of free places ... it is while grouping simultaneous 'placements' and 'displacements' ... that the subject is led to conceive space as a container or as a system of references independent of its content." G.S. 109. [Co Ge 79–80]

"Euclidian space consists of coordination of the objects themselves; then, since objects or their figures are mobile or subject to displacement ... the essential of this coordination consists in relating positions, distances, and displacements as a function of an immobile 'container' of which the structuration permits reference to mobile 'contents.' This distinction between container and content, essential to representation in Euclidian space is at the very source of systems of coordinates..." G.S. 504. [Co Ge 404–405]

2.1 **Space, physical and**
2.2 **Space, geometrical**
(2.1) "... the possibility of constructing triangles ... teaches the subject the existence of physical space, constituted by interactions between macroscopic solids [2.2] as well as the ones of geometric space tied to the actions of construction and to joining of angles." G.S. 269.

"Space occupies a special situation, being either physical and

163

mathematical [2.1] at the same time, or mathematical only [2.2], according to whether it involves simultaneously the object and the action, or the action in its coordinations alone." E.G. II 342.

3.   **Space and group of displacements**
According to H. Poincaré, space "derives psychologically from a group of displacements constituted in the experimental fashion by each subject as function of perceived movements on the objects and their proper displacements." M.V. 264. [Mo Sp 287]

4.   **Space, sensory-motor**
"... a single perceptual field would not suffice to determine a space, since space is the possible passage from one field to another."
"... there exists, on the level of perception, a perceptual activity consisting in regarding, comparing, and analyzing, etc. but the constitution of space is far from depending on these alone and presupposes its relation with the totality of other actions." E.G. I 164.

5.   **Space, empty non-intuitive**
"If 'intuitions' remain disjointed, it is that the relations between successive intuitions are not in themselves possible objects of intuition, because they have not been distinctly perceived; therefore, we have these empty, non-intuitive spaces. It is the role of operations to fill them by means of a system of reversible transformations." M.V. 15–16. [Mo Sp 16]

6.   **Space, projected**
"... projected space is constituted mainly by the group of transformation (and, before there can be mathematized group, by qualitative grouping), of which the psychological expression is the representative, and not the perceptual, system of perspectives which are worked through by the child in the course of his four sub-stages..." R.E. 289. [Ch Co Sp 245]
"... the essence of projected space is to be found in the sensory-motor coordination, then operational, of the points of view." R.E. 291. [Ch Co Sp 246]

1.   **Speed**
Speed is the correspondence between specialized actions of the subject and the resistances of the objects. E.G. II 53–54, 30.
"Speed of actions does not constitute a result of the activity of a subject but a characteristic of his actions considered as objects." E.G. II 51.

2.   **Speed, intuitive**
"Speed is the passing, that is, a reversal of the order of respective

positions, of two moving things in the course of displacement." M.V. 271. [Mo Sp 293] Cf. M.V. 123, 128, 150, 215.

"The intuitive starting point of the notion of speed seems to be based upon a sensory-motor schema appropriate to the activity of the subject: the one of arriving at the head of the line or may simply be expressed as winning." M.V. 164. [Mo Sp 176]

"... language, which often uses infantile logic, says without differentiation 'faster' for 'faster in moving' (surpassing in time) and for 'faster in getting there' (surpassing in space)." M.V. 136. [Mo Sp 145]

"$r = d/t$, [is the] mathematical expression of the qualitative grouping of codisplacements." M.V. 172. [Mo Sp 185]

It is the "overtaking in time and not in space, that is, the inversion of temporal and not spatial order ... we can almost say 'potential speed'." M.V. 135. [Mo Sp 145]

3.1 **Speed, frequency**

3.2 **Speed, movement**
"A number of given changes in a unit of time is thus a speed ... [3.1]. We think that the most general law is that of a relation between duration and speed and not between duration and the number of changes, even though these intervene effectively in the particular case of frequencies." M.P. 347. [Me Pe 277]

4.1 **Speed, qualitative** (intensive)
1. by Asymmetric relations of order, and 2. by Partitive addition.

4.2 **Speed, measured**
"... the notion of time rests in that of qualitative speed and consists of placing in relationships different qualitative speeds. Once time is constructed by that coordination, it serves to define measured speed." E.G. II 33.

5.1 **Speed, absolute**
"Absolute speed is related to a stationary observer." M.V. 183. [Mo Sp 197]

5.2 **Speed, relative**
"Relative speeds are those observed by a moving observer." M.V. 183. [Mo Sp 198]
Relative speed is the "coordination of two speeds in an apparently unique speed." M.V. 150. [Mo Sp 186]

Spheres of reality (*See* **Zones of reality**)

Stability of equilibrium
"Df. A state of equilibrium is the more stable the more transforma-

tions in question are compensating one another." E.E.G. II 42. (*See* **Equilibrium.**)

1.   **Stage** (Definitions)
The stages are the 'sections' in the genetic evolution which satisfy the following conditions:
(1) It is necessary that the order of the various acquisitions be constant. (For example: the acquisition of the notion of volume is always after that of the notion of weight.)
(2) Each stage is characterized by a structure and not by a single juxtaposition of properties.
(3) The structures constructed at a given age become a part of the structures of the age following. (Integration of the inferior structures into the superior ones.)
(4) In each stage we distinguish a moment of preparation and a moment of accomplishment.
(5) We ought to distinguish the processes of creation and the final forms of equilibrium (always relative). Cf. S.E.A.
"The stages are to be understood as the successive phases of the regular processes, which are reproduced like rhythms, on the super-imposed levels of behavior and consciousness." J.M. 61. [Mo Ju 85]
"There do not exist global stages defining the totality of the psychological life of the subject." J.M. 61. [Mo Ju 85]
The study of stages has to take into account: (1) the Functional Continuity and (2) the Differences of the structures to be observed.

2.   **Stages and periods** (Classification in the development of the intelligence of the child)
(I) *Period of sensory-motor intelligence* (0–2 years)
Stage I: Exercise of reflexes (0–1 month)
Stage II: First acquired adaptations and primary circular reaction (1–4 months)
Stage III: Proceedings to make interesting sights last and the secondary circular reaction (4–8 months)
Stage IV: Coordination of the secondary schemas and their application to new situations (8–12 months)
Stage V: Discovery of new means for active experimentation and the tertiary circular reaction (12–18 months)
Stage VI: Invention of new means by mental combinations (after 18 months)
(II) *Period of preparation and organization of concrete operations.*

166

Subperiod IIa: Preoperational representation
Stage I: Symbolic function (2–3.6 years)
Stage II: Simple regulations (to 5.6 years)
Stage III: Articulated regulations (to 7 or 8 years)
Subperiod IIb: Concrete operational
Stage I: Simple operations (to 9 or 10 years)
Stage II: Complex operations (for example construction of spatial coordinates) (to 11 or 12 years)
(III) *Period of formal operations*
Stage I: (to 13 or 14 years)
Stage II: (Adolescence)

3.   **Stages of moral development**
The psychologist asks "how consciousness comes to respect rules." J.M. 1. [Mo Ju 13(2)]
In the evolution of the practice of simple rules, such as those used in the play of children (for example, marbles), we distinguish 4 stages.

3.1   **Stage, motor individual (0–2 years)**
Stage "purely motor and individual, in the course of which the child manipulates the marbles as function of his own desires and his own motor habits." J.M. 12. [Mo Ju 26]

3.2   **Stage, egocentric (2–5 years)**
"The child receives from outside the example of codified rules ... but in imitation of these examples the child plays either totally alone without being concerned with finding partners, or with others, but without trying to win. In neither case does he want to make the different ways of playing uniform." J.M. 12. [Mo Ju 27]

3.3   **Stage of initial cooperation (to 7–8 years)**
"Each player tries now to win over his neighbors, and this creates concern for mutual control and unification of rules." J.M. 13. [Mo Ju 27]

3.4   **Stage of the codification of rules (to 11 or 12 years)**
"The games are from then on regulated with fussy detail of the procedure, and the code of rules to be followed is now known to the whole society." J.M. 13. [Mo Ju 27]

States of consciousness and covert behavior
"... the states of consciousness and covert behavior do not originate in causality and they form systems of meanings exclusively or signifying actions, and the meanings are thus interrelated by 'implication' in the larger sense of the term." M.P. 11. [Me Pe xxiii]

167

Story

"There is a story ... when the events, still depending in part one upon the others as in the first of these systems, thus are in part fortuitous because of the crossing over of causal series." E.G. II 188.

"... a story cannot be deduced itself much as it is composed of events which do not repeat themselves." E.G. II 189.

1. **Structure** (*See* **Equilibrium**)

"... the logical structures constitute not *a priori* forms nor the products of experience with objects, nor the social conventions, but the forms of equilibrium toward which the intellectual coordinations of the subject tend..." E.E.G. II 27, note 1.

"Each structure ought to be understood as a particular form of equilibrium, more or less stable in its restrained field and becoming unstable at its limits." P.I. 12. [Ps In 7]

"To say that a structure is 'achieved,' even if it is not 'final,' means that it reaches the state of equilibrium such that it can be integrated, without being modified in ulterior structures which have already been constructed." E.E.G. XV 12.

"It is a form of organization of experience." (8) 149.

"It is taking into consciousness or a 'reflection' always approximating the function itself." (8) 152.

"The structure is only a momentary crystallization, always surpassed in fact by the mind in its functioning." (8) 160.

The structures "do not exist because of distinct notions in the consciousness of the subject, but constitute only the tools for his behavior." E.E.G. XIV 195.

1.1 **Structure and energetic**

"Contrary to energetic, structure is defined without making appeal to strength or to weakness, to the more or to the less." A.I. 9.

1.2 **Structure and function**

"Structure could be the result of a functioning, but this functioning supposes the preexistence of structures." A.I. 9.

1.3 **Structure and content**

"It is often impossible to distinguish, in the course of development, structures from their content, because structures are differentiated only progressively." A.I. 9.

2. **Structure and totality**

The most important characteristic of a structure "is that of closure. A structure is a closed group." A.I. 10.

"We say that there is a structure ... when the elements are reunited into a totality presenting certain properties as totality and when the properties of the independent elements depend, entirely or partially, on the characteristics of the totality." E.E.G. II 34.

Df. 5. "We call 'structures' all logical connections susceptible of, alternatively or simultaneously, playing the role of form and content." T.L. 42.

2.1 **Structure, mathematical**

2.2 **Structure, genetic**

We call "'M structures' those of mathematicians and 'G structures' those of the subject studied genetically. While being less general than M structures, G structures bear nevertheless elements of very different natures.

What Bourbaki calls 'relations' constituting the M structures correspond to what we call 'operations' of G structures, for example, the law of composition $z = x\tau y$ of a 'group'."

"The 'conditions' of these relations in M structures are what we call 'laws of composition' characterizing the G structure as a system of a group; examples: reversibility by inversion for structures of classes and by reciprocity for those of relation." E.E.G. XIV 201–202.

3. **Structure and deduction**

"Once the operations are constituted into structures, deduction will become possible and experience useless." E.E.G. XIV 251.

3.1 **Structure, partial or quasi-structure**

"Before structures appear with their habitual criteria one could find quasi-structures (intuitive articulations ending in certain situations as judgments equivalent to the structural inferences) or of partial structures (structures already organized as such, but being applied only to a limited domain), etc." E.E.G. XI 50.

The "partially indetermined structures [are] like the not entirely closed groups with reference to an operator (which would lead beyond to an algebra *sensu stricto*), etc." E.E.G. XV 11.

3.11 **Structures, sensory-motor (Example)**

Sensory-motor structures could "play the double role of regulators in respect to perceptual activities (special case of sensory-motor activities) and of formation in respect to the representative activities and later operations (rising from the interiorization of these sensory-motor structures and of their structuration on the symbolic level, which permits thus the prolongation into new constructions)." M.P. 412. [Me Pe 331]

Subjectivity opp. **Activity**
There is an essential duality which "opposes one against the other subjectivity, as taking into egocentric consciousness, and activity of the subject as operational coordination decentering the action able to adapt it to the object." E.G. II 15.

Subjectivism
"The phenomenism of immediate perception is nothing but subjectivism." N.I. 154. [Or In 173]

1.1 **Subject, psychological**
1.2 **Subject, epistemic**
The psychological subject is centered on its conscious self; the epistemic subject is the "common part of all the subjects at the same level of development..." E.E.G. XIV 329.

"Reflexive abstraction apart from actions does not reach an empirical interpretation in the psychological sense, for the actions with which it is concerned are not particular actions of the individual subjects (or psychological subjects): they are the most general coordinations of the systems of actions, translating thus that which is common to all subjects and making reference to a universal or epistemic subject and not to an individual subject. From the beginning of mathematizing activity appears thus as ruled by internal laws and as avoiding the arbitrariness of individual wills." E.E.G. XIV 254–255.

"The epistemic subject (in contradistinction to the psychological subject) is that which all subjects have in common since the general coordinations of actions contain a universality which is that of biological organization itself." E.E.G. XIV 304–305.

2.1 **Subject, individual**
2.2 **Subject, collective**
Neither individual nor collective subjects are "determining the evolution of operational structures."

2.2 The collective subject is the result "of social and cultural factors (language, etc)." E.E.G. XIV 261. Cf. E.E.G. XIV 262.

Substance or **Matter**
Substance is "the quantity in general." D.Q. 257.

It is "the matter as such, that is to say, an undifferentiated quality and consequently quantified before all the others." D.Q. 24.

"Quantity of matter or of substance is the simplest form of quantities." D.Q. 333.

"It constitutes an undifferentiated and global quality, completing on the conceptual level those of the sensory-motor object." D.Q. 20.

170

"This notion of substance or matter is that of a general schema of quantification; that means the simplest and least differentiated physical *quantum*." D.Q. 21.

The notion of substance is to be considered "as a prolongation of that of the object." D.Q. 21.

"The substantial quality will thus be no longer such and such quality directly visible or perceptible (length, size, weight, color, etc.) but the quality proper to the permanent support of these characteristics perceived or conceived as variables." D.Q. 22.

Substance is on one hand, "a sort of formal regulator" and on the other hand, "substance remains an undifferentiated quality serving as content to this general *quantum*, which without it would remain empty." D.Q. 23.

"Substance is before its conservation only the simple undifferentiated quality which serves as support for the others." D.Q. 29.

Substitution of behaviors

"Df. 32b ... a behavior *B* is substituted for a behavior *A* or derived from the substitution of *A'* to *A* if *B* or *A'* preexists to *A* (or exists next to it before entering into relationship with it) or if *B* or *A'* constitutes the exclusive manifestation, or almost, of a source of influences preexisting to *A* (or existing next to it before the junction)." E.E.G. IV 77.

Superego

"The superego is the simplest example of what I will call the schemas of reaction ... The superego is the product of an assimilation ... The superego is on the other hand, a schema susceptible of generalization." A.I. 98.

1. **Symbol and sign**

"The symbol is the necessary but not sufficient condition for the appearance of signs. The sign is general and abstract (arbitrary). The symbol is individual and motivated." J.M. 19. [Mo Ju 34]

"Symbol and sign are nothing but the two poles, individual and social, the same elaboration of meanings." N.I. 170. [Or In 191]

"Symbol is an image evoked mentally or a material object chosen intentionally to designate a class of actions or objects." N.I. 170. [Or In 191]

"It is a concentration of ideas and of diverse feelings in a single image which summarizes all of them." (1) 56.

"It is thus an embryo of concept still charged with affectivity." (1) 57.

2. **Symbol, ludic**
    The ludic symbol is the "union *sui generis* of the deforming assimila-
    tion, principle of play itself and a sort of representative imitation."
    F.S. 108. [Pl Dr Im 102]
    "In the ludic symbol, imitation is not connected to the object present
    but to the absent object which has to be evoked and thus imitative
    accommodation remains subordinated to assimilation." F.S. 110.
    [Pl Dr Im 103]

3. **Symbol unconscious**
    "The unconscious symbol is an image of which the content is as-
    similated to the desires or the impressions of the subject, and the
    meaning of which remains not understood by him. Thus, the image is
    explained by earlier accommodations of the subject, assimilation of
    the real to the self. Primarily the actual accommodation is common
    to dream-like and ludic symbolisms and the unconscious character
    of the symbol stems entirely from the primacy of assimilation which
    goes as far as eliminating any actual accommodation. Thus it ex-
    cludes even the consciousness of the self and the becoming conscious
    of assimilatory mechanisms." F.S. 219. [Pl Dr Im 205]

1. **Syncretism**
    Is the "nondiscursive character of thought, which goes directly from
    the premises to the conditions in a single intuitive action and without
    passing through deduction." It is "the use of imaginary schemas and
    of schemas of analogy." L.P. 131. [La Th 127]
    It is the "spontaneous tendency of children to perceive through
    global vision instead of discerning details, to find immediate an-
    alogies, without analysis, between the object or among unfamiliar
    words, and to connect two natural heterogeneous phenomena, to
    find a reason for every event, however fortuitous. In brief, it is the
    tendency to connect everything to everything else. Syncretism is
    thus an excess." J.R. 13. [Ju Re 4]

1.1 **Syncretism of verbal comprehension**
    When "the elements themselves [of the] propositions are distorted
    in the functioning of a schema of a group." L.P. 139. [La Th 138]
    The child "lets escape, in a given phrase, all the difficult words, then
    he relates the understood words to the point of building collective
    schema, which, afterwards, permits him to interpret the words he
    does not understand." L.P. 148. [La Th 152]

1.2 **Syncretism of reasoning**
    "There is syncretism of reasoning when two isolated understood

172

propositions are implied in the eyes of the child, thanks to the collective schema into which they merge." L.P. 139. [La Th 138] Cf. L.P. 136.

Synthesis of elementary structures

"Each structure is distinguished by its own postulates; the synthesis of two structures into a third is obtained thus by modification of the postulates of the components, and this modification consists either in generalizations due to the extension of domains, or in suppression of limiting postulates, made possible by virtue of the synthesis itself." E.E.G. XV 8.

Example: There are two forms of "junction" between the elementary structures: (a) In the genesis of the Notion of Number we observe a veritable "synthesis" (without intermediaries), between the structures of inversion (grouping of classes) and the structures of reciprocity (grouping of relations) into a unique structure. (b) In the genesis of the Notion of Logical Proposition ("to know how to reason on a proposition considered as hypothesis independently of the truth of its content") we observe a "combination" by stages (4 stages and 10 substructures according to Grize's formalization) between the elementary structures of classes and relations. E.E.G. XV 1–23, 25–63. Cf. E.E.G. XV.

1.   **Synthetica I**

"Df. 30. Synthetica I is all action manifesting a belief the adoption of which has not as a sufficient condition the meaning of the subactions which compose it." E.E.G. IV 70.

2.   **Synthetica II**

"Df. 31. Synthetica II is any action manifesting a belief the adoption of which does not have as a sufficient condition an inference starting from the meaning of the subactions which compose it." E.E.G. IV 70.

T

Teleology (*See* **Finalism**)

Things opp. **Objects**

"We say 'things' in the most general sense of perceptual presentations, before constitution of 'permanent objects'." E.E.G. II 74, note 1.

1. **Thought**
It is a "composition of operations more and more rich and coherent which prolong actions by interiorizing them." E.G. I 34.
"Natural thought is, from the synchronic point of view, essentially circular and, from the diachronic point of view, engaged in a succession of constructions from which the efferent structures recoil, to the genetic analysis, and an infinite regression. The afferent structures are always open toward new constructions which will enlarge the circles without ever breaking them." E.E.G. XIV 299.

1.1 **Thought, non-directed or autistic**
It "is unconscious, i.e., that the aims which it pursues or the problems which it poses are not present in consciousness ... It is not adapted to exterior reality, but creates for itself a reality of imagination or of dream; it does not tend to establish truths, but to satisfy desires, and it remains strictly individual without being communicable through language." L.P. 42. [La Th 43]
The characteristics of symbolic thought are: 1. absence of logical sequence; 2. predominance of image over concept; and 3. unconsciousness of the connections which relate the successive images. (2) 273.

1.2 **Thought, directed or intelligent**
"Directed thought is conscious, i.e., it pursues the ends which are present in the thinker's mind; it is intelligent, i.e., it is adapted to reality and it tries to act upon this latter; it is susceptible to truth and error (empirical or logical truth) and it is communicable by language." L.P. 42. [La Th 43]

2. **Thought, egocentric**
It is the thought which "tries to adapt to reality by not communicating." L.P. 43. [La Th 45]
"That thought always remains autistic in its structure, but ... its interests do not seek organic or ludic satisfaction only, as pure autism, but already intellectual adaptation, like adult thought." J.R. 166. [Ju Re 205]
(1) From the point of view of structure, it is thought without norms.
(2) From the point of view of content, it is the beginning of proper perspective. (6) 100.

3. **Thought, intuitive** (4–7 years)
"It supplies to unachieved operations a semi-symbolic form of thought, which is intuitive reasoning; and it controls judgment only by means of intuitive 'regulations'." P.I. 154–155. [Ps In 129]

4. **Thought, logical**

The "essential characteristics [of logical thought] is in the operational, i.e., of prolonging the action by interiorizing it." P.I. 45. [Ps In 34]

4.1 **Thought, concrete**

Contains the "operations in the first degree, interiorized actions becoming combinable and reversible." P.I. 177. [Ps In 148]

"Does not contain opposition between the static situations and their transformations: the first are now subordinated to the second, in the sense that each state is conceived as the result of a transformation." L.E.A. 217. [Gr Lo Th 248]

4.2 **Thought, formal**

"Consists in reflecting the (concrete) operations, thus in influencing the operations or their results and consequently in grouping of the operations of the second degree." P.I. 177. [Ps In 148]

"The principal characteristics of formal thought depend without doubt on the role which it assigns to the possible in relation to real observations..." L.E.A. 215. [Gr Lo Th 245] Cf. L.E.A. 220–222.

"We have up to here defined formal thought as the capacity to reason on several systems at a time ... and as being specific reasoning which bears on the possible." I.H. 243.

"It is precisely the power of formal thought which can satisfy these two conditions at the same time, by surpassing reality with a hypothetico-deductive reconstitution which permits at will to think of simultaneity as successive and reciprocal." M.V. 105. [Mo Sp 114]

"Formal thought, thanks to its hypothetico-deductive mechanism, allows to translate simultaneity into succession, then succession into simultaneity." M.V. 107. [Mo Sp 116] Cf. M.V. 183.

"Formal operations add nothing to concrete operations as far as they are operational: they simply translate them on a new level, which is that of assumptions or hypotheses." M.V. 108. [Mo Sp 117]

5. **Thought, verbal**

"Verbal thought of the child consists in progressively being conscious of the schemas constructed by action." J.M. 88. [Mo Ju 117]

"For the child, to think is to manipulate words. Three confusions are implied in this belief and three dualisms will derive from the elimination of these confusions. First of all, there is the confusion of sign and thing: thought is considered as tied to the object. There is the confusion of internal and external: thought is considered as situated on the one hand in the air and the other in the mouth. There is finally the confusion between matter and thought: thought is considered as a material body, a voice, a breath, etc." R.M. 66. [Co Wo 86]

1. **Time**

Time is "the coordination of movements; they may be physical displacements or movements in space, or those internal movements which are simply outlined actions, anticipated or reconstituted through memory, but the result is itself also spatial. Time plays in regard to actions the same role as space in regard to immobile objects ... Space is an instantaneous taking on of time, and time is space in movement..." N.T. 2.

"What we call the 'course' of time is nothing other than the succession of events, but if the notion of time constitutes a collection of relations of co-placement and of co-displacement which unite these events, the temporal correspondence, as relation, is reversible since an order can be noted in two directions and only the contents succeed each other in one direction." N.T. 63.

"Time is ... a coordination of speeds." M.V. 162. [Mo Sp 173]

1.1 **Time, psychological**

"Psychological time constitutes a coordination of speeds of actions..." E.G. II 43.

"... 'more time' expresses a greater amount of work accomplished. It is accomplished work (of which traversed space is a particular case) which is, at first, the true criterion of time, and of psychological duration as physical time." E.G. II 26–27.

"Psychological time [is the] connection between work accomplished and activity (force and rapidity of action)." N.T. 44.

"Immediate psychological time is ... the time of action in process." N.T. 241.

"Like physical time, psychological time depends upon two distinct fundamental systems, of intuitions at first, and then of operations. The order of succession of events and the nesting of durations which connect them. The single difference is that it is concerned with living events, either exterior and interior at the same time, or purely interior. It concerns not only events observed independently of the action — the difference, as immediately apparent, is simply of degree and not of kind." N.T. 260. Cf. (13) 185.

1.2 **Time, physical**

"Physical time is a coordination of exterior speeds." E.G. II 43.

"Physical time has the form $t = d/r$." N.T. 44.

2.   **Time, origin of**

2.1   **Time, primitive, proper, egocentric, subjective, or sensory-motor**

"The child constructs his notion of subjective time according to the model of time which he attributes to things, as well as the inverse." E.G. II 27–28.

"Time ... does not derive from the subject's becoming conscious, but it proceeds from the action of the subject upon the object, which is not at all equivalent ... That is, perceived or conceived in the object it remains relative to the intuitions of space and speed determined by the activity..." E.G. II 28.

"Time proceeds from the organization of movements and that is why it is dominated from the start by spatial coordinations; but it is differentiated from space to the degree that speeds intervene. It is thus a connection between specialized actions of the subject and the resistances of objects whatever their size." E.G. II 30.

"... Time itself is plastic; it expands according to the deceleration or contracts according to acceleration of action..." N.T. 51.

"Time is confused at its point of departure with the impressions of psychological duration inherent in the attitudes of expectation, effort, and of satisfaction: in brief, in the activity of the subject." C.R. 281. [Co Re 321]

"Primitive time [is not] a time perceived on the outside, but a duration felt in the course of the action." "... time itself ... [is] the simple feeling of an unrolling and of successive directions in states of consciousness." C.R. 285. [Co Re 326]

"... primitive time is neither interior nor even purely endogenous, but results from indifferentiation between the time of objects and that of the subject..." N.T. 207.

2.2   **Time, practical**

"How thus is sensory-motor intelligence disengaged from practical time; that is to say, how does he get a correct sequence of the events upon which his action bears, [from the] initial egocentric series? ... It is the coordination of successive actions which, in engaging or bringing anticipations and practical reconstructions into play (= connected to the entire action and not only the movements of regard) will permit the grouping of exterior movements into a practical group of displacements. It is this organization of successive movements of something mobile ... which constitutes exterior space, that will become at the same time the foundation of physical time of a practical order, thus an order of the successions necessary to the action." N.T. 124.

2.3 **Time, perceptual**

"Perceptual time bears uniquely on what is distinguished as successive or fused as simultaneous, but independent of the understanding
of these notions, the same way that the ear can distinguish a chord
as a simple note without intelligence knowing that the first is formed
from two or more notes and the second of a single one." N.T. 89.

2.4 **Time, intuitive**

Intuitive time is "limited to the correspondences of succession and
of given durations in immediate perception, external or internal."
N.T. 2.

"... it is concerned with a gradual 'decentration' which leads the
subject from the initial 'centered' time of the action or the isolated
movement, to coordinate time which relates several points of view
and finally constitutes a system of co-displacements." N.T. 97.

2.5 **Time, operational**

"There is an operational time consisting of relations of succession
and duration based upon the operations analogous to logical operations ... Operational time could be qualitative [2.51] or measured
[2.52] according as the operations which constitute it remain analogous to those of classes and logical relations or which introduce
a numerical unit." N.T. 2.

2.51 **Time, qualitative**

"... qualitative time conserves, if it becomes operational, a much
greater practical role within measured time than is the case, for
example, of qualitative weight in connection with the measure of
weight. But this difference is explained by the existence of an internal duration..." N.T. 75.

2.52 **Time, measured**

"Measured time is both ordinal and cardinal: in the temporal order
or ordinal succession of the points of reference, duration or cardinal
value corresponds to intervals between these points." N.T. 37.

"... even more than qualitative time, measured time presupposes
both geometry, cinematics and mechanics, since in addition to correspondence between the work accomplished and its speed already
taking part in synchronization, it presupposes constant speeds
(rectilinear and uniform movements or regular periodicity)." N.T.
83.

2.6 **Time, rational**

The three fundamental attributes of rational time are homogeneity,
continuity, and uniformity. N.T. 291.

178

2.61 **Time, homogeneous**

"Homogeneous time is time common to all phenomena and is thus in opposition to local time of initial intuition. But homogeneity does not imply uniformity of successive durations..." N.T. 292.

3. **Time, and causality**

"It is from causality [that time] draws its order of succession, since causes are necessarily prior to their effects, and it is causality which expresses their durations, since duration is only the correspondence, qualitative or measured, between traversed space and speed." N.T. 83.

Time is "inherent in causality: it is to explicatory operations what logical order is to implicatory operations." N.T. 6.

Totality, virtual

"When the child sees a portion of the object emerging from a screen and postulates the existence of the totality of the object, he does not thus consider that totality as constituting the all 'behind' the screen. He admits simply that it is in the process of being constructed starting at the screen." C.R. 32. [Co Re 31]

Transduction

Transduction is "a sort of mental experience ... these representations do not constitute general concepts, but simply mentally evoked schemas of action." F.S. 248. [Pl Dr Im 234–235]

If transduction "succeeds in practice, it is only because it constitutes a sequence of actions symbolized in thought, a 'mental experience' in the proper sense of the word." P.I. 154. [Ps In 128]

"Primitive reasonings, which do not proceed by deduction [nor by induction], but by immediate analogies." P.I. 153. [Ps In 128]

"Stern has named this procedure transduction as opposed to induction and deduction." J.R. 150. [Ju Re 184]

"We could not characterize transduction better than as a primitive combination of imagination of relations which reality presents us." J.R. 154. [Ju Re 190]

"Pure transduction is a primitive 'mental experience,' ... that means a simple imagination or imitation of reality as it is perceived, i.e., irreversible." J.R. 155. [Ju Re 191–192]

"... Transduction could be defined as a combination of relations woven between things and the organism by the action (by the movements of the organism), without this action being conscious of its own processes, and consequently without thought being able to become conscious of its existence." J.R. 159. [Ju Re 197]

1. **Transport, perceptual** (*See* **Centration, Coupling, Decentration, Transposition**)
    "When it is a question of confronting objects too distant for being able to be included in the same centrations, perceptual activity is prolonged in the form of 'transports' in space, as if the vision of one of the objects were applied upon the other." P.I. 98. [Ps In 81]
    "In comparing two sizes A and B ... regard is given ... to one kind of measure ... and that measure contains two essential moments. On the one hand, there is a sort of approximating of elements of comparison, that is of virtual displacement of one of them in the direction of the other, accompanying the real displacement of regard (we call this virtual approximating 'transport'). On the other hand, in case of inequality, there is a decomposition of a larger element B into a part equal to A and a difference A', with a possible relating of A and A' (again by 'transport'...)." G.S. 42. [Co Ge 28–29]
    The transport T_P is not an entity for it is reducible to "some complexes of relations." "The transport consists in relating at a distance a connection with these centrations." M.P. 9. [Me Pe xxi]

1.1 **Transports, double and simple**
    "These transports which thus constitute the (potential) approximations of centrations give way to 'comparisons,' in the proper sense of the word, of double transports decentering by their goings and comings the deformations due to transport in one direction." P.I. 98. [Ps In 81]

2. **Transport, manual**
    Manual transport consists "in approximating objects which have to be compared, not by visual comparisons at a distance, but right in the same group of objects applied one against the other." G.S. 45. [Co Ge 31]

3. **Transport, bodily**
    When "instead of transporting the object itself, the child transports the gesture of the hand or of the arm that was first intended to grasp or to embrace the object." G.S. 45. [Co Ge 31]

1. **Transposition**
    "We shall speak of 'transpositions' when the transport matches, not only the dimension (or the direction) of an element, but a group of relations, for example, the difference between two elements L_1 and L_2 (matched on L_3 and L_4)." M.P. 227. [Me Pe 176]
    "It is a 'transport' of correspondences, as opposed to that of an isolated value." P.I. 102. [Ps In 84]

    180

"One of the criteria of 'good form' is precisely the possibility for perception of recognizing the same structure when we change the absolute values of the figure" (transposition). R.E. 379. [Ch Co Sp 321]

1.1   **Transposition, internal**
The internal transpositions are "transpositions on the inside of the same figure." E.E.G. V 75.
"The internal transpositions permit the recognition, on the inside even of the figures of correspondences which are repeated, the symmetries ... etc." P.I. 102. [Ps In 84]

1.2   **Transpositions, external**
"External transpositions are transpositions of multiple relations of one figure to another." E.E.G. V 75.
Traversed way (*See* **Road traversed**)
Trial and error (*See* Groping)

1.1   **Truth, external or empirical** opp.
1.2   **Truth, internal, or logical of coordinations**
We have to "distinguish external or empirical truth of conclusions [1.1] from internal truth or logic of coordinations ... [1.2]." G.S. 248.

U

Unconscious
"The unconscious is only the expression of impotence of our introspection. There are no two mental domains separated by a border, but only one and the same working of the mind, of which even in the most lucid states we perceive only one very small part (centered on the obtained results and not on the processes as such), and which escapes us almost completely when we have no more close control over it." E.E.G. XIV 214.
"An unconscious thought is a series of operations, no longer effective and at hand, if you like, but potential and sketched by the organism." J.R. 120. [Ju Re 145]
Understanding (*See* **Comprehension**)
Unforeseen and unforeseeable
"... the unforeseen, which the child states simply by contrast with the expected regularities, is not at all to be confused with the unforeseeable, that is to say, with the modifications conceived as irreducible to a possible deduction." I.H. 231.

Unit

"Unit is the part that may be both displaced or substituted for any other, as opposed to the qualitative part the dimensions of which are known only by correspondence with those of the whole." G.S. 164. [Co Ge 123]

Unit is elaborated "by synthesis of the partition and of displacement." P.I. 173. [Ps In 145]

Universe of presentation (*See* **Perceptual picture**)

"There is at the beginning [of the child's thought] neither an exterior world nor an interior world, but a universe of 'presentations' of which the pictures are charged with affective, cinesthetic and sensory-motor, as well as physical, qualities." C.R. 185. [Co Re 259]

"The universe of the child is still only a collection of pictures, emerging from nothingness by reason of his action, only to go back there at its extinction." C.R. 41. [Co Re 43]

Unitarist (*See* **Hypothesis, psychophysical**)

V

1. **Value**

"Value is the product of feeling. It is the feeling projected into the object, attributed to the object." A.I. 156.

"We could characterize it as the enrichment of action. Objects and persons have value when they enrich the action ... it is above all a functional enrichment. A valued object or person can be the source of new activities." A.I. 39.

"Value is an affective characteristic of the object, that is, a collection of feelings projected on the object. It constitutes thus a connection between the object and the subject, but an affective connection." A.I. 41.

Value is "a general dimension of affectivity, and not ... a particular and privileged feeling." A.I. 29.

2. **Value and quantification**

"It is the value of a goal which determines the energy to be used for reaching it and not the energy at his disposal which determines the value or the non-value of the goal." A.I. 69.

"... there is heterovaluing in the exchange with others and auto-valuing in the action itself, but the values could be qualitative or quantitative ... as soon as they are quantified according to measured or extensive quantity they take on an economic aspect..." A.I. 91. "In the case of an energy system we have to make a purely quantitative system; there are forces present with intensity, but without qualities. On the contrary, in the system of autovaluing we deal with a qualitative system, where we have intervening values with qualitative content and not solely with intensity." A.I. 89.

3.1 **Values, practical (practical intelligence)**

3.2 **Values, indifferent (indifferent intelligence)**
"... impartial values appear to lead not to an enrichment of action of the subject, but, on the contrary, to sacrifices. The problem here shows an exact parallel on the plane of cognitive functions. Practical intelligence, oriented toward realization of the goal, will succeed an indifferent intelligence, representative and gnostic, presupposing decentration the aim of which is understanding." A.I. 39.

4.1 **Values, intra-individual**

4.2 **Values, inter-individual**
"Similarly, to intra-individual values involving the action will succeed inter-individual values, which are the values of exchange presupposing reciprocity." A.I. 39.

5.1 **Values, real or actual**
The negative or positive values "constitute the real or actual values, that is, those which correspond to the perceptual affects or to those feelings relative to regulations of the action..." A.I. 78.

5.2 **Values, virtual**
"The virtual values: ... disappearance of feelings almost immediately after the perceptual disappearance except for a momentary need to make pleasure last." A.I. 78.

6.1 **Values of utilization (need for success)**
"The values of utilization or of success: in the function of primary needs (to attain nourishment, to manipulate an object, etc.)." E.E.G. VII 48.

6.2 **Value of knowledge (need for understanding)**
"Values of knowledge or of understanding: testifying to derived needs..." E.E.G. VII 48.

Velocity (*See* **Speed**)

Verbalism
Is the "automatic use of words deprived of all sense." L.P. 133. [La Th 130]
It is "the joint product of the method of oral authority and of syncretism belonging to egocentric language of the child." J.M. 326. [Mo Ju 402]

Verification (need)

"It is surely the shock of our thought with that of others which produces in us the doubt and the need to prove ... It is the social need to share the thought of others, of communicating our own and of convincing which is at the origin of our need for verification. The proof is born out of discussion." J.R. 164. [Ju Re 204]

1.   **Virtuality**

"The notions of the virtual and of the potential are the correspondences of operational equivalence of which the criterion of legitimacy is at the interior of a group of well-determined compositions and is indispensable to the reversability of this system." E.G. II 89.

2.1   **Virtuality of repetition**

2.2   **Virtuality of new composition**

"... all formation action of an operation brings about by its very performance two sorts of virtualities, i.e., while 'engaging' in the activity of the subject, it opens two categories of new possibilities: on the one hand, the possibility of effective repetition, or of reproduction of thought, accompanied by a determination of characteristics which are so far implicit in the action [2.1]; on the other hand, a possibility of new compositions, virtually carried along by the execution of the initial action [2.2]." E.G. I 34–35.

1.   **Volume, interior**

"Physical volume, once quantified and detached from its qualitative appearance, will be defined for the child as correspondence between the quantity of matter and its compression or concentration." D.Q. 64.

"... we will call interior volume ... the quantity of matter ... surrounded by the frontal surfaces..." G.S. 454. [Co Ge 359–360]

2.   **Volume, occupied**

"We will call occupied volume ... the place taken up by the total volume of an object in relation with those objects which surround it..." G.S. 454. [Co Ge 360]

3.   **Volume, global**

"Global volume corresponds to its exterior surface and is equal to the volume of united [corpuscles] plus the volume of the empty spaces between these [corpuscles]." D.Q. 130.

4.   **Volume, total**

"The total volume, or the total corpuscular volume, is the sum of the volumes of the particular grains, without taking into account the interstitial spaces." D.Q. 130.

W

Way traversed (*See* **Road traversed**)
1. **Weight**
"Weight appears at first as a concrete quality characteristic of matter." D.Q. 317.
2. **Weight, intuitive**
"... weight consists of absolute qualities depending in reality on the activity or on the self." D.Q. 276. Cf. D.Q. 30, 40, 45.
Why (principal types)

Forms of the question			Matter of the question
1. Explanation (causal)	{	1.1 Cause ... (because)	Material objects
		1.2 Goal ... (for)	
2. Motivation		Motive	Psychological actions
3. Justification	{	3.1 Justification as such	Usage and rules
		3.2 Logical reason	Classification and relation of ideas

L.P. 161. [La Th 171]
1. **Will and conservation of values**
It is the "affective involvement, thus energetic, bearing on higher values, and making them susceptible to reversibility and to conservation (moral feelings, etc.)." P.I. 10. [Ps In 5]
"Will is thus simply the conservation of values." A.I. 132.
"... will will be only one of the particular cases of decentration which weaken the initially strong tendency, not because we need a new force to weaken it but simply because its force was residing only in the limited situation of the moment and because by enlarging the field the connection of these forces will be transformed." A.I. 128. Cf. (12) 21.
2. **Will and regulation**
"Pierre Janet based elementary feelings on the economy of behavior and defined them as a regulation of forces at the disposal of the individual: one can conceive will as a regulation of elementary regulations." A.I. 2.
3. **Will** (conditions)
"We will say that there is will in the case where the two following

185

conditions are present: The first condition: conflict between two tendencies; a single tendency does not constitute a voluntary act ... Second condition: when these two tendencies are of unequal force, when one begins by being weaker than the other and in the course of the act of will, there is a reversal; that means the weaker becomes thus stronger and the stronger is overcome by that which was initially the weaker." A.I. 121.

Z

Zones of reality or **Spheres of reality**
"... to distinguish the zones or spheres of reality means to distinguish among the totality of known realities (physical, social, subjective, etc. reality) or conceivable realities (world of ideas), that reality which one wishes to characterize and give it existence to the extent that it supports valid demonstrations." E.E.G. XIV 160.